16.75
9107

SO-AJV-860

Inventing America

Oklahoma Project for Discourse and Theory

OKLAHOMA PROJECT FOR DISCOURSE AND THEORY

SERIES EDITORS

Robert Con Davis, University of Oklahoma
Ronald Schleifer, University of Oklahoma

ADVISORY BOARD

INVENTING
A·M·E·R·I·C·A

Spanish Historiography
and the Formation of Eurocentrism

José Rabasa

University of Oklahoma Press : Norman and London

To the memory of my father, Josep Rabasa

Published with the assistance of The Program for Cultural Cooperation
Between Spain's Ministry of Culture and United States' Universities, and
The McCasland Foundation, Duncan, Oklahoma.

Rabasa, José, 1948–
    Inventing America : Spanish historiography and the formation of
Eurocentrism / by José Rabasa. — 1st ed.
        p.   cm. — (Oklahoma project for discourse and theory; v. 11)
    Includes bibliographical references and index.
    ISBN 0-8061-2495-4
    1. America — Early accounts to 1600 — History and criticism.
    2. America — Discovery and exploration — Spanish — Historiography.
    I. Title.   II. Series.
    E141.R23   1993
    970.01'6'072 — dc20   92-34510
                                                                      CIP

Inventing America: Spanish Historiography and the Formation of Eurocentrism is Volume 11 of the Oklahoma Project for Discourse and Theory.

The paper in this book meets the guidelines for permanence and durability
of the Committee on Production Guidelines for Book Longevity of the Council on Library Resources, Inc. ∞

Contents

Contents

Figures

Figures

Series Editors' Foreword

The Oklahoma Project for Discourse & Theory is a series of interdisciplinary texts whose purpose is to explore the cultural institutions that constitute the human sciences, to see them in relation to one another, and, perhaps above all, to see them as products of particular discursive practices. To this end, we hope that the Oklahoma Project will promote dialogue within and across traditional disciplines — psychology, philology, linguistics, history, art history, aesthetics, logic, political economy, religion, philosophy, anthropology, communications, and the like — in texts that theoretically are located across disciplines. In recent years, in a host of new and traditional areas, there has been great interest in such discursive and theoretical frameworks. Yet we conceive of the Oklahoma Project as going beyond local inquiries, providing a larger forum for interdiscursive theoretical discussions and dialogue.

Our agenda in previous books and certainly in this one has been to present through the University of Oklahoma Press a series of critical volumes that set up a theoretical encounter among disciplines, an interchange not limited to literature but covering virtually the whole range of the human sciences. It is a critical series with an important reference in literary studies — thus mirroring the modern development of discourse theory — but including all approaches, other than quantitative studies, open to semiotic and post-semiotic analysis and to the wider concerns of cultural studies. Regardless of its particular domain, each book in the series will investigate characteristically post-Freudian, post-Saussurean, and post-Marxist questions about culture and the discourses that constitute different cultural phenomena. The Oklahoma Project is a sustained dialogue intended to make a significant contribution to the contemporary understanding of the human sciences in the contexts of cultural theory and cultural studies.

The title of the series reflects, of course, its home base, the University of Oklahoma. But it also signals in a significant way the particularity of the *local* functions within historical and conceptual frameworks for understanding culture. *Oklahoma* is a haunting place-name in American culture. A Choctaw phrase meaning "red people," it goes back to the Treaty of Dancing Rabbit Creek in Mississippi in 1830. For Franz Kafka, it conjured up the idea of America itself, both the indigenous Indian peoples of North America and the vertiginous space of the vast plains. It is also the place-name, the "American" starting point, with which Wallace Stevens begins his *Collected Poems*. Historically, too, it is a place in which American territorial and political expansion was reenacted in a single day in a retracing called the Oklahoma land run. Geographically, it is the heartland of the continent.

As such—in the interdisciplinary Oklahoma Project for Discourse & Theory—we are hoping to describe, above all, multifaceted *interests* within and across various studies of discourse and culture. Such interests are akin to what Kierkegaard calls the "in-between" aspect of experience, the "inter esse," and, perhaps more pertinently, what Nietzsche describes as the always *political* functioning of concepts, art works, and language—the functioning of power as well as knowledge in discourse and theory. Such politics, occasioning dialogue and bringing together powerfully struggling and often unarticulated positions, disciplines, and assumptions, is always local, always particular. In some ways, such interests function in broad feminist critiques of language, theory, and culture as well as microphilosophical and microhistorical critiques of the definitions of truth and art existing within ideologies of "disinterested" meaning. They function in the interested examination of particular disciplines and general disciplinary histories. They function (to allude to two of our early titles) in the very interests of theory and the particularity of the postmodern age in which many of us find ourselves. In such interested particulars, we believe, the human sciences are articulated. We hope that the books of the Oklahoma Project will provide sites of such interest and that in them, individually and collectively, the monologues of traditional scholarly discourse will become heteroglosses, just as such place-names as *Oklahoma* and such commonplace words and concepts as *discourse* and *theory* can become sites for the dialogue and play of culture.

ROBERT CON DAVIS
RONALD SCHLEIFER

Norman, Oklahoma

Acknowledgments

This book would have been impossible to conceive outside the intellectual climate of the History of Consciousness Program at the University of California, Santa Cruz. I was especially fortunate as a graduate student to have James Clifford, Jorge Klor de Alva, and Hayden White coincide as faculty when I first began working on this project. I thank all those who have contributed to my project—some for making devastating criticism, other for offering useful suggestions. For critical readings of chapters and earlier versions of this book, I would like especially to thank Rolena Adorno, Ronaldo Balderrama, Amy Burse, Karen Caplan, Catherine Durand, Marta Morello-Frosch, Walter Mignolo, and Sidney Monas.

I am grateful for fellowship support from the Graduate Opportunity Program at the University of California, Santa Cruz, and the University Research Institute at the University of Texas at Austin.

The following chapters have appeared in other publications. Chapter 2 is a slightly modified version of "Columbus and the New Scriptural Economy of the Renaissance," *Dispositio* 14:36–38 (1989). Chapter 3, "Dialogue as Conquest in the Cortés–Charles V Correspondence," is a revised and enlarged version of "Dialogue as Conquest: Mapping Spaces for Counter-Discourse," *Cultural Critique* 6 (1987), reprinted in Abdul JanMohammed and David Lloyd, eds. *The Nature and Context of Minority Discourse* (New York: Oxford University Press, 1990). Chapter 5, "Allegories of Atlas," appeared in a very early form as "Allegories of the *Atlas*," in Francis Barker et al., eds., *Europe and Its Others*, 2 vols. (Colchester: University of Essex, 1984). I thank the editors of *Dispositio* and *Cultural Critique* for permission to reproduce my revised essays on Columbus and Cortés.

JOSÉ RABASA

College Park, Maryland

Inventing America

Le Roy, à demy rosty, fut emporté de là, non tant par pitié (car quelle pitié touchajamais des ames qui, pour la doubteuse information de quelque vase d'or à piller, fissent griller devant leurs yeux un homme, non qu'un Roy si grand et en fortune et en merite?) mais ce fut que sa constance rendoit de plus en plus honteuse leur cruauté. Ils le pendirent depuis, ayant courageusement entrepris de se delivrer par armes d'une si longue captivité et subjection, où il fit sa fin digne d'un magnanime prince.

Michel de Montaigne, *"Des coches"* (c. 1586)

La cual suplico se reciba en el mismo ánimo que yo la presento, y las faltas que lleva se me perdonen porque soy indio, que a los tales, por ser bárbaros y no enseñados en ciencias ni artes, no se permite que, en lo que dijeren o hicieren, los lleven por el rigor de los preceptos del arte y ciencia, por no los haber aprendido, sino que los admitan como vinieren.

El Inca Garcilaso de la Vega, La Florida del Inca (1605)

Or le nom propre, dans ce jeu, n'est qu'un artifice: il permet de montrer du doigt, c'est-à-dire de faire passer subrepticement de l'espace où l'on parle à l'espace où l'on regarde, c'est-à-dire de les refermer commodément l'un sur l'autre comme s'ils étaient adéquates.

. . . Il faut donc feindre de ne pas savoir qui se reflétera au fond de la glace, et interroge ce reflet au ras de son existence.

Michel Foucault, Les mots et les choses (1966)

The Critique of Colonial Discourse: An Introduction

Inventing America seeks to underscore the ongoing process of colonization and decolonization implicit in the writing, interpreting, and critiquing of early visual representations of and writings on the New World. The gerund *inventing* foregrounds the assumption that what we say about European expansionism, conquest, and colonization of the world in the early modern period implies a position on issues pertaining to neocolonialism and Eurocentrism today. The term *New World* should be understood, not solely as that imaginary geographic space that emerged in the European wish-horizon of ideal landscapes in the sixteenth and seventeenth centuries, but also as the constitution of the modern conception of the world that results from the exploration of the globe—and, by extension, the metaphorical use of "new world" among such philosophers and painters as Francis Bacon and Jan Vermeer to speak of new fields of vision and inquiry. Indeed, already in Columbus's descriptions of nature we find a sense of opening up new worlds of nature, of carving out new parcels of reality. It is not a coincidence that Columbus and voyages of discovery in general are preferred metaphors for scientific inquiry and innovation among such modern and contemporary philosophers as Bacon, Vico, Bentham, Engels, and Althusser.[1]

The notion of the invention of America first appeared in the title of a book by Hernán Pérez de Oliva, *Historia de la invención de las Yndias* (c. 1528), where the term *invención* reflects the Latin *inuenire*, to discover. More recently, the Mexican historian Edmundo O'Gorman wrote a book with precisely the title *La invención de América* (1958; 1977) in which he argues that America was not discovered but invented. For O'Gorman, the

3

idea of a discovery of America is in itself part of the process of invention. However useful O'Gorman's critique might be, his distinction presupposes stable definitions and values of the terms *invention* and *discovery*. Indeed, it assumes a truth about an American reality from which we can differentiate inventing from discovering, and ultimately define "the historical structure of the being of America and the sense of American history," as he titles part 4 of his book.[2] The title of Pérez de Oliva's book, furthermore, would call for a history of the semantic differentiation of the two terms. Moreover, a number of recent usages of *invention* as a paradigm to understand the emergence of mythology, cultural processes, daily life, and also racism provide alternative perspectives to O'Gorman's narrow definition of *invention* in opposition to discovery (e.g., Marcel Detienne, *L'invention de la mythologie* [1981]; Roy Wagner, *The Invention of Culture* [1981]; Michel de Certeau, *L'invention du quotidien* [1980]; and Christian Delacampagne, *L'invention du racisme* [1983]).

Roy Wagner's understanding of invention as a semiotics of cultural processes and Michel de Certeau's as the oppositional practices of everyday life enable us to understand how the Indians' invention of European culture constitutes forms of reinventing their own and articulating a counterdiscourse. On the other hand, Marcel Detienne, by showing how rationality constituted itself by consigning whole fields of experience to myth (lies), makes manifest the philosophical tradition from which Indians are invented as myth-ridden. And Christian Delacampagne, by tracing a history of the birth of racism in the European construct of the barbarian, of the illusion (indeed with very real consequences) of the perverse foreigner, foregrounds the propositions underlying the definition of Indians as biologically inferior to Europeans. My use of the concept of invention seeks to explore further these kinds of semiotic and deconstructive areas of inquiry, rather than the epistemological distinction O'Gorman establishes vis-à-vis discovery.

We should keep in mind, however, a recommendation O'Gorman made to historians a number of years ago, in his introduction to Joseph de Acosta's *Historia natural y moral de las Indias*, that recent literary critics have taken as a point of departure.[3] There O'Gorman expressed the need to rectify the emphasis that

4

positivist historiography had placed on the exclusive appraisal of the histories of the Indies as sources of information. If O'Gorman underscored that we ought to read and study the epistemological and ontological as well as rhetorical suppositions informing the historiography of the New World, literary critics of Spanish-American colonial literature have moved from a first instance where the so-called chronicles (*las crónicas*) were read merely as fiction to more refined analyses of their artistic qualities.[4] In this study, however, we will not be concerned with defining the literary value of the "chronicles," but will follow up O'Gorman's suggestions with Michel Foucault's concept of discursive formation. The generic differences between histories, chronicles, and *relaciones* (accounts) correspond to rules that do not merely reflect aesthetic formulas but define who has the authority to speak and what is legitimate knowledge.[5] Moreover, one can also distinguish *relaciones*, chronicles, and history in the strict sense of the term on the basis of narrative structures; for example, *relaciones* and chronicles call for a weak plot that highlights the particularity of its contents and, above all, lacks the "moralistic" resolutions that lend universal significations to history.[6] These genres would differ, then, according to how explicit they make their *allegoresis*, that is, the degree to which "the historical narrative endows sets of real events with the kinds of meaning found otherwise only in myth and literature."[7] Under this perspective, narrative forms would purvey, not exclusively aethestic or rhetorical formulas prevalent in sixteenth-century historiography, but also generic strictures determining the kinds of meanings that might be conveyed under specific legal, political, or religious constrains.

If the humanist historiographical model in the sixteenth century prescribed a providential concept of history, eloquence and good tone, a courtly morality, and an elegant style, to insist too much on these aesthetic formalisms would lead us to ignore their function within the colonial enterprise: that there are new values, meanings, and functions in the providential schemas, for instance, among millenarian Franciscans, where the ultimate referent of history is no longer Europe; that the good tone and courtly morals convey, beyond rhetorical formulas, another mode of violence and conquest; or that the elegant style implies a cultural appropriation of narrative forms that follow other poetics.[8] At any rate, the tasks would no longer be how or to what degree New World histories approximate the ideals of humanistic historiography, but rather to read them as instances of a colonial process.

As a study of the invention of America in the sixteenth century, this book shows how a thesaurus of New World motifs (e.g., exotic fauna and flora, cannibalism, the noble savage, the legendary kingdom of Tenochtitlan, and millenarian interpretations of an until then unheard-of humanity) was constituted in personal letters, official accounts, encyclopedic histories, and world atlases. My emphasis on the production of America as something "new"—that is, semiotically created—challenges the view of the New World as a natural entity, discovered, revealed, or imperfectly understood. Consequently, I am less interested in issues regarding a distortion or misrepresentation of the New World than in how a new region of the world was invented, and how fiction (literary or otherwise) and history constitute complementary forms of understanding the "West" and "the Americas."

Conventional approaches presuppose an accurate and realistic representation of America against which Spanish-American historiography can be measured. Rather, we ought first to question the rhetorical as well as the epistemological grounds that underlie authorized versions of America. My study begins and ends, therefore, with examples of typical iconographical and cartographical documents and images that represent the European conception of the world toward the turn of the sixteenth century. Thus the first and last chapters provide a frame for an investigation into the structure of the invention of America's text and the emergence of Eurocentrism during that crucial historical moment. Looking first at Jan van der Straet's (better known as Stradanus) allegory of "America" (c. 1600) and ending with the allegories, motifs, and maps in the 1636 English version of Gerhard Mercator's *Atlas* (1595), I argue that by the early seventeenth century these and other equivalent images had already coalesced into a fully constituted Eurocentric worldview. Indeed, the production of America is coterminous with the formation of the "Europe and its Others" cultural complex in the early modern period. Although the ramifications of this worldview span four centuries, my analysis concentrates on early

6

documents written in Spanish under the auspices of the Spanish crown—a corpus of texts describing the New World on a first-hand basis. I am especially concerned with the force and effectiveness of images that fabricated new realms of reality that are still influential today.

The timing of this study is the Columbian quincentennial. Its purpose is to intervene in what "promises" to be a celebratory occasion with little room for criticism. As a critical reading of early Spanish-American writings on the New World, this study attempts to elaborate an alternative understanding of the colonization and conquest of the Americas to the Eurocentric version that will inevitably prevail among the official circles.

Let us briefly consider the recent debates over the appropriate term to be adopted in the quincentenary commemorations of Columbus's voyage. Indian leaders have preferred the term *invasion* over *discovery*, which clearly reduces the indigenous peoples of the Americas to objects whose reality depends on the European gaze, and over *encounter*, which suggests a symmetrical relation of power in exchanges between Europeans and Amerindians. The objection to the latter would be obviously not over its valorization of native cultures, but rather over a tendency to ignore the Europeans' opportunistic exploitation of conditions favoring a military and political occupation. On the other hand, *invention* would be opposed by the proponents of *discovery* and *encounter* on the grounds that it negates an ontological primacy to the New World.[9] But as Pierre Chaunu already showed many years ago, European expansionism from the thirteenth to the fifteenth century, and beyond, can be truly called a geographic invention of the world insofar as it involved developing technologies, establishing commercial routes, and constructing intellectual frameworks.[10]

The notion of an invention of America that I am advancing here would seek to test the grounds on which Europeans devised strategies for invading indigenous territories, the categories and suppositions that underline an understanding of the contact as a discovery, and the possibility of reversing the centrality of European history by recalling how ongoing encounters during the last five hundred years have been asymmetrical, but also by underscoring the endurance of Amerindians. For we know that there was an Indian invention of the Europeans in the early contacts. We can reconstruct today the Indian vision of the conquest in spite of the imposed silence on Indian historians of the conquest for more than three hundred years until their retrieval from the archives last century. Moreover, we must recall that the pioneer work of Angel María Garibay K. and Miguel León-Portilla in Mexico, and of José María Arguedas and Jesús Lara for the Andean region, has only very recently, in the last thirty or so years, revaluated and legitimated their historical expression. And indeed, we must insist with Michel de Certeau that the Indians, "dominated but not vanquished . . . keep alive the memory of what the Europeans have 'forgotten'—a continuous series of uprisings and awakenings which have left hardly a trace in the occupiers' historiographical literature."[11]

I use the term historiography in its most general sense of writing the real. As de Certeau has reminded us in *The Writing of History*: "Historiography (that is, 'history' and 'writing') bears within its own name the paradox—almost an oxymoron—of a relation established between two antinomic terms, between the real and discourse."[12] This definition enables us to understand the real as a product of discourse, rather than as an adequation of writing to a preexistent object. Under this definition, historiography comprises truthful accounts of the past and the present as well as of the realms of nature and culture. Accordingly, then, the invention of America pointed the way to a unified, univocal world picture. As has often been remarked, the emergence of America completed the European image of the planet; beyond that, however, it also established the universality of European history and subjectivity. Such a universality is not limited to matters of geographic location, but includes the inauguration of modes of thinking that define a global reality. This study is thus concerned with the colonization of subjectivity implicit in the formation of a dominant, expansive culture. Its emphasis on the invention of America is strategically designed to debunk a contemporary complacency with the historic, geographic, and cartographic rudiments underlying our present picture of the world.

As I envision it, a critique of dominant and established modes of understanding the New World calls for an opening of factualism to a paradoxical terrain that precludes closure. Let us define *factualism* with the following remarks about modern scholarship

8

by Friedrich Nietzsche in *The Use and Abuse of History*: "The measurement of the opinions and deeds of the past by the universal opinions of the present is called 'objectivity' by these simple people. They find the canon of all truth here: their work is to adapt the past to the present triviality and they call all historical writing 'subjective' that does not regard these popular opinions as canonical."[13] The quote speaks for itself; my only remark is that such a "canon of all truth" must be dismantled as a preliminary task toward a decolonization of subjectivity. However, it is not a dismantling by factual contradiction—that is, by establishing that early versions of the New World were "wrong," imposed, or distortions of reality—but rather by destabilizing the ground of factuality itself. It is a counterfiction as a means of trying the dominance of Western institutional fictions that is of interest here, and definitely not a straightening out of the record.

This study builds on recent work in discourse analysis and a critique of representation that is developing in such varied fields as anthropology, literature, history, and cartography. My basic premise is this: verbal texts, maps, icons, and other cultural products should be taken as rhetorical artifices and not as depositories of data from which a factual truth may be construed. Rhetoric, in this sense, is not simply an art of persuasion, but also implies strategic moves that constitute forms of subjectivity and produce what Roland Barthes called an "effect of the real."[14] Let us briefly look into the relevance of Barthes's analysis of "reality effects" for a critique of colonial discourse.

In "The Discourse of History," Barthes isolated two operations in the production of the "real" in historical discourse. A first operation separates the "referent" from discourse and gives it an extralinguistic existence—events are constituted as *res gestae* and discourse as *historia rerum gestarum*; in other words, it is presumed that facts have extralinguistic existence and that discourse merely tells their meaning. A second operation enmeshes meaning, the signified, with the referent; thus the discourse of history creates a semantic schema with two terms: the signifier and the referent. The elimination of the signified in history prompts the "effect of the real" with an insistent repetition: "it happened." And also claimed, by extension, is a direct access to reality and a referential plenitude in representation. We can foreground two implications Barthes's analysis of "the effect of the real" has for a study of sixteenth-century historiography of the New World. On the one hand, it should alert us to how contemporary readings might project our "real(s)" with no attention paid to their production, nor to their often paradoxical expression in sixteenth-century texts. We must indeed attend to the artificiality and the blind spots that early modern practitioners of *conceit* were so fond of displaying in their apparently closed and coherent historical, iconographical, and cartographic representations. On the other hand, we must underscore that it is not only the production of mere reality effects that comes into play in the colonial writing of the world, but also the subjugation of indigenous knowledges that accompanies the emergence of a Eurocentric worldview. But here again the zeal of the inquisitor-ethnographer to register every detail about native culture—its understanding of the self and the literal as well as symbolic dimensions of language—constitutes an invaluable testimony of resistance and of the ever-present alternative readings and usages of European modes of representation.

It should be obvious by now that I am interested here, not in defining and then applying a cogent theory, but in exploring some of the new dimensions of Western poststructuralist thinkers within the general area of a critique of "colonial discourse." The transformations poststructuralist theories undergo in displacements of geography manifest instances of what Angel Rama called "transculturation" and Edward Said has more recently charted with the apt metaphor of "traveling theory."[15]

The term "colonial discourse" in itself reveals transformations in poststructuralist thought as it grafts colonial situations and cultural artefacts into the analysis of discourse as defined by Hayden White, Roland Barthes, and especially Michel Foucault. Edward Said's definition of orientalism as a discursive formation is perhaps the earliest formulation of colonial discourse, though it is not yet named as such. Orientalism (i.e., colonialism understood as a form of discourse) suggests a whole set of questions that point to how Europe systematically produced large portions of the non-European world, in our case the New World, through political, military, ideological, scientific, and imaginative kinds of writing and imagery.[16] Yet Said not only borrows but also transforms Foucault's dissolution of the subject and call for a history without proper names: "Yet unlike Michel

Foucault . . . I do believe in the determining imprint of individual writers. . . . Accordingly my analyses employ close textual readings whose goal is to reveal the dialectic between individual text or writer and the complex collective formation to which his work is a contribution."[17]

By taking into account the agency of individual writers, Said would ultimately seek to override Foucault's formulations of discourse and power, which make insufficient allowances for resistance.[18] But Said's insistence on individual texts also opens the possibility of understanding the specific interaction of writers and texts with the discursive formation that defines who has the authority to speak and what is legitimate knowledge. This appeal to dialectic spaces of intervention suggests ways of reading how texts vary, alter, and challenge, if not subvert, the rules of a hegemonic discourse. Said's call for historical agency, for something beyond the reach of dominating systems, is not extraneous to the "personal dimension" that charts, at least partially, the study of orientalism as "an attempt to inventory the traces upon me, the Oriental subject, of the culture whose domination has been so powerful a factor in the life of all Orientals."[19] However, there is a danger here of conflating the predicaments of a Third World elite and its decolonizing agenda with the interests of disempowered or marginalized groups. It borders with a self-ascription of otherness and thus constitutes the temptation, in Gayatri Spivak's diagnosis, of aligning oneself with the subaltern.[20]

And yet we should not reduce subalternity to some kind of privileged perspective on power and oppositional consciousness. Equally dangerous, as Spivak has pointed out, are Foucault's and Gilles Deleuze's transparency when they argue that subalterns "know far better than [the intellectual] and they certainly say it very well."[21] To the question, Can the subaltern speak?, Spivak answers in the negative, and if pressed with examples she would retort by questioning our authority to stage speaking subalterns. Spivak's negative, however, would not necessarily exclude such instances of colonized subjects defracting power as those Homi Bhabha has isolated in the case of India,[22] and those that can be amply documented with numerous colonial texts from Peru and Mexico. For instance, Rolena Adorno has analyzed the semiotic and discursive stratagems developed by the Peruvian

Indian historian Felipe Guamán Poma de Ayala to appropriate and subvert, if not violate, the pictorial spatial code, alphabetical writing, humanist historiographical precepts, and a Western sense of linear history: "The violation of the pictorial spatial code denies again and again the notion that justice and order could rein under the Spanish colonial regime." But these forms of resistance ultimately partake of Guamán Poma's "failure to believe in its [language's] power to communicate; his use of the language of persuasion stands sentinel over his lack of belief in its power."[23] Moreover, as Frank Salomon has shown, indigenous histories are fundamentally "chronicles of the impossible" precisely because they try to reconcile two incompatible understandings of history, where the European conceptualization thwarts the pursuit of a genuine native historiography.[24]

In chapter 3 I attempt to hint at how the informants of the Franciscan missionary-ethnographer Bernardino de Sahagún managed to inscribe their ethnicity in spite of (and as a result of) a tension that arises from the need to use European discourse to express ideas foreign to it. The obscurity to which sixteenth-century indigenous histories were condemned until very recently manifests their incapacity to "speak" (their speech was interrupted by a censure that disqualified the validity of their discourse as well as that of such interlocutors with the crown as Sahagún);[25] consequently, we should be weary of posing ourselves as transparent intellectuals and heed Spivak's questions about our position as we "stage" or tease the "meanings" of their actions. To paraphrase Roy Wagner, in the act of inventing Indian historiography we invent our own, and, in fact, we reinvent the notion of historiography itself. In the process we should aspire to a disappearance of the thinking that silenced Indian historians and confined them to the status of subalterns.

As Spivak has reminded us in her discussion of how Foucault's notion of the dissolution of the Subject betrays "a Subject of the West . . . that presides by disavowal," Derridian deconstruction entails a relentless questioning of what enables one's knowledge and authority.[26] In studying Indian historians and European visual and literary cultural artifacts that self-consciously court paradox, we should practice an affirmative deconstruction. Perhaps nothing is less difficult than to "demonstrate" the traces of colonization in native texts that in one way or another had to conform to the colonial order of ideas. Such a deconstruction, by placing its emphasis on a reading of the texts as bearing the "influence" of the colonizers, would neutralize them and reiterate their evaluation as lacking coherence or being imperfect imitations of European texts. An affirmative deconstruction, as I understand it, would trace how under the veneer of a (commonly judged unsuccessful) imitation of Western historiography, indigenous texts elaborate alternative modes of representation and historifying. On the other hand, we should also inventory the blind spots and undecidables that European practitioners of *conceit* have traditionally been fond of displaying in apparently closed, totalizing representations and interpretations of reality.

But let us look at how Derrida's concept of undecidability and endless interpretation in "The Double Session" undergoes profound modifications in Homi Bhabha as it gives place to the question of the ambivalence of colonial authority and to a mapping of colonialist strategies of disavowal, "a discrimination between mother culture and its bastards, the self and its doubles, where the trace of what is disavowed is not repressed but repeated as something *different*—a mutation, a hybrid." We can further refine our initial comments on Barthes's "effect of the real" and the subjection of native knowledges; now the issue is the incapacity of colonized subjects to reproduce the cultural system of the metropolis. It is not a question, as in Derrida or Barthes, of how an "effect of presence" fixes contents in plenitude, but of how the structured gaze of power imposes its authority and introduces a differential sense of order. For Bhabha the specificity of colonial power would call for "a theory of 'hybridization' of discourse and power that is ignored by Western poststructuralists who engage in the battle for 'power' as the purists of difference."[27] If for Foucault it is the omnipresence of power that needs to be accounted for, if in the metropolis a small group is representative of the whole, then Bhabha reminds us that in colonial situations it is also a part that rules over a whole, but the representation is now based on its radical difference (through various modes of discrimination, e.g., cultural, racial, administrative).

The dichotomy "dominant/dominated" is, of course, too simplistic—but for reasons very different from those expressed by Foucault and from the intact extrapolations by such colonial historians as Serge Gruzinski.[28] For hegemonic power, the discourse of Europe's unity vis-à-vis the rest of the world always remains the discourse of a possibility. Furthermore, there are indeed whole sets of variations in the colonial order. For one, the exercise of power is not a simple exercise of commands but a subjugation of indigenous knowledges and a definition of problematic neophytes to Western culture and religion. But colonial power thus constitutes the hybrid, the ambivalence of an undecidable and elusive subject that seems to reiterate, to mime colonial authority, but in the end only reveals (blinds) the eye of power in its subversion. Hybridity would thus enable displacing the quandary of most postcolonials, who, as Spivak has put it, "are still interested either in proving that they are ethnic subjects and therefore the true marginals or that they are as good as the colonials."[29]

I have insisted on these theoretical underpinnings and exemplary readings of colonial texts to foreground and illustrate the "hybridity" inherent to a critique of colonial discourse.[30] It is not a preference for some sort of eclectic approach that is at stake in such a critique, but a predicament not unlike that of Salomon's "chroniclers of the impossible." Moreover, colonial situations, as Walter Mignolo has pointed out, call for diatopical, if not pluritopical, understandings.[31] Readings of colonial texts are comparativist insofar as they are required to trace the intersection of two or more cultures and attend to different conceptualizations of the world and the self. Attending to pluritopical cultural spaces necessarily exposes Eurocentrism as a construct. While fully cognizant of thinking and writing within a poststructuralist intellectual milieu that quite often has overlooked its Eurocentricism, the critique of colonial discourse, as I envision it in this study, would ultimately attempt to construe alternative histories. I must add that the history of Latin America can be read as the constant construction of alternative histories and subjectivities. And in this respect Jean Franco's *Plotting Women*[32] is worthy of mention as an exemplary instance of rewriting history, of construing another subjectivity. Therefore, the "use" of poststructuralist theories (as well as others available in the theoretical marketplace today) does not consist of adopting and applying a menu of (what for some would seem incompatible) methods, but to experiment with their propositions, question their epistemological grounds, suspend claims to universality, and taunt requirements of theoretical purity or demands of consistency. The object of study relevant to a critique of colonialism and imperialism often leads us to question the claims and assumptions of theories formulated exclusively with Western texts, categories, or historical situations in mind.

In chapter 1 a methodology is introduced. I establish a contrast between a seventeenth-century paradoxical reading of an allegorical representation of America by Jan van der Straet and a series of contemporary reductive factual captions and commentaries. From this contrast I critique binary and scientistic oppositions between the real and the fantastic, the historical and the allegorical, and the written and the oral. I show how the possibility of comprehending this allegorical representation presupposes an encyclopedic thesaurus of motifs—a thesaurus whose production can be charted in terms of four main moments. As such, the moments are not so much defined by the awareness of the participants or epistemological capabilities as by the body of knowledge and forms of discourse that emerge in the course of the sixteenth century. These knowledges and discursive modes of organizing and articulating America's "reality" will imply a transformation of the conditions of possibility of writing about the world in general. These moments in the invention of America structure chapters 2–5 of this book. They should be seen as sequential, but also as overlapping. For in the end what is important about the sequence of moments is less a diachronic staging than the cultural system that defines each moment and makes the specific texts possible.

Chapter 2 elaborates the first of these moments by examining how Columbus's writings create the notion of a *new world* intimately bound to the production of examples of newness. Simile and metaphor rule the task of describing phenomena without precedent. On the basis of marvelous phenomena (which not only comprise unheard-of natural and anthropological particulars but also invoke a benevolent climate and the belief in a higher region of the world in the vicinity of Paradise), the New World is first conceptualized as a different ontological region. The age-old themes of the exotic, the millenium, and the noble savage mediate a process of differentiation between the new and the old. This chapter also traces Columbus's projections of

Marco Polo into the American landscape, as well as the problems Columbus faced when describing phenomena without precedent in the European stock of knowledge. Chapter 2 thus provides a detailed study of how Columbus's writings constitute an inaugural moment in the invention of the New World. The crucial task is not so much how Columbus draws from the old to inform about the new but the predicament of describing the new in its own terms precisely because he did not find the lands visited by medieval travelers. Chapter 2 attempts to point out how a new text of the "Far East" surfaced in conjunction with the concepts of a *new man* and a *new world*.

The second moment in the invention of America sees a reduction of the notion of a *new world* into a geographic concept denoting and naming a new region of space. This process is most visible in the initial reception of Amerigo Vespucci's letters (c. 1500). As an example of this moment, chapter 3 studies the production of "Mexico" as an object for conquest in Cortés's letters to Charles V (1519–26). It attempts to differentiate the discourse of conquest from that of exploration. Whereas the explorer projects the "city" into an ideal garden, the conquistador finds in Tenochtitlan the code of the garden registered in the mode of the market, the botanical garden, the zoo, the book, and so on. For the conquistador the codification of the land is no longer exclusively that of natural phenomena, but involves appropriation of the indigenous text he finds in the city. Chapter 3 also provides an analysis of Cortés's representation of his dialogue with Moctezuma in the light of Hegel's famous passage on the Master/Slave relation in *The Phenomenology of Mind*. Beyond this representation of the encounter between the two cultures, the indigenous version of the conquest in the *Florentine Codex* reveals the other side of the dialogue. Within a broader historical panorama, this chapter makes a larger claim as it attempts to show how Cortés's understanding of dialogue as conquest constitutes an overarching determinant of the modern anthropological enterprise.

In the third moment of invention we see the accumulation of data under the rubric *New World* from which particular encyclopedic compendia eventually take form toward the middle of the sixteenth century. These *summas* constitute coded thematic blocks drawn from those originally motivating the notion of a *new world*. For example, the exotic predominates in the descriptions of the crown's official chronicler and settler of Hispaniola Gonzalo Fernández de Oviedo, the millenarian is spotlighted by the Franciscan ethnographers of Mesoamerican civilizations, and the noble savage figures prominently in the polemical writings of Bartolomé de Las Casas. Chapter 4 analyzes how these dominant themes are invoked to reconstitute an original New World. But the *new time* of the encyclopedias defines description as concerned not solely with items but with a whole √ field of reference, of registered facts and opinions. The European presence in the New World becomes an integral element in the descriptions. The encyclopedias also provide alternative (conceptual) *narratives* of a corruption, a fall from an original full presence implicit in the two earlier moments. This reconstitution is analyzed against the background of chapter 4, which provides a historical overview of the effect that colonization had on the indigenous population.

As I have already pointed out apropos of Stradanus's allegory, the fourth moment consists of a virtual thesaurus in the complex of particular encyclopedias from which unlimited combinations of motifs can be elaborated. Beyond Spanish-American historiography, chapter 5 concentrates on the appropriation and reorganization of Spanish data in Gerhard Mercator's *Atlas*. Indeed, the *Atlas* undoes the semantic closure imposed by a Spanish historiography increasingly preoccupied with Spain's retention of its domains. In Mercator's text, an ideal universal subject constructs an "objective" picture of the world, where an equally ideal universal plurality of readers can project their interests without altering the stability of a whole. In the analysis of the *Atlas*, the rise of secularism as well as the universality of European history and subjectivity emerge as examples of a Eurocentric worldview still influential today. In the last analysis, however, the universal plurality of subjective appropriations includes the possibility of reinventing the world from a non-European perspective.

Secularism does not constitute, therefore, a new moment, but √ a specific strategy within the fourth moment. Whereas Spanish historiography must establish a semantic register of its dominions, a secular version must subject Spanish data to syntactical rearrangements. Such a secular rearrangement is an instance of the fourth moment. The rise of secularism is part of the invention of America; it is not a consequence. In order not to be trapped by the universality of reason, in the Hegelian sense of the term, we must analyze secularism as one more example of invention, however powerful it turns out to be in the context of a Euro-centric worldview.

I must emphasize again that by Eurocentrism I do not simply mean a tradition that places Europe as a universal cultural ideal embodied in what is called the West, but rather a pervasive condition of thought. It is universal because it affects both Europeans and non-Europeans, despite the specific questions and situations each may address. As Bryan S. Turner has amply documented in *Marx and the End of Orientalism*, Marxism itself is plagued with Hegelian, Eurocentric conceptual devices. Turner's study is not only a critique of Eurocentric approaches "but in large measure a work of personal de-colonization."[33] Although the critique of Hegelianisms in Marx is indissoluble from the question of colonization, I would like to underline the call for a decolonization of subjectivity. Since our investigation concentrates on an earlier period, our concern with Hegel is anachronistic; thus as we trace moments in the invention of America, we must not only avoid imposing a Hegelian grid but also destroy the ground upon which Marx, Hegel, and all models of "development" or acculturation build their historical stages.[34]

After Jacques Derrida we read prefaces as a kind of chitchat. We avoid them, or we call them other names, or we weave them with ironic moves that signal their posterior production and mock their traditional role of defining how to read the main body of the text. But there is something more to introductory remarks. For if prefaces say what is realized at the end, that ending might very well be an oral text that we have elaborated all along but have chosen to leave out in the process of writing. Writing cannot be reduced to that silent, private affair that I am engaging in right now. It also involves a public space where we converse, participate in conferences, discover audiences, witness growing literatures — events that shape to a great extent the type of texts we produce. Thus introductions also function as sites for a reinscription of one's enterprise within an evolving field of discourse.

I began my research on the invention of America in 1979, when I came to the United States from Mexico to do graduate studies in the History of Consciousness Program at the University of California at Santa Cruz. At that time there was little talk about a Columbian quincentennial, Tzvetan Todorov's *Conquest of America* had not been published yet, and Said's *Orientalism* was about to inaugurate a new situation in studies of colonialism. As I have already pointed out, Foucault's work played a fundamental role in the definition of Said's questions. Given my concern with sixteenth-century historiography of the New World, the most immediately suggestive, related text of Foucault for my project was *Les mots et les choses*, translated as *The Order of Things*. That text, however, presented many inconsistencies with respect to the writing of America. The conjunction of the three epigraphs to this book sum up what caused for me a certain quizzical distance from the dominant, mutually exclusive epistemes of the Renaissance and the Classical Age.

All three passages raise questions about the status of proper names. Foucault ignores proper names as a method. Although in the context of Montaigne's essay we learn that *le Roy* is Mexican, Montaigne fails to tell us he is Cuauhtémoc, the last Aztec ruler. El Inca, as he signals his mestizo origins by juxtaposing this epithet to his father's surname, Garcilaso de la Vega, renders problematic the reception of his history in a society that identifies truthfulness with being an Old Christian [*cristiano viejo*], that is, on purity of blood [*limpieza de sangre*]. Moreover, El Inca, in his history of De Soto's expedition, identifies himself with Indians in Florida and thus demonstrates the interiorization of the term *indio* and an identification with all Amerindians regardless of cultural differences. However learned and skilled El Inca is in European letters, his subject position in the text reminds us how important proper names were in the sixteenth century, especially in colonial situations. Specifications of this nature led me to question Foucault's formalist proposal.

It would make a great difference if, for instance, the man at the doorway in *Las meninas* was not an anonymous unknown—not El Inca, for he was dead by 1656, when Diego Velázquez painted *Las meninas*—but another *indio* weaving his way through the palatial hallways of the crown. We could hardly resist interpreting this figure as a symbol of cultural intervals. Likewise, it is important to know who the king is in Montaigne, and that it is not

19

Humanist tradition, est. authority thru citation.

Cuauhtémoc who is reflected in the mirror behind Velázquez. Montaigne and El Inca foreground European expansionism, a total absence in Foucault's archeology of the human sciences. Montaigne is indeed too concerned with writing and exploring his subjectivity to be reducible to a dominant episteme. Foucault quite correctly reminded us that "Man" was a recent invention of Western culture; but his history unfolds as if the European colonization of the world never took place, as if the formation of Eurocentrism did not play a role in the emergence of the human sciences, as if talk about the dissolution of man was not complicitous with a definition of European subjectivity as universal.

I would like to ignore the fact that I am writing in English, to pretend that no one would question my language choice, to pass unperceived as a Mexican who has adopted a foreign, often oppressive tongue to Spanish America. If this was a book in the social sciences or even in formalist literary criticism, or if the intent of this book was to explain sixteenth-century Spanish-American historiography to an English-speaking audience, an excursus on language motivation would be superfluous; however, it behooves the critic of colonial discourse to be accountable for her or his usages of natural as well as theoretical languages. To write in English is hardly a casual affair in Latin American history. As the Nicaraguan poet Rubén Darío reminded us at the turn of the century, in his poem "A Roosevelt," Spanish is perhaps the last bastion of U.S. colonization of Spanish America, "de la América ingenua que . . . aún habla español" [of the ingenuous America that . . . still speaks Spanish]. The adoption of English by a Mexican, at best, would suggest someone who is courting the English-speaking establishment; at worst, it would convey someone who has sold out, a *pocho*, a Mexican who has adopted North American manners and values. But there is a colonialist impulse in those perceptions that would have Chicanos as their most immediate target, often forgetting that to exist in the intervals of cultures and languages is not a choice. For better or for worse, this book testifies to English as the lingua franca of our time.

One could perhaps shun value judgments by evoking Caliban's curse of Prospero. But the Caliban gesture (as a Spanish-versus-English dilemma) would obviate accounting for the Spanish colonization of the indigenous peoples of the Americas; and consequently, it would also tend to confuse the territory I can claim as a Spanish-speaking Latin American with the field of a discipline that should include a plurality of non-European tongues and territorial perspectives laying equally valid claims.[35] Such distinctions, however, are of very recent vintage and by and large reminiscent of decolonizing agendas among Third World intellectuals in a postcolonial condition of thought. My positioning as postcolonial might seem mystifying to Latin American readers accustomed to a lengthy independent history. If I adopt the denomination *postcolonial* usually favored by Indian, Middle Eastern, African, Australian, New Zealand, and Canadian intellectuals, as well as by writers from the Anglo and Francophone Caribbean (and others), it is to acknowledge their contributions to the field and situate my immediate audience as one engaged in one form or another, in one language or another, in the critical study of colonialism, in minority discourse, or in the deconstruction of Eurocentrism.[36] English is indeed also a means to reach a more general audience concerned with issues and topics related to the European colonization of the globe that results from Columbus's inaugural voyage in 1492.

Beyond an investigation of Spanish-American historiography and the nature of America's text in general, this study aspires to elaborate an essay in countercolonial thinking. I prefer the prefix *counter-* to *anti-* because it does not necessarily suggest a position outside colonialism, but one attempting to work its way out from within. Whereas *anti-* implies the formulation of an alternative master discourse, *counter-* pursues the terrain of a minor form of discursivity. As a Mexican, my writing in English would further reinstate the notion of countering from within. To adopt English as a means, then, implies not simply a preference for a vehicle but also the possibility of altering the tenor. For if, as Talal Asad has argued, the anthropological enterprise is vitiated by an inequality of languages, then a starting point, a point of contention, is the weakening of stronger languages.[37] The culturally complex New World is in itself a product of stronger European languages (obviously not just English), which constitute territories for colonization as well as subject its peoples to cultural translations whereby they come to resemble Europeans. Thus America is from the start orientalized, and not simply because Columbus mistook it for India, but on account of his reduction of its different peoples to Indians (good or bad pending their function within his schemes) and his implementation of a colonializing process whose long-lasting effects rebound in today's Third World.

and First, if intro is to hold up. And, what about lumping all colonized together?

CHAPTER 1

The Nakedness of America?

THE THESAURUS IN PARADOX

Jan van der Straet (1523–1605), better known as Johannes Stradanus, is well known among Americanists for the engraving representing Amerigo Vespucci and "America" (fig. 1, pt. 1), an
engraving that is in itself a variation of an original drawing (fig.
1, pt. 2). As the credits for the engraving and printing of the
drawing point out at the bottom of the plate, Stradanus worked in
close collaboration with Theodore Galle and Phillipe Galle. The
Galles, a family of artists, engravers, and printers from Antwerp,
were not only responsible for the copper plates but also for the
first captions to the drawings Stradanus sent them from Florence.
In the process of engraving they subjected the drawing to a series
of alterations; for instance, the positions of Amerigo and America were inverted and they erased the word *America*, written
backwards as if uttered by Vespucci. These alterations suggest
that the Galles took Stradanus's geographic orientation as a
playful mirror effect marked by the word *America*. They also
added the emblematic Southern Cross to the banner and erased
the written identification of Vespucci as a Florentine: thus, the
allegory gains ambiguity by reducing information.

In the hands of the Galles, the allegory appears in two
different printing formats. The first was designed as a wall
decoration. The second appears in a collection of prints in a book
format entitled *Speculum diversarum imaginum speculativarum*
(1638). *Nova reperta* and *America retectio* comprise two main
sections of the collection. The engraving of Vespucci and America

23

Ioan. Stradanus invent.
Theodor Galle fecit.

Figure 1. Vespucci's "tearing" of the veil would suggest an awakening of America from a slumber akin to that of the sloth. Part 1 (above). *"America." In Jan van der Straet, Nova reperta (1638). Courtesy Burndy Library, Norwalk, Conn. Part 2 (below). "Discovery of America: Vespucci Landing in America," Flemish, sixteenth to seventeenth century. Courtesy The Metropolitan Museum of Art, Gift of the Estate of James Hazen Hyde, 1959. (1974.205) All rights reserved, The Metropolitan Museum of Art.*

forms part of the *Nova reperta* that gathers together a series of twenty plates representing modern discoveries.

Stradanus's late sixteenth-century allegory of the Old World's encounter with the New is, in itself, but a speckle in the archive. The engraved version assumes monumental import, however, in its recurrence as an iconographic example, or illustration, in a series of texts about the exploration of the New World.[1] In the first part of this chapter I give a sort of Geertzian, thick description of the allegory—a phenomenology of its leading, eliciting features—and examine it in the light of a paradoxical caption written by the Galles in the seventeenth century. The second part of the chapter is concerned with contemporary commentators who write reductive and naïve captions that tend merely to repeat what they take to be the "obvious" meaning of Stradanus (as it were, thin descriptions that fail "to sort winks from twitches and real winks from mimicked ones").[2] The problem with these latter-day captions is that they transform the allegory into a repository of true statements about the discovery. The playful mirror effect manifest in the drawing ultimately confirms the ironic and paradoxical import of the engraving. As a critique of dominant contemporary understandings of America, this chapter, then, provides a sort of prolegomenon to the analysis of the New World as an invention.

An apparent opposition between "discoverer" and "discovered" surfaces as we trace a temporal movement from the entering caravel in the upper left-hand corner to the quizzical glance of the beast (an anteater) in the lower right-hand corner. These two motifs point to opposite organizing principles in the allegorization of the encounter: while the entering ship symbolizes the course of history, the strange beast betokens the naturalness of America. They lend support to the contrast between Vespucci (an individual historical figure) and America (an abstract). In between, the astrolabe and the gold band on America's calf mark other possible key motifs for reading the allegory. But as one's gaze returns to the center of the tableau, America's pointing index finger reorganizes the play of forces; it signals conceit and jest in its conception. Simultaneously, it points to Vespucci and to a background scene of anthropophagi cooking a human leg; in the background, the finger calls our attention both to this New World commonplace and to the vanishing point constituting the illusive three-dimensional space that highlights the casting of Vespucci and America in the foreground, as if within a theatrical stage.

As one returns to the interlocutors, a most naïve reading of the tableau in terms of a dressed navigator and a nude Amerindian proves irresistible. The traces of epistemological, moral, and aesthetic agencies disappear under the spell of a lifelike representation. As an allegory, by definition, it conveys a literal as well as a figurative meaning. The discriminating reader will, of course, see through the *allegoresis* and observe that America is a figurative feminization of the land, or even a sublimated representation of ubiquitous testimonies in New World accounts of erotic and voracious Amerindian women. And yet this sort of figurative reading does not necessarily exclude a literal meaning that credits Vespucci for the "discovery" since after all he "named" her. But as we become seduced by its realism, America loses its abstract quality. The same spatial prominence of Vespucci and America blurs the threshold separating the event from its allegorical representation. Indeed, it becomes just an "allegory" of Vespucci's discovery of America. The limen distinguishing the figurative from the historical disappears when we ignore America's finger pointing at the "discoverer."

Thus surfaces an apparent opposition between nature and culture, not only in relation to the nude and the dressed, but also in the supporting materials for representing the central interlocutors. The essence and destiny of Europe is symbolized by the historical actor, whereas the American continent is confined to a series of separate, individual representatives wandering without direction or meaning. The significance of American motifs is thus reduced to the context of a European abstraction of the New World. This hierarchization of the two continents subsumes the depicted dialogue under the monotonous murmur of a European monologue fantasizing a New World. Accordingly, the naturalness of America is a mere mirage of European culture and its exploits. The emergence of America marks its loss of identity. It becomes merely a "naked body" for the inscriptions and longings of a European imagination.

As we imagine the American motifs lending support to the notion of a nude America, we encounter, besides the anteater, other beasts suggesting a state of enervation. Hanging from the tree is a sloth, whose contours are barely recognizable. And right under the sloth is a hybrid depiction of a tapir that displays a European inclination to represent and classify American fauna within the monstrous. Along with the monstrous (which must be specifically American so that hybrid traits do not blend with specimens contained in Old World bestiaries and teratologies), there is a tendency toward a formalization of particular features first derived from oral and written sources. The familiarity and authority of these prior texts lend credibility to the depiction of New World animals as they pass from source to source.

A well-known example is the correspondence between the opossum described by Vicente Yáñez Pinzón and Martin Wald-seemüller's drawing of an opossum in the *Carta marina* (1516). As Wilma George points out: "This particular animal of Wald-seemüller was traced off on to many later maps, sometimes facing one way, sometimes the other and becoming progressively formalized."[3] From George's remark we may speak of an errancy of features from four perspectives (not exclusively with respect to the animals, but also with respect to the anthropophagi, the hammock, and the paddle casually resting against the tree). First, verbal comparisons take features from Old World proto-types for the constitution of a new animal. Second, the crystal-lization of similes into images erases the "like" of the compari-sons. Third, the process of formalization makes less prominent the juxtaposition of different species by accentuating a particular feature at the expense of others. Fourth, as particular features become readily recognized in the process of formalization, they take different significations according to the particular contexts in which they occur.

For an allegorist such as Stradanus the inclusion of an animal becomes a means for imprinting a symbolic "newness" upon a representation of the New World. We must observe that the sloth does not simply correspond to a depiction of one more animal, but functions symbolically to suggest a sense of torpor in the fauna. This quality ultimately congeals into a languid quiescence in the depiction of America just discovered napping in a ham-mock.

All the American motifs appear slightly out of focus if one compares them to the supporting emblems surrounding Vespuc-ci. The astrolabe, the sword, and the caravel set the inscriptional power of Vespucci, as well as being instruments of discovery and conquest. Among the American motifs, on the other hand, the lack of focus reinforces notions of a nude America, dependent on the supporting emblems for its identification. But the southern cross on the banner testifies that America was never subject to an empirical glance. Moreover, this detail erases the dichotomy between supportive motifs; Vespucci can be identified only with a New World symbol. Thus the allegory generates a transparent view of the event by means of a careful arrangement of features. This transparency of the event is further reinforced as the sleepy attributes of the sloth induce a "veil" over the representation of America and its supportive motifs. Vespucci's "tearing" of the veil would suggest an awakening of America from a slumber akin to that of the sloth.

As New World specimens appear in the context of an allegory, the renderings of Americana become descriptive motifs with symbolic value. Their symbolic function within an allegorical terrain, moreover, presupposes a thesaurus for their more or less ready identification as examples of novelties found in the New World. The drawing of the sloth, which for instance does not appear in sixteenth- and seventeenth-century maps,[4] introduces an interpretative subtlety. In early descriptions of unprecedented phenomena one finds thingamajigs (something hard to classify, a fortiori to depict, whose name is not known) and monsters (hybrids, whose combination of parts from known specimens jeopardize novelty by being subsumed under patterns prefigured in medieval teratologies). The process by which the descriptions gain resolution and become descriptive motifs as sine qua non for representing the New World seems to be allegorized as an awakening of America. The formation of a cluster of motifs associated with Brazil also suggests the production of a New World that Vespucci first set in motion but which can only be associated with his name retrospectively.

My aim here is obviously not to deny the empirical veracity of a land first discovered by Vespucci in favor of another contender to the title (Columbus, the Vikings, or the Chinese, among others), but to question the formation of such statements about a first discovery and the criteria that constitute them as historical truths. This study attempts to avoid the powerful illusion generated by a rhetoric based on scientific truth; the crediting of

Vespucci tends to be ideological because it confuses a form of understanding the voyages of discovery with the contents of its proposition. Vespucci's voyages can certainly be understood and reconstructed from our conception of the world. By crediting Vespucci, however, one transforms the explorer into a proto-scientist who enunciates geographic claims that anticipate our criteria of scientific truth. If the reconstruction of Vespucci's voyages in terms of our own geographic conceptions appears as a valid method among others for tracing the territories he ex-plored, having Vespucci pass judgments in terms belonging to our understanding of scientific observations establishes a tele-ological validation of our fabrications of the real. The production of the real in contemporary historiography has been likened by Michel de Certeau to the trompe l'oeil of the baroque, but as de Certeau quickly adds, this is profoundly different "from the trompe l'oeil of old in that it no longer furnishes any visible signs of its theatrical nature or of the code whereby it is fabricated."[5]

This is a most pertinent observation for analyzing Stradanus's playful allegory and contemporary naïve readings. As one moves back and forth between captions written in the seventeenth century and our own, one cannot fail to notice that contemporary commentaries tend to adhere to factual statements within an all too certain historical vantage point. Our dull readings, not exempt from a lofty assurance of superiority, find themselves enclosed and overdetermined by an allegorical game. As a result, our factual reductions of the discovery of America mani-fest ideological variations on features that became available for allegorical representations of the New World toward the end of the sixteenth century.

A closer look at the conditions and implications of writing a paradoxical caption to Stradanus in the seventeenth century will prepare the ground for a critique of the scientific and binary oppositions that modern commentators have inscribed on the margins.

Stradanus, though born at Bruges, settled in Florence, where he remained until his death, which perhaps explains his admira-tion for Vespucci among the many illustrious children of that city.[6] We may presume that Stradanus realized, along with the commercial benefits to be derived from a mass production of his work, the sociopolitical domain of influence opened up by the printing press. Moreover, the importance of iconography for carrying out ideological battles within the baroque period cannot be overstressed in the context of the increasingly predominant visual mental habits that Walter Ong and more recently Johannes Fabian have analyzed apropos of the diffusion of Peter Ramus's teachings.[7] The sophisticated, self-conscious use of images remains unsurpassed up to our day. Indeed, it has often been remarked that in comparison with baroque extravaganza, our use and consumption of images seem undeveloped.

As I have pointed out at the beginning of this chapter, the allegory of America forms part of the *Nova reperta* in which a series of twenty plates praise such diverse modern discoveries as sugar cane, olive oil, the printing press, gunpowder, and the astrolabe (fig. 2). Curiously enough, this last plate represents not an astrolabe but Vespucci observing the Southern Cross, holding an armillary sphere. It also includes a quotation from Dante's *Divine Comedy* where the Florentine poet speaks of a constellation of four stars in "Purgatory":

> I turned to the right and set my mind
> on the other pole, and I noticed four stars
> never seen except by the first people. (1.23–27)

As Antonello Gerbi has pointed out, this passage is not only quoted by Vespucci but also suggests a reading of passages in Vespucci in the context of Dante's descriptions of Paradise in the last cantos of "Purgatory."[8] The assessment of a correspondent symbolism between Dante and Vespucci need not concern us here; it is important, however, to see how within the allegory literary space is translated into a visual representation.

Following Jacques le Goff's analysis of the birth of purgatory in the twelfth century in terms of a spatialization of thought, we may construe the reference to Dante as bespeaking an epistemological precondition of the invention of America and in particular to Stradanus's allegorical interpretation.[9] Intimately bound to a tendency starting in the thirteenth century to geographically locate the otherworldly (not only in Dante but in travelers such as Sir John Mandeville, Marco Polo, Giovanni da Pian del Carpini, and Willem van Ruysbroek) is, in Fabian's phraseology, a denial of coevalness.[10] The Southern Cross in

Figure 2. Curiously enough, this plate represents not an astrolabe but an armillary sphere. *Astrolabium.* In Jan van der Straet, Nova reperta *(1638). Courtesy Burndy Library, Norwalk, Conn.*

Vespucci's banner implies the allusion to Dante's stars, "never seen except by the first people." As we return to the depiction of America, she surfaces as a fallen Eve, emerging fully dressed, in leaves surrounding her hips. And the contrast with the naked anthropophagi in the background betrays both an anthropological and a historical statement. Not only does it constitute a common human lineage with reference to the "first people," but at the same time, by spatially locating the first men, it identifies a historical gap separating the Old and the New World.

Although a further anthropological distinction can be established between people with and without history — as if Vespucci planted a seed of time in the New World — we should be cautious not to fall into a binary trap. The caption written by the Galles, while it would seem to confirm the above interpretation, does so by forbidding a simple reduction of the allegory's signification: "America. Americen Americus retexit—Semel vocavit inde semper excitam" (America. Americus rediscovers America—he called her but once and thenceforth she was always awake [translation in Bern Dibner's edition]). Amerigo is seen as a temporal beginning, but whether he brings about the fall remains ambiguous, or more precisely it is unclear what the significance of the fall might be. The ample circulation of Fray Bartolomé de Las Casas's and Girolamo Benzoni's histories of the destruction of the Amerindian cultures would undoubtedly, by midcentury, taint the awakening. From another perspective, however, there is a play between the first part of the caption, which speaks in terms of rediscovery, and the attribute of a beginning in the awakening. The implicit reflection between Amerigo's name and the success of the name America for the continent further reinforces the paradox in specular circularity: Amerigo's significance and the meaning of America depend upon and mirror each other as they constitute together an ensemble of motifs. We can further document Stradanus's playfulness with Peter Hulme's remark that as Vespucci "utters" the word America, "he recognizes or speaks *her* name, which is *his* feminized."[11] Without getting entangled in possible mythological allusions to Narcissus and Echo, we can conclude that for the Galles the allegory called for a paradoxical caption.

Let us further clarify the implications of a paradoxical caption with a remark on paradox by Rosalie Colie: "The very 'infinite-

ness' of paradox, its open-endedness, is balanced by its tautology, for all paradoxes (especially those of self-reference) are
self-enclosed statements with no external reference point from
which to take a bearing upon paradox itself. Self-limited, they
deny limitation." If open-endedness and closure coexist in paradox, then, we may trace at least two possible readings of
paradoxes in general: one would merely repeat its tautology; the
other would seek to understand how self-limitation (the absence
of external reference) denies limitation. Modern commentators
betray a dull wit in their desire for closure without surprise; they
actually invert and lose sight of the delight to be derived from
paradox as Colie succinctly puts it: "The satisfactions of paradox
depend upon the frustrations of satisfaction in the ordinary
sense, then; the successful paradox can only satisfy by surprise,
by its twist, its gimmick."[12] The gimmicks of old are still
effective today, not for generating delight in conceptual play, but
for infusing blindness. The flaw, the blindness is in the audience,
and obviously not in Stradanus's tableau.

One may thus trace in the allegorical instant a murmuring past
that would reveal the conceptual mechanisms by which it produces its motifs, a present paradoxical reading in the context of
the seventeenth century, and the promise of a deliverance from
the entrapments of colonial discourse by a critique. As we trace
captions (along with contextual relocations) that have been
appended to the allegory in the course of history whereby the
meaning of the allegory is implicitly or explicitly defined, there
arises a whole arena where variant interpretations of the discovery of America confront one another. It consequently becomes
futile either to pursue the intentions of Stradanus or even to
unmask an ideology. It is not by chance that Vespucci is constantly portrayed as a protoscientific observer of natural and anthropological phenomena. Nor is it fortuitous that we remain enclosed by America's index finger pointing at Vespucci. America
signaling at her discoverer marks Stradanus's allegory as ironic
in terms of Quintilian's definition in the *Institutio oratoria*:
"That class of allegory in which the meaning is contrary to that
suggested by the words involves an element of irony, or as our
rhetoricians call it, *illusio*" (8.6.54).

The tableau is pregnant with an infinitude of possible contrary
meanings. America's pointing at Vespucci betrays a fallacious *post*

hoc, ergo propter hoc accreditation of Vespucci's discovery. As she points to the background, her significance is bound to the anthropophagi and the vanishing point enabling the three-dimensional representation of space. Thus, semantic *illusio* conjoins a reflexive display of the pictorial conventions that fabricate the spatial illusion. A spatial vanishing point converges with a vanishing point in history. This confluence of geometry and time marks the inseparability of the newness that characterizes the region from the geometric demarcation of the territory. Figural/literal, spatial/temporal, and symbolic/iconic dichotomies dissolve their oppositional character in Stradanus's location of the vanishing point on the roasting leg. Ultimately we may lend to the signaling America one of Charles Peirce's favorite quotations from Emerson, where the sphinx answers our queries: "Of thine eye I am eyebeam."[13]

Tentatively let us presume an acquaintance by Stradanus with Leonardo's theory of perspective in the so-called notebooks. As is well known, for Leonardo the structure of perspective corresponds with the structure of the eye.[14] Furthermore, Leonardo builds his theory of perspective on a curious notion of errant images traveling through the atmosphere; accordingly, the task of the painter is to discover new realms of reality. Leonardo's notion is compatible with the errancy of motifs I have outlined above.[15] On the one hand, Stradanus displays Leonardo's pictorial techniques for rendering a realistic representation. Stradanus also situates the eye of the observer within an ideal point in the north (playfully concealed in the mirror effect). Outside and inside correspond in the vertical flow from the eye to the vanishing point. On the other hand, the horizontal line extending from east to west in the foreground reiterates and thus reinforces (or questions in the mirror effect of the original drawing) Western conventions of reading and writing and, ultimately, of the course of history. He gives the technical unveiling of spatial illusion an unexpected turn as it highlights the dominant motif (anthropophagi become a commonplace after the early printings of Vespucci's letters), making the other, more obscure supporting motifs recognizable as samples of Americana. As such, Stradanus discloses not only a structured eye in the act of perception but also a structured cultural complex of American motifs in the act of conception. In passing, we may also remember that Leonardo wrote backward, as is the case with Stradanus's word "America" in the drawing. The grounds for differentiating the real from the fantastic collapse into a play of mirrors and cross-references. Furthermore, by merging the grounds of the iconic and the symbolic and by dissolving the dichotomy between subject and object, Stradanus displaces "otherness" from America to an origin of history and humanity—that is, to an alterity encompassing the ancestors of the observer. Along with the first men of Dante's "Purgatory" emerges the historical incarnation of the lost vision in a now privileged northern eye, perhaps the glimmer of a coming Eurocentric order of the world:

> The heavens seem to rejoice in their light.
> O region of the north widowed!
> Since you are denied that view. (1.25–27)

Vespucci's observation of the Southern Cross is slightly translocated from the mirage of an American landscape to an ambivalent rendering of Europe's historical chimeras. These interlacings of literary passages, technical devices, and a cluster of New World motifs that make up the means of representation of the allegory suggests Foucault's observations about the binary definition of the sign in the Classical Age: "From the Classical age, the sign is the *representativity* of the representation in so far as it is *representable*."[16] But the symptoms of a binary system in Stradanus's allegory belongs to the "games" the age of resemblance has left behind, rather than to a full correspondence of content and representation dictated by a science of order:

Games whose powers of enchantment grow out of the new kinship between resemblance and illusion; the chimeras of similitude loom up on all sides, but they are recognized as chimeras; it is the privileged age of *trompe-l'oeil* painting, of the comic illusion, of the play that duplicates itself by representing another play of the *quid pro quo*, of dreams and vision; it is the age of the deceiving senses; it is the age in which the poetic dimension of language is defined by metaphor, simile, and allegory.[17]

From this perspective, at least from the Galles' reading, Stradanus may be seen as an accomplished ironic allegorist. The symbolic import of his representation opens the interpretation of the allegory to infinity. But the same play between obvious and contrary meanings lays out the terrain where binarism will crystallize; this is the same terrain where our contemporaries project final interpretations: America is undressed, and a distinction between the real and the fantastic is superimposed on a symbolic play of errant features.

These ironic and paradoxical traits we have traced in the readings by the Galles, obviously, should be taken not as a unique representation of America but as a moment in the invention of America where newness is produced by means of discursive arrangements of more or less readily recognized descriptive motifs.

In passing we should observe that some of the commentators we will examine shortly write their captions to a version derived from *America pars decima* of the *Collectiones peregrinationum in Indiam orientalem et occidentalem*, otherwise known as the *Great and Small Voyages*, assembled by Théodore de Bry and his sons. The de Bry family's decision to exclude the caption from their printing of Stradanus's allegory partly explains the need to write a caption anew. As the allegory recurs in the context of de Bry's collection, it is juxtaposed with a series of plates illustrating passages from Vespucci that reveal his participation in the cruelty of the Spaniards toward the Amerindians. In the context of *America pars decima*, the negative appraisal of Vespucci is furthermore juxtaposed with benevolent versions of English voyagers in the New World: the opposition between Spaniard and Englishman translates into an appropriation of Stradanus in the context of a religious battleground where Catholicism is ultimately denounced as responsible for cruelties in the New World, if not in Europe as well. The de Bry collections were placed in the *Index exporgatorius*, within a class of books that could be read only after offensive passages had been deleted: matters dealing with religious questions were made illegible in censored versions.[18] Let these facts stand as one more indication of the ideological implications that accompany the writing, erasure, and rewriting of a caption as well as contextual reaccommodations.[19] While the seventeenth century took delight in reflexive works of illusion and propagandistic manipulations, we get entangled in their rhetorical virtuosity.

AMERICA UNDRESSED

The image of awakening America can be paralleled to a tendency Urs Bitterli has traced in the interpretations of voyages of discovery, from Columbus to David Livingstone, as creative deeds whereby the recently found territories are not merely discovered but actually come into existence in the act of their discovery. Following this notion of discovery as bringing into being, Bitterli appropriately diagnoses the symptoms of an invention of territories for appropriation: "The cultural chauvinism that has always concealed itself behind that manner of seeing things was also exercised in the terrain of international law, with the 'right of finding': in hoisting the flag, the discoverer tends to validate a claim of national sovereignty solely based on the factum—frequently difficult to prove—of an act without precedents."[20] But Bitterli limits himself to a denunciation of a cultural chauvinism that asserts the primacy of discovery to validate jurisdiction. The simplicity of this ideological unmasking (in the last instance an epistemological aberration in Bitterli's analyses), however, ignores the relationship between power and knowledge. Thus Bitterli proposes an evaluation of the history of exploration and ethnographic description from the standpoint of modern science: "Although since Vespucci there were always intents of scientific planning and realization of voyages, in the second era of discoveries appears more clearly than ever the type of the explorer properly speaking."[21] Vespucci accordingly becomes a protoscientist. For Bitterli the rise of the scientific method dates a second phase of voyages of exploration during the eighteenth century. Vespucci anticipates the properly called voyage of exploration of the second phase, which becomes possible only after "the intellectual and historical revolution effected by Descartes and Newton."[22] The program of Bitterli's history of European expansionism is succinctly put as follows: "This process will be examined from the basic question of whether those implicated in the aforementioned expansionism pretended to arrive at an understanding of the alien culture; and, if that was the case, by what means and to what degree of success; and, if they did not achieve it, what was the cause of their failure."[23] In Bitterli's history of expansionism three criteria evaluate registered data during the voyages: the intention to

comprehend other cultures, the epistemological means of comprehension, and the reason for their failure when that would be
the case.

Thus Bitterli disentangles the scientific knowledge of other
cultures from the colonialist penetration into Africa and Asia in
the nineteenth century: "But, in spite of everything, it is indis-
putable that the scientific labor of the imperialist epoch has great
importance."[24] Bitterli presumes that a scientific methodology
guarantees objective representations despite the imperialistic
context: science is taken at once as a panacea for overcoming
distortions and for evaluating premodern figures. I do not believe
such comfortable grounds for clearing up the historical archive
of Europe's colonial enterprise are any longer possible in the light
of Edward Said's *Orientalism*. From Said, one learns how the
notion of the "Orient" was constructed by Europeans, and that
the acquisition of knowledge about the entities populating the
Orient is immersed in power relations: "My contention is that
without examining Orientalism as a discourse one cannot possibly understand the enormously systematic discipline by which
European culture was able to manage — and even produce — the
Orient politically, sociologically, militarily, ideologically, scientifically, and imaginatively during the post-Enlightenment period."[25] The debate takes another form, no longer centering on an
appraisal of scientific objectivity, but on the pretended autonomy
of science from politics. Science itself becomes a mode of
producing the Orient for specific political purposes. Moreover,
Said's reference to a post-Enlightenment period does not necessarily undermine the power of objectification in earlier periods;
rather, it highlights the specific epistemological matrix that
informed and enabled nineteenth-century global imperialism.

As Bitterli moves on to document the "importance" of scientific observation in the "imperial epoch," he unwittingly opens
up a more complex penetration. Scientific research during that
time is important "to a great extent for having managed (by
means of exact descriptions, structural analyses, and the fixation
of an oral tradition) to leave a record of the ways of life of ethnic
groups immediately prior to technico-industrial cultural shock
of latter times, and, in many places, to have interested the same
inhabitants overseas in the inquiry — the scientific research about
their history and existence."[26] Along with the laudatory evalua-

tion of scientific observation runs an unconditional praise of "natives" beginning to study themselves. The universality of European history and subjectivity assumes a final hegemonic mode in the form of an orientalism from within. Domination thus achieves impunity and becomes imperceptible in the generalized validity of science as the ultimate achievement of mankind.

Such a scientific approach does not appear so clearly and innocuously objective when we take into account recent critiques of anthropology by James Boon, James Clifford, Johannes Fabian, and others.[27] The scientific apparatuses informing voyages from the Enlightenment on do not achieve a simple epistemological refinement, but rather produce two fields of observation that Daniel Defert characterizes as follows: "The identities of people were divided up with reference to the question of the state; there were people who inhabited states, and people who inhabited Nature. The opposition between Nature and Culture is not a grid which permits one to understand the origins of society; it is an historical division that the West erected between itself and the others."[28] The grounds for defining anthropology as the scientific study of peoples "without history" lie precisely in the given binary opposition between nature and culture. And this is the epistemological terrain where the theme of the noble savage (by means of an interiorization of the grid) crystallizes as a fetish, according to Hayden White's study.[29] The eighteenth century cannot provide a privileged point of reference, either moral or scientific. Moreover, the opposition between nature and culture that one could pursue in Stradanus's tableau itself reflects a later demand for closure in the allegory.

As Bitterli suggests a preference for Vespucci over Columbus as the true discoverer, he recapitulates Stradanus's celebration of "Amerigo the awakener of America" with an unreflective assertion of scientific veracity as the ultimate criterion for a timeless meaning of the term *discovery*.[30] Although Bitterli's study of European encounters with other cultures does not specifically address Stradanus's allegory, his otherwise highly informed and suggestive text conforms with such commentators as Jean Amsler and Hugh Honour. As the latter draw a distinction between fantastic and realistic elements in the allegory, they ignore the symbolic function of the motifs and indeed succumb to the illusion deftly elaborated by Stradanus. Take for instance this indication by Amsler: "Different animals from the New World—tapir, anteater, sloth—are treated with a touch of fantasy."[31] Honour provides a similar distinction: "At about the same time Stradanus must have found in the Tuscan Grand Ducal collection the models for the sloth and the anteater which he incorporated into his otherwise fantastic evocation of the discovery of America."[32] In a spirit analogous to Bitterli's scientism, Amsler and Honour pursue the objectivity of the representations without questioning whether the fantastic traits of the fauna bear a symbolic import; as with the sloth they would be preoccupied with its realism and not with the symbolic effect (a generalized state of enervation in the American motifs) its attributes infuse into the tableau.

The captions written by these commentators replay a naïve reading of an "obvious" meaning without apparently paying attention to the rhetorical strategies organizing the allegories. Honour's caption reads, "Vespucci 'discovering' America."[33] The hesitant quotations over *discovering* seem to question more the identity of the act than the credit given to Vespucci. Amsler's caption merely repeats the events represented and the historical destiny of the name America for the continent: "Bearing the cross on the banner and having descended from the ship, Amerigo awakens a nude female savage, asleep in a hammock, and who will receive the name America after him."[34] Here again the caption states an apparently blatant meaning and treats a series of temporal elements as if they were "factual" events; how "the nude female savage" (*sauvagesse nue*) comprises the attributes of the continent remains untouched—it is neither hinted at nor problematized. Unwittingly the caption reinforces, along with its repetition of a factual version of the archive, the reductive categories of savagery and nudity as natural givens. Curiously enough a most naïve reading recurs in a caption by Michel de Certeau: "L'explorateur (A. Vespucci) devant l'Indienne qui s'appelle Amérique" [The explorer (A. Vespucci) facing the Indian woman named America].[35]

From so sophisticated a thinker as de Certeau, one would expect an ironic turning of this assertion of fact, but in the opening statements of *The Writing of History* he apparently confirms the commonplace: "Jan van der Straet's staging of the disembarkment surely depicts Vespucci's surprise as he faces this world, the first to grasp clearly that she is a *nouva terra* not yet existing on maps—an unknown body destined to bear the name, Amerigo, of its inventor."[36] Stradanus proves irresistible, as de Certeau not only credits Vespucci but also uses modern cartography authoritatively. It remains to be seen whether it was an uncharted land that Vespucci had in mind, or whether he was appealing to a geographic tradition dating back to Isidore of Seville, as W. G. L. Randles has claimed.[37] Beyond a philological point, the debate calls for an analysis of how newness is produced in the invention of the New World. The writing of the new, in turn, must be observed in conjunction with a reading of the old in the new lands.

De Certeau must be credited for taking in a new direction Bitterli's denunciation of the cultural chauvinism prevalent in the interpretation of discoveries. He accomplishes this by emphasizing that what is at stake in the creative deeds is "a colonization of the body by the discourse of power." However, we must beware of de Certeau's simile of the colonizing process as a "blank, 'savage' page [*page blanche (sauvage)*] on which Western desire will be written."[38] De Certeau has refined this image of a "blank page" in *The Practice of Everyday Life*.[39] From that later essay let us note the following. The notion of a "blank page" does not simply pertain to the "Other" as absence of culture, but forms an integral condition of the Renaissance. To be sure, the blank page quite literally means the proper place of "writing," of producing the world anew. But it is also the place where writing transforms a received tradition as well as the influx of exterior phenomena into a new order. Accordingly, it appears appropriate to me, at least from the perspective of the Spanish colonization,[40] to speak of a European pursuit of a New World that bears the imprint of native and ancient texts whereon the West discovers or fabricates its imperial destiny. The pursuit obviously implies an appropriation of indigenous texts, but that is very different from reducing the encounter to "blank page" versus "Western desire."

Despite these factual and metaphorical slippages into commonplace, de Certeau's studies of the production of knowledge, space, and time in historiography, and in particular his comparison of Stradanus's America and Botticelli's Venus in his essay on Jean de Léry's *Histoire d'un voyage faict en la terre du Brésil* (1578), provide categories for an archaeology of modern ethnology. My reservations about the "blank, 'savage' page" simile and the uncritical adherence to factual givens are corrective in view of possible reductive readings that would ignore the complexity and fruitfulness of de Certeau's work.[41] Beyond the scientistic tendency that we have observed in Amsler and Honour, and that is indirectly associated with the allegory in Bitterli, de Certeau attempts to dismantle the naturalness of the binary oppositions he finds operative in Stradanus: "Amerigo Vespucci the voyager [*le Découvreur*] arrives from the sea. A crusader standing erect [*debout*], his body in armor [*vêtu*], he bears the European weapons of meaning. Behind him are the vessels that will bring back to the European West the spoils of a paradise. Before him is the Indian "Ameriga," a nude woman reclining [*femme étendue, nue*] in her hammock, an unnamed presence of difference, a body which awakens within a space of exotic fauna and flora."[42]

This description of Stradanus's allegory opens Michel de Certeau's *The Writing of History* and furnishes a leitmotif to his analyses of modern historiography. It also forms part of the history of commentaries, captions, and textual translocations that have subjected the allegory to variant interpretations. Such semantic supplements also carry the imprint of a historical moment. De Certeau's caption to Stradanus and his reading of Léry form part of a full-fledged critique of structuralism that emerged in the late 1960s. His archeology of ethnology is clearly associated with Foucault's archeology of the human sciences, as are the problems implicit in a dissociation from structuralism— the danger of repeating the categories of the method under criticism with an illusive detachment.[43]

The key oppositional words in de Certeau's description are *étendue* (reclining) and *debout* (standing). These spatial terms provide an irresistible transparence to the other binary pairs that follow: *vêtue* versus *nue*, "the European weapons of meaning" versus "an unnamed presence of difference," and so on, are carefully juxtaposed in the description. A studied casualness pervades this critical strategy of organizing features in the allegory into pairs. Thus the word *étendue* gains an epistemological signification as it recurs in de Certeau's chapter 5. "Ethnographie. L'oralité, ou l'espace de l'autre: Léry." It forms the basis for drawing an archeology of ethnology: "The 'difference' implied by orality and by the unconscious delimits an *expanse of space* [*découpe une* étendue], an object of scientific activity. In order to be spoken, oral language waits for a writing to circumscribe it and to recognize what it is expressing."[44] As de Certeau italicizes *étendue*, he refines the initial literal meaning into a concept for elucidating the production of a historical *place* where writing inscribes the meaning of the oral.

De Certeau traces back to Léry Lévi-Strauss's well-known distinction between ethnology and history in terms of the oral and the written, the conscious and the unconscious. As de Certeau reminds us, the separation of those disciplines had already been fixed in the eighteenth century, even though Jean Jacques Ampère first used the term *ethnologie* in the nineteenth century. Lévi-Strauss's differentiation loses its givenness, however, as the reading of Léry manifests the production of an oral and unconscious savage and the space for constituting ethnology as a modern science.

Since a self-reflexive statement by de Certeau problematizes his reading of Léry's *Histoire*, we need not get entangled with analytical details, nor with evaluating the adequacy of his interpretation. De Certeau lucidly historicizes his approach: "Concerning ethnological discourse, I would like to explain what it articulates in exiling orality outside of the areas which pertain to Western work, in transforming speech into an exotic object. But even so, I do not escape the culture that has produced this discourse. I only reduplicate its effect."[45] This brilliant move at once questions the validity of his reading of Léry and highlights modern ethnology as the "true" object under criticism. What is important is the *effect*, what Lévi-Strauss (and Ampère, among others) could "find" in Léry and other travel accounts. For instance, Lévi-Strauss not only calls Léry's account a "masterpiece of Anthropological literature" but walks into the field with the text: "in my pocket I carried Jean Léry, the anthropologist's breviary."[46] But this cultural situation, the "circum-scription" as de Certeau calls it,[47] leads de Certeau to project a binary logic on Léry as well as on Stradanus.

De Certeau cannot avoid defining the modernity of Léry retrospectively even though "his text is based on a long medieval tradition of utopias and expectations."[48] Would it not be more correct to say that by 1578, when the *Histoire* was first published, Léry presupposed almost a century of writing on the New World? Is de Certeau bypassing earlier writings in his definition of a break, or simply reducing all previous literature on the New World to a medieval tradition? After all, Léry quotes Francisco López de Gómara to validate his observations of the Amerindian's fear of writing and poses his task as an amplification of the topic: "whoever wishes to amplify this matter here has a handsome topic."[49] Léry thus travels into a fully constituted geographic New World with a corresponding thesaurus of motifs and discursive variants against which he writes: for example, André Thevet's *La cosmographie universelle*. My point is not to oppose different versions of the event, but to ask, who is not a modern at this time? Or better, what particular discursive variant is more representative of modernity? It seems that it all depends on our definition of *modernity*. Moreover, de Certeau suggests that the production of the *étendue* was already present in Vespucci in the mode of an inaugural *writing that conquers*: "This conquering and orgiastic curiosity, so taken with unveiling hidden things, has its symbol in travel literature: the dressed, armed, knighted discoverer face-to-face with the nude Indian woman. A New World arises from the other side of the ocean with the appearance of the Tupi females, naked as Venus born in the midst of the sea in Botticelli's painting."[50]

Vespucci face to face with America, the dressed and the nude, constitutes a symbol of travel literature and the unveiling of the hidden. In brief, Vespucci is the true discoverer because he represents some sort of empirical curiosity about the world. The linking of America and Venus leads to another example of how modernity is projected: "Like the Indian woman's naked body, the body of the world becomes a surface offered to the inquisitions of curiosity."[51] Along with a questionable transposition of the nudity of Botticelli's Venus into America, there is an equally questionable interpretation of Botticelli's nude that suggests an empirical, "fresh" look at the world. At any rate, the nudity of America has its match in a "naked" glance (a direct and empirical look) on Vespucci's part. To the extent that these features signify the interpretation and extraction of timeless truths by commentators, we find here the pattern by which modern scholarship examines the past to find the origin of a later, ideal mode of apprehending the world.[52]

Discovery — must be empirical, not imaginative
?

Instead of taking "nature," "nudity," and "exoticism," like "west" and "modernity," as matters of fact, we must taken them both as products of writing, and as formal categories that appear in earlier representations of the New World. We must consider "newness" itself as a production. Thus we may be able to overcome the impasse de Certeau defines as a "circum-scrip-tion" by timeless truths that have crystallized in history: the project of an archeology of structuralism winds up imposing a binary logic on Stradanus's allegory.

De Certeau's insistence on binarism overshadows his brilliant analysis of the different stages in what we might call—evoking Freud—the *textwork* of Léry's *Histoire*. Indeed, de Certeau reads the *Histoire* in the guise of a Freudian analysis of the dreamwork: "In this respect the reading of texts has much to do with an interpretation of dreams."[53] This is not the place to discuss in any detail specific examples in de Certeau's analysis that would correspond to condensation, displacement, means of representation, and secondary revision in Freud. I will just point out that an ethnographic text about the Tupinambas is written in the interval that separates an initial condensation expressed in terms of a Self and an Other—"the separation (between 'over here' and 'over there') first occurs as an oceanic division"[54]—and the secondary revision that reinstates a series of oppositions as a result of a return of the repressed that irrupts in the ethnographic text in the mode of eroticized speech—the primitive as a *body of pleasure*: "By way of hypothesis we can say that in an esthetic and erotic fashion, he [primitive man, *le sauvage*] is the return of what the economy of production had to repress in order to be founded as such."[55] Beyond an ideal primitivism and an antiprimitivism (i.e., de Certeau's "blank page" or, in other words, the common-place of a rhetoric of negativity—an absence of government, clothing, money, writing, sexual restrictions, and so on),[56] Léry's *Histoire* constitutes a space for the inscription of "objective" data. Here is a production of knowledge where the subject and the object of ethnology emerge as separate entities. In this regard, two planes coexist in the *Histoire*:

> On the first is written the chronicle of facts and deeds by the group or Léry. These events are narrated in a *tense*: a *history* is composed with a chronol-ogy—very detailed—of actions undertaken or lived by a *subject*. On the

second plane *objects* are set out in a space ruled not by localization or geographic routes—these indications are very rare and always vague—but by a taxonomy of living beings, a systematic inventory of philosophical questions, etc.; in sum, the catalogue raisonné of a knowledge.[57]

Far from being a unique aspect of Léry's *Histoire*, this distinction between a "subject" and an "object" of knowledge can be further corroborated with Spanish sources from Columbus, if not before, onward. In the writing of the New World, which was already in place when Columbus sailed, we can trace the emergence of Western subjectivity as universal. This epistemic mutation constitutes a new form of writing that, on the one hand, provides a "catalogue raisonné of a knowledge" (a system for inscribing knowledge that can be resumed by other historians) while, on the other, entails a constant self-clarification and verification of premises (an ongoing reflection about the significance of events, writing, and earlier texts). The redefinitions of both the "subjective" and the "objective" planes presuppose a "blank page" where data is processed into knowledge. This processing of information manifests a will to truth that has nothing to do with reducing the New World to a "blank page." Moreover, beyond the invention of the "savage," either in the form of ideal primitivism or an antiprimitivism, we can observe that sixteenth-century accounts and histories of the colonization include, quite as matter of course, representations of Europeans that embody the worst forms of barbarism and ignorance (not only in Las Casas, but in Columbus, Cortés, Oviedo, and so on). Indeed, we may read into the awakening of America the beginning of a chapter in the history of the West. As Las Casas never failed to remind Charles V, among the "marvels" of the "discovery of America" one should include the unheard-of atrocities, massacres, and destructions of entire peoples. *but this includes*

From the paradoxical caption written by the Galles we have learned that the binary oppositions we may trace in Stradanus's allegory correspond to the illusion of a tautology in paradox; consequently, it is a tautological reading that ignores openendedness. Captions written either from a scientific or from a binary point of view reveal a will to closure that falls prey to playfulness. My intention is not to call for an indiscriminate form of play, but to avoid being "played" by the same artifacts that, assuredly, we reduce to a univocal meaning. Furthermore, an open-endedness suggests a way out from within Eurocentrism. By placing ourselves within a *paradoxical terrain*, we may avoid a detachment that ends up in repetition.

In appraising the participants in the "discovery" and the "conquest," de Certeau partakes of a congenital tendency in New World historiography to assure our contemporary understanding of America. For better or for worse, the knowledge of America presupposed by traditional scholarship constitutes an integral element of what one might call, following the philosopher Karl-Otto Apel, our institutional fictions.[58] When considering the discovery of the New World, such fictions are particularly difficult to overcome; it is not only America that is at issue, but also the universality of European history and subjectivity.

CHAPTER 2

Columbus and the New Scriptural Economy of the Renaissance

Jacques Heers opens his indispensable biography *Christophe Colomb* by affirming the historicity of the famous mariner: "Christopher Columbus, of course, is not a myth."[1] In support of this factual statement, Heers mentions the innumerable sources that name Columbus without ambiguity, and points out that few enterprises ever had such celebrity during the lifetime of a hero as Columbus's first voyage to the Indies. Heers goes on to assert that the printing of Columbus's letter announcing his discovery was the first typographical success of a living author.[2] One paragraph later, after telling us that legends overshadow certainty with respect to the personality as well as the national identity of Columbus (Italian, Portuguese, Jewish *converso*, Catalan, and whatnot according to different authors), Heers states that "Columbus is not a historical personage."[3] The latter assertion, however, does not keep Heers from elaborating a more-than-six-hundred page biography. Ellipses (. . .) punctuate areas where silence must be kept because documentation is lacking, and a *via negativa*, which dismantles the legends, defines the probable.

Heers's antithesis on the historical status of Columbus posits a gap where historians write plausible stories. These initial gestures would first inscribe a distance from the past, and historians would then proceed to discover a structure in the fragments of information. Heers's specifications on the archive, however, betray a will to restrict the significance of documents and thus to reduce the status of Columbus (i.e., Columbus is neither a myth nor a historical personage), which from the start mars the

definition of historical alterity (the myth versus history opposition is taken for granted and hence naturalized as a universal).
These observations on Heers's opening moves obviously could be
extended to other readings of Columbus and, in general, to a
historiography that overlooks the conversion into documents,
collections, and data of objects with another significance and
distribution. In these introductory remarks, by way of comments
on Heers, Tzvetan Todorov, Michel de Certeau, and others, I will
identify and critique some dominant commonplaces in the secondary literature. We must first rid ourselves of some deep-
seated assumptions and categories that inform our understanding
of Columbus before we try an alternative reading of his writings.
I will argue that in Columbus we can trace the production of a
new man (as forms of subjectivity), a *new world* (as parcels of
reality and image of the globe) and a *new scriptural possibility*
(as modes of description) that we have come to identify with
modernity.

Heers complements the above methodological precautions
with a theoretical postulate on the art of biography. "But what
has mainly guided me is a care not to reduce everything to the
man and his anecdotes: to evoke a great figure from the past, it is
obviously to talk about his time."[4] Biography merges into a
history of mentalities organized around the name "Columbus."
The task of the biographer can be compared to that of a semioti-
cian: Columbus is a sign whose significance depends on the
structure to be found in the clusters of signs where the names
"Columbus" and "the New World" are immersed. In Heers's
biography, however, the terms *New World* and *Columbus* function
as full signs, as natural entities—not as empty signifiers, to
adopt Roland Barthes's distinction in *Mythologies*.[5]

Thus Heers entitles a chapter of his book "Le refus du
Nouveau Monde" [The Refusal of the New World], attributing
questionable semantic stability to Columbus and the New World.
The name "New World," however, had not gained enough
currency during Columbus's lifetime for such a rejection to make
sense. Only by transposing a referent from our standpoint can we
speak of Columbus rejecting a *natural entity*.[6] In fact, as I shall
establish in the pages which follow, Columbus actually invented
the very notion of a *new world* that has determined the latter
significations imputed to the New World as a proper name.

Columbus's use of the term *new world* does not refer any longer to one more discovery among others, as in the literature of the exploration of Africa and the Canary Islands, but to a notion with aesthetic, historical, and mystical dimensions.[7]

Heers manifests a tendency in traditional scholarship to separate the image of a modern Columbus armed with a "rational" or "scientific" geography from the image of a medieval Columbus endowed with a "mystical" or "poetic" imagination. This split has led scholarship to evaluate the modernity of Columbus's writings by comparing his geographic ideas with more recent understandings of the New World. Whether negative or positive, this kind of appraisal ignores the myth-shaping powers of Columbus, as well as the inseparability of aesthetic, historical, and mystical significations from the geography and cosmology informing Columbus's invention of a *new world*.[8] How we characterize Columbus's place in history ought to depend, not on mental or attitudinal traits that modern scholars have defined as medieval or modern, but on a determining structure that circumscribes writing on the New World within modernity. It ultimately does not matter whether Columbus utters "medieval" or "modern" statements, since their significance depends neither on his intentions nor on his beliefs, but on the system in which they become meaningful. As we will see later on, Columbus himself, for different reasons, was very much aware of the semantic gulfs that separated writing from reading about a *new world*. This chapter argues that the Age of Exploration and its corresponding colonial discourse are determined by a larger event, which I shall define, following Michel de Certeau, as the new scriptural economy of the Renaissance.[9]

The most salient feature of this new scriptural economy is the transition from a history that purports to register exemplary lives and to keep a record *of* events or natural phenomena to a history that seeks to valorize an individual subject and to provide a record *for* the appropriation as well as the transformation of a territory or a social body.[10] If all cultures practice forms of writing that inscribe laws into the body (ranging from tattoos to the regulation of vocal cords) with the intent of reproducing a social order, it is only in the Renaissance that writing defined itself as labor, in opposition to nonproductive orality. This scriptural economy reduced Amerindians to "savages" without culture, hence to apprentices of Western culture, and the New World to a "state of nature" that eventually would yield valuable products once a rational order was implanted. The Renaissance as a historical period, moreover, defined itself in opposition to the scribes of the Middle Ages precisely for the purpose of remaking history and using the recently reinvented printing press to establish texts in exact copies. The printing press thus facilitated private collections of books and maps that not only made information more accessible but also laid out the world on surfaces ready to be "explored."[11] Indeed, it was this recently available stock of knowledge and objectification of the world that defined the place from which Columbus wrote and that empowered him to appropriate the territories he encountered.

I would like to overturn the assumption of the "discovery" of a natural entity by tracing the simultaneous production of various Columbus "personas" and a *new world* in the writings of the mariner. Columbus's reticence toward giving autobiographical information does not prevent the proliferation of self-portraits that are juxtaposed with or immersed in the descriptions of the *new world* and of the enterprise itself. Following Michel Beaujour, one might further remark that "literary description is never 'objective': it always points to the semiotic system which is meant to provide a mimesis of the visionary mind. . . . Description is Janus-like, always facing at once in two opposite directions."[12] Beaujour's entailed subjectivity in description suggests a reading of Columbus wherein we may trace how a *new world* and a *new man* both surface from an encounter with the unknown. I am concerned not with setting out the deep or correct meaning of Columbus, nor with documenting the colonial order he imposes on the new territories, but rather with observing the emergence of forms of subjectivity still influential today. Modern refinements in the description of landscapes and cultures tend to blind us to originating forms underlying our thinking and sensibility toward nature.

Given Tzvetan Todorov's interest in semiotics and the representation of otherness, his chapter on Columbus in *The Conquest of America* would apparently offer a point of entry to the production of a *new man* and a *new world* in Columbus's writings. But Todorov also assumes the external reality of the New World in the opening lines of *The Conquest of America*: "(My subject—)

the discovery *self* makes of *other*."[13] From the English version, which leaves out "the" before "self" and "other," one might suspect Todorov of some sort of ironic play, but the French reveals that the proposal is in earnest: "Je veux parler de la découverte que le *Je* fait de l'*autre*." While the "self" here obviously refers to an all-too-universal European subjectivity, Todorov posits the "other" as an empirical item. This move obviates a self/other dichotomy supposedly discovered during Columbus's journey to America; moreover, it sidesteps questions about how specific historical configurations can produce variant modes of "othering" and, in particular, the emergence of the "Europe and its others" cultural complex. In addition, Todorov is exclusively concerned with Columbus's correct or mistaken interpretations of signs, and not with the production of a New World code.[14] Consequently, in Todorov's reading, a matter-of-factness about Columbus's "errors" and his "medieval" mentality forbids the comprehension of the complex artifice Columbus constructs. Take for instance:

> There is nothing of a modern empiricist about Columbus. . . .
> Every day Columbus sees "signs," and yet we know that these signs were lying to him. . . .
> He always perceives names as identified with things: the entire dimension of intersubjectivity, of the reciprocal value of words . . . of the human therefore arbitrary character of signs, escapes him. . . .
> What he "understands," then, is simply a summary of the books of Marco Polo and Pierre d'Ailly. . . .
> Columbus speaks about the men he sees only because they too, after all, constitute a part of the landscape.[15]

My point in listing these quotations is obviously not to prove Todorov wrong; statements such as these are commonplaces for depicting a medieval Columbus. But they do not help us see how Columbus fabricates a desirable and intelligible notion of a *new world* that would convince the crown to finance a second journey, as well as entice the imagination of his contemporaries. Instead of typifying Columbus as lacking interest in the peoples he encounters because he merges them with the landscape, it seems to me that we should trace the emergence of people with the landscape in the discourse of exploration Columbus invents. After all, as Todorov himself points out, it is in Columbus's attitude toward nature that we find the traces of a "modern" mentality.[16]

In order not to dissolve the uniqueness of the event into abstract terms defined from our privileged historical perspective, we must see how Columbus's writings produce a new discourse out of the shreds of medieval and native texts. We must attend to Columbus's refurbishings of the map at hand with new landmarks. Instead of construing the typicality of the explorer by measuring his accounts against the discourse of the conqueror or the missionary, we ought to consider the specificity of Columbus's situation in which he encountered unprecedented peoples and natural phenomena. The specificity of Columbus's situation, however, should not be trivialized by reducing it to some kind of typical problem, apparently common to all narratives of discovery, of how to describe the new in terms of the old. One can actually invert the question and say that Columbus's problem is how to suggest the old when all there is to describe is the new—to reinvent the India of Marco Polo and others, specifically the borderlands, those places that medieval travelers passed by and about which they provided little information. The traditional form of posing the question inevitably leads to evaluating accuracy in Columbus's descriptions of "new" things, which I have dismissed as irrelevant since it presupposes the notion of the New World as a natural entity and not a product of writing or of material colonization. Moreover, Columbus is much more ambitious than that: his voyage seeks to inaugurate a new man, a new world, and a new history. Exploration manifests itself as a bringing forth of new parcels of reality and forms of subjectivity. As we read Columbus we must pursue what Daniel Defert calls to mind about travel literature in general, "one must rediscover which techniques constituted the art of travelling."[17]

A SEMIOTIC OF ERRANCY

For Columbus, the breakdown of the code (an inherited encyclopedia of knowledge about the East) implies the need to produce new signs for registering unheard-of peoples and things. And it is precisely in this breakdown of information that errancy (in the etymological sense of errare, to wander, to stray) may illuminate Columbus's mode of traveling. Though the destination of the voyage is the "Far East," the inauguration of a new sea route entails the need to keep a record of the unknown, of phenomena never before observed. The discourse of exploration thus surfaces as a constant movement from the familiar to the unfamiliar; in this movement the known is constantly reconstituted in order to accommodate the unknown. It is not simply a question of following (or simply "understanding," as Todorov puts it) the image of the world derived from Pierre d'Ailly or Marco Polo, but of reinventing the world. Indeed, Columbus has to fabricate a frame of reference so that the production of information about the new makes sense to a European reader. To be sure, such compendiums as Marco Polo's *Divisament dou monde* and Pierre d'Ailly's *Ymago mundi* provide Columbus with an image of the world by which to imagine his whereabouts. But once immersed in the insular world of America, Columbus has no alternative but to stray from one island to another. For him, the pursuit of the known (be that Cipango, or gold and spices) assumes the mode of a wandering through new territories, "y por esto no fago sino andar para ver de topar en ello" [and for this I do not do anything but wander about to see if I come upon it] (Friday, 19 October 1492).[18]

We may tentatively characterize Columbus's art of traveling with the paradoxical notion of a semiotic of errancy. By paying attention to Columbus's reflections on writing we can trace both an interpretation and a production of signs. My insistence on errancy seeks to give greater weight to the productive side — that is, to highlight the Columbus who writes the new rather than the one who reads the old. Thus the notion of errancy does not provide an all-encompassing explanation, but rather isolates an often ignored aspect of Columbus—his inauguration of new topics.

Over against an all-too-reductive, mistaken Columbus, we will pursue a Columbus who conceptualizes his task as writing a *new world* in his *Diario*, letters, and nautical charts—indeed, imposing a new order on the European image of the planet. In Michel de Certeau's words, within the new scriptural economy of the Renaissance, "writing" assumes the following characteristics: "I designate as 'writing' the concrete activity that consists in constructing, on its own blank space [*un espace propre*]—the page—a text that has power over the exteriority from which it has first been isolated." Writing operates on a "blank space" that is

why separation? 55
or, why insist on separation? point here?
refusal of totality (totalitarianism?

"proper," in the dual sense of being "clean" of ambiguities and of providing the locus for the appropriation of an exterior reality. As the page separates the subject from the object, it provides "the field for an operation of his own." Writing thus bears the power to construct a *text* and impose an order on the world. De Certeau's notion of a "blank page" refers not only to the absence of a record and the task of writing about unheard-of subject matter but also to a "place" that enables the writer to transform a received tradition: "The island of the page is a transitional place in which an industrial inversion is made: what comes in is something 'received,' what comes out is a 'product.'" The new scriptural economy of the Renaissance is capitalistic and conquering insofar as it combines "the power of *accumulating* the past and that of making the alterity of the universe *conform* to its models."[19] There is, moreover, a felicitous parallelism between sailing into uncharted waters and broaching topics on a "blank page." The ship's rostrum and the pen's stylus draw patterns on surfaces devoid of earlier traces. This lack of precedents, the fiction of a "blank page," enables the writer and mariner, as in the case of Columbus, to claim "ownership" of both text and territory.

Tentatively we may differentiate this understanding of Renaissance writing as the production of a new order and its imposition on the world from medieval scriptural writing, which contains the Word, whose teachings must be "heard and understood" by a reader. Even when we find Columbus supposedly in the medieval "listening" mode, he is not so much interpreting the Bible as privileging his persona and enterprise as keys for an interpretation of the course of history.

From the beginning, in the "Prologue" to his *Diario*, Columbus infuses his voyage with millenarian undertones as he pairs the historical importance of his voyage with the expulsion of the Jews and the conquest of Granada in 1492; moreover, he tells us that he was sent ". . . á las dichas partidas de Yndia, para ver los dichos prínçipes y los pueblos y tierras y la disposiçión d'ellas y de todo, y la manera que se pudiera tener para la conversión d'ellas á nuestra santa fe" [to the said parts of India, to see the said princes and the countries and peoples and lands and the disposition of them and everything else, and the manner one should follow for their conversion to our holy faith]. The

"said princes" refers to Marco Polo's account of the Gran Can—
the great khan—and how the khan and his antecedents had asked
Rome to send them doctors in the faith. Implicit to this discussion are the diplomatic missions of such Franciscan missionaries
as Giovanni da Pian del Carpini, Willem van Ruysbroek, or
Odoric of Pordenone.[20] Neither their journeys nor Marco Polo's
ever had Columbus's intent to conquer and fully convert the
peoples of Asia. Indeed, Columbus sailed not as diplomat or
merchant but with the full power of Admiral of the Ocean Sea
and a viceroy of all territories that he would discover and gain for
the crown.[21] Reading the *Diario*, we must attend to the simultaneous emergence of a *new man* and a *new world*. One finds a *new
man* not exclusively in terms of his prophetic individuality or the
guerdoning of the admiralcy upon his successful return, but also
with respect to forms of sensibility that continue to mediate the
West's experience of the exotic.

The scriptural inscription of a *new world* is implicit in Columbus's decision to adopt the form of a diary in the "Prologue"
to his *Diario*: "y para esto pensé de escrevir todo este viaje muy
puntualmente, de día en día, todo lo que hiziese y viese y
passasse, como adelante se veyrá. también, señores príncipes,
allende de escrevir cada noche lo qu'el día passare y el día lo que
la noche navegare, tengo propósito de hazer carta nueva de
navegar" [And for this I thought to write down upon this voyage
in great detail from day to day all that I should do and see and
encounter, as hereinafter shall be seen. Also, lord princes, in
addition to noting down each night what has happened during the
day, and each day what was sailed by night, I intend to make a
new chart of navigation]. This methodical registration of data on
a daily basis bifurcates into two simultaneous operations. On the
one hand, the *Diario* produces an objective, cartographical
record of the new territories within the abstract temporal frame
of hours and days while, on the other hand, it registers subjective impressions of particulars that substantiate the uniqueness
of the event within a historical paradigm. The "objective" and
the "subjective" are not opposite forms, suggesting right and
wrong, or some kind a medieval-versus-modern paradigm, but a
Janus-like coexistence of objectification and subjectivity in all
"literary" description. As Antonello Gerbi has reminded us,
"Columbus's diary or *Journal*, possibly the oldest 'diary' in liter-

57

ary history, . . . by virtue of its very nature . . . unfolds the miracle of the discovery with the steady rhythm of each passing day."[22] Let us further define these two operations, which produce a subjective along with an objective record of the voyage.

First, the *Diario* alters cartographical paradigms as it systematically maps uncharted waters with Spanish or hispanicized terminology. Though Columbus's mapping is sufficiently precise to guarantee the reiteration of the journey, the imperfect instruments available at the time introduce subjective observations. For instance, Columbus's dependence on sandglasses constantly frustrates the exactitude of his data: ". . . halló que passaron veynte ampolletas, que son de á media ora, aunque dize que algo allí puede haber defecto, porque ó no la buelven tan presto ó dexa de passar algo" [He found that there passed twenty *ampolletas*, which are half-hour glasses, although he says that there could be some fault, because either they do not turn them so promptly or some [sand] fails to pass through] (Thursday, 13 December 1492). In the transcript by Las Casas, speculation about the technical difficulty explainable as human error is followed by a second possibility, which suggests an eerie stoppage of the flow of time. Notwithstanding the problems of producing an objective record, Columbus manipulates time by keeping two records of the crossing; not only does this duplicitous distortion of time alleviate the crew's anxiety before the sighting of land, but it also enables Columbus to affirm himself the sole possessor of the secret route to the Indies toward the end of the *Diario*. He has maintained a second record, ". . . por quedar él señor de aquella derrota de las Yndias, como de hecho queda, porque ninguno de todos ellos traýa su camino çierto, por lo cual ninguno puede estar seguro de su derrota para las Yndias" [in order to remain master of that route of the Indies, as in fact he remained, since none of them was certain of his course, therefore nobody could be sure of his route to the Indies] (Monday, 18 February 1493). The pretense lends a secretive element to the *Diario*, leading Las Casas at one point to remark, "si no está mentirosa la letra" [if the log is to be trusted] (Monday, 8 October 1492). The indeterminacy of the data for a contemporary like Las Casas prompts the semblance of two, at times indiscernible, Columbuses. The technical impasse conjoins with a deceiving Columbus to produce a "secret" chart of the route.

Second, in the *Diario*'s account of exploration, the inscription of minutiae at "random" reveals a subjective record of an increasingly unfamiliar reality. As the first voyage penetrates further into the territories, the randomness of the data reveals a narrative pattern; the particular events bespeak a providential design and the emergence of a land of promise. Columbus registers information as if the most insignificant detail would reveal the coming of new times: ". . . no sé adónde me vaya primero, ni me sé cansar los ojos de ver tal fermosas verduras y tan diversas de las nuestras" [I do not know where I will go first, nor do I know when my eyes will tire of seeing such beautiful foliage and so different from ours] (Friday, 19 October 1492). We must therefore separate the random registration of details from the narrative in which they appear, so that we can discern the innovations they introduce into the narrative paradigm; for Columbus, the discovery of the new territories implies anticipation, yearning, and also the advent of change and a unique historical configuration.[23]

In what follows, I set aside Columbus's art of cartography and concentrate solely on the subjective register. I touch on two questions that deviate from Todorov's matter-of-factness: first, I observe how an inherited stock of knowledge constitutes a thesaurus for the invention and description of a desirable *new world*; next, I attempt to show how descriptions of unprecedented phenomena transform extant paradigms as the *new world* gains a new semantic substance. A metaphorical appropriation of the new territories zigzags between drawing similitudes with Europe or precedent descriptions of the East, on the one hand, and the fabrication of images that produce the sense of a new land, on the other. Columbus's discourse at once brings together elements of the old in a new fashion and invents new topics as his descriptions carve out new parcels of reality.

SCRIBBLING ORIENTAL TOKENS

In Columbus's writings the word *maravilla* (marvel) competes with *oro* (gold) for supremacy: Columbus's expectation of Oriental cities effervescent in splendor and wealth is met by a paradisiacal land where lushness and eccentricity enchant him beyond speech. At the same time that Columbus traces a pattern of signs derived for the most part from Marco Polo's description of

59

Cathay (China) and Cipango (Japan) among other regions of the "Far East," he attempts to describe phenomena without precedent in medieval literature. His communication with the crown (the "old world") depends on established, familiar indices first constituted in antiquity to characterize the Orient. Against this symbolic field of reference, however, a sense of the marvelous erupts, as his descriptions both reiterate the code and evoke the new.

After his first voyage, Columbus asserts in the letter to Santangel the novelty of his discoveries: ". . . porque aunque d'estas tierras hayan fablado ó escripto, todo va por conjetura sin alegar de vista, salvo comprendiendo a-tanto que los oyentes los más escuchavan é juzgavan más por fabla que por poca c[osa] d'ello" [For although others have talked about these lands, it was all by conjecture, without reasoning from having seen them; barring understanding so much that listeners would mostly hear and judge what was said more as fable than as anything else] (*Racc.*, pt. I, 1:130). Columbus sees his voyage as the one that finally transforms fable into fact. Moreover, he inscribes a privileged persona in an intimate dialogue with God: ". . . Dios Nuestro Señor, el cual da á todos aquellos que andan su camino victoria de cosas que parecen imposibles . . ." [God Our Lord, who gives all those that follow his path victory over things that seem impossible . . .] (*Racc.*, pt. I, 1:130). Implicit in this passage is a millenarian theme that constantly haunts Columbus's interpretation of his voyage and selfhood. The historical import of the voyage displaces previous accounts of the islands based on conjecture or hearsay.

Conjecture or hearsay are not suspect from a cognitive point of view; the islands are there, after all. It is also beside the point that Columbus is the first to navigate across the ocean. What is important, it seems to me, is the vagueness of the "fables" — what makes them susceptible to Columbus's reelaboration. The merging of the fabulous and the real depends on the possibility of tracing the signs of the former onto the latter. Such a process of recognition implies a reading of the islands, as well as a confirmation of legend, in the medieval Latin sense of *legenda*, "things for reading."[24] But Columbus finds more than the legends to decipher. Ultimately, he fashions a "borderline region" to the lands visited by medieval travelers, ". . . y dize que cree que estas islas son aquellas innumerables, que en los mapamundos en fin de oriente se ponen" [and he says that he believes that these islands are those innumerable ones that on the world maps are placed at the end of the Far East] (Wednesday, 14 November 1492).

My own reference to medieval cartography is not intended as an account of a Columbus "library," but merely indicates a semiotic repertoire available to Columbus. I have pointed out how the imagery of the "Far East" derived from medieval sources constitutes a symbolic field of reference for charting the horizon of a Cathay and Cipango near at hand. We must see now how images drawn from these previous descriptions of the Orient function as indices: Columbus's imagination transmutes natural phenomena, linguistic expressions, and cultural traits observed in the New World into Oriental motifs well stocked in European registers of Eastern things. For Columbus and for the European imagination in general, the descriptions of Marco Polo are a primary authoritative source.[25] As far as Columbus is concerned, the object under survey, the content of his descriptions, corresponds to the Orient of Marco Polo; the product, however, is a *new India*.

contradict *p. 59*

While Cathay remains on the horizon, Marco Polo's description of Cipango lacks a precision that would forbid an easy identification of the new land with Japan. Even when Columbus identifies the island of Española (Hispaniola) with Cipango during his first voyage, or when he makes the members of his crew state under oath that the coastline of Cuba corresponds to that of mainland China during the second voyage, or when in the course of the fourth voyage he identifies the coast of Central America with the province of Mangi described by Marco Polo in the vicinity of Cathay, all these tentative locations remain on the fringes of the territories dearly pursued. Columbus still faces the need to describe the borderlands of the legendary civilization of the great khan. These regions are merely alluded to by Marco Polo, or systematically excluded from his writings because they lack commercial activity and civilization. Commerce and courtly life, after all, are Marco Polo's favorite topics; by comparison, his descriptions of natural phenomena are scant and insipid.[26] Here and there we find his attempts to rationalize fabulous phenomena, but for the most part natural colors, landscapes, and

61

Colón differs - describes
amazing flora + fauna +
potential of market / raw materials
[other than gold + spices] ← a new OTHER
what shapes the writing. Audience, expectations

peoples are absent. For instance, the legendary unicorns lose their charm: "This is a passing ugly beast to look upon, and is not in the least like that which our stories tell of as being caught in the lap of a virgin; in fact 'tis altogether different from what we fancied." Rationalization dissolves the idyllic image of the unicorn by investing it with the image and habits of the rhinoceros: "They have hair like that of a buffalo, feet like those of an elephant, and a horn in the middle of the forehead, which is very black and very thick."[27] Columbus himself produces parallel rationalizations of mythical beings. Mermaids, in Columbus's *Diario*, suffer an analogous transformation: ". . . dixo que vido tres serenas, que salieron bien alto de la mar; pero no eran tan hermosas como las pintan, que en alguna manera tenían forma de hombre en la cara" [He said that he saw three mermaids who rose very high from the sea; but they were not as beautiful as they are painted, because to some extent they have the face of a man] (Wednesday, 9 January 1493). Mermaids, perhaps manatees, in this passage expurgated by Las Casas, retain their reality, and as in the case of the unicorn they lose their beauty. But the mixture of feminine and masculine features (*cara de hombres*) ultimately reinforces accounts of the luring song and deadly seduction associated with sirens.

Besides a common tendency to parody earlier texts in these transformations of imagery, Marco Polo and Columbus have few stylistic points in common. In Marco Polo's text, the rationalizations of fables betray a disregard for landscapes or peoples without the traits of civilization: "There is nothing else to mention except that this is a very wild region, visited by very few people." These scanty descriptions are not a result of Marco Polo's inability to describe, but merely stem from his lack of interest. There are incidental passages of idolaters with gruesome customs, allusions to monstrous races, and descriptions of wild men with tails, but for the most part they are marginal commonplaces lacking color and precision: "Now you must know that in this kingdom of Lambri there are men with tails; these tails are of a palm in length, and have no hair on them. These men live in the mountains and are a kind of wild men. Their tails are about the thickness of a dog's."[28] This passage closes a brief enumeration of the natural resources of Lambri. Marco Polo offers nothing specific about the mountains where these wild men live, and the whole description centers on a quantitative appraisal of the tail, perhaps an association with the satanic. In general, such reiterations of monstrous races (among other commonplaces representative of the Orient since antiquity) constitute the ambiance of the "exotic" in Marco Polo. Inhabitants and things representing the insular world of the tropics do exist in the available repertoire, but there are no motifs at hand for the depiction of its exotic landscape.

Columbus can draw only isolated pieces of information from the series of commonplaces—signs emblematic of the "Far East"—constantly recurring in earlier literature. From this symbolic field of reference Columbus derives a code for interpreting and organizing the phenomenal chaos of the real, and for fabri- ? cating a semblance of the new lands that suggests the legendary Orient. Thus Columbus mentions men with tails on his return from his first voyage in the letter to Santangel: ". . . me quedan de la parte de poniente dos provincias que yo no he andado, la una de las quales llaman 'Avan,' adonde naçe la gente con cola" [there remain on the western side two provinces that I have not reconnoitered, among them the Indians call one "Avan," where the people are born with a tail] (*Racc.*, pt. 1, 1:128). Marco Polo's Lambri disappears from the horizon, but its particularizing signs are inscribed onto Avan. Native proper names become full signs that connote the legendary, and legends may also travel from one island to another, acquiring new semantic investments. Consequently, both the names and the contents of medieval maps undergo a transformation. Furthermore, we must underscore that Columbus uses indigenous place names, however inconsistently, rather than merely relying on Marco Polo's geographic terms.

In a map of the island of Hispaniola drawn by Columbus during his first voyage (fig. 3), Civao appears as one of its provinces, while in the *Diario* Civao, or Çybao, is identified with Cipango: ". . . entre los otros lugares que nombravan, donde se cogía el oro, dixeron de Çipango, al cual ellos llamaban 'Çybao;' y allí affirman que hay gran cantidad de oro, y qu'el caçique trae las vanderas de oro de martillo, salvo que está muy lexos, al leste" [Among the other places that they were naming where gold was procured, they spoke of Cipango, which they were calling "Çybao," and they affirm that there is a great quantity of gold

Figure 3. In a map of the island of Hispaniola Civao appears as one of its provinces. *Chart of Hispaniola (1494), Christopher Columbus. Courtesy Newberry Library.*

there, and that the cacique bears banners of beaten gold, but that it is very far to the east] (Monday, 24 December 1492). Çybao, according to Columbus, is the native name for Cipango. The possible assonances between the two worlds could in itself have generated the identification in Columbus's mind. The *Diario* does not mention a palace paved with gold, but according to the Amerindians, Çybao is a source of gold as was the Cipango of Marco Polo. And the mirage of a civilization appears in the cacique with banners of beaten gold. Interestingly enough, it is not a king, as in Marco Polo's narrative, that the admiral expects to find in Cipango, but a cacique.

In tracing a lack of consistency in names and locations, especially when these refer to fantastic peoples, I have tried to find a clue to understanding the role identifiable passages from Marco Polo and other medieval sources play in Columbus's narratives. The *Diario* and other documents are sprinkled with allusions to peoples with one eye, bald heads, or dog faces, and to an island inhabited only by women (the Amazons are described, but not named). These fantastic commonplaces, along with signs of gold (to be taken here as a shorthand for pearls, spices, lignaloe, brazilwood, etc.) function in the communications as indices of the "Far East." I have also pointed out how the introduction of native information brings forth a transformation of this code. Beyond an assimilation of what he observes with previous descriptions of Asia, the writings of Columbus suggest the fabrication of a new region in space. A new language, a new historical moment, and a new world are in the offing in Columbus's metaphors, which conjoin legends with an indigenous knowledge of the territories.

It is beside the point that the Amerindians might have confirmed such expectations in the course of what must have been an obtuse, gestic, discursive exchange of symbolic forms. Columbus's almost verbatim reiteration of commonplaces from medieval travel literature are not inspired by the so-called "ignorance" of the Amerindians, as some historians have argued in order to justify his immersion in an epistemology where the fantastic and the real cannot be isolated. As far as knowledge is concerned, the sixteenth century had no grounds for discriminating between the real and the fantastic.[29] Fables (made-up stories) are opposed to history (real events), but the same fantastic entities may appear in both genres.

65

Furthermore, when "factual" information about the anthro-pophagy of the Caribs,[30] the so-called cannibals, merges with traditional tales of monstrous peoples, Columbus dismisses and rationalizes it: "toda la gente que hasta oy a hallado, diz que tiene grandíssimo temor de los de Caniba ó Canima, y dizen que biven en esta ysla de 'Bohío.' . . . y dizían que no tenían sino un ojo y la cara de perro; y creýa el almirante que mentían, y sentía el almirante que debían de ser del señorío del gran can, que los captivavan" [All the people that he found hitherto he says show tremendous fear of those of Caniba or Canima, and say that they live in this island of "Bohío." . . . And they said that these people had but one eye and had dogs' faces; and the admiral believed they were lying, and felt that those who captured them must be from the dominion of the great khan.] (Monday, 26 November 1492). The Amerindians' fear seems to call forth Columbus's speculation on the sonorous affinities of *Caniba* and *Can*. One may wonder how Columbus gained his information about the facial deformities of the Caribs, but one thing is for certain, they need no collaboration from native sources for their production. Their monstrosity is a mere reiteration of features common in medieval teratologies, while *can*, "dog," rings with dog faces and Caniba. Did Columbus carry representations of these monsters and show them to the Amerindians? We will proba-bly never know for certain, but it is interesting that Columbus repeats the description to the Amerindians and thus confirms European expectations, even if he refutes them and brands them as liars. Although Columbus gainsays the truth about the Amer-indians' gestures, the discursive exchange is woven in the context of a code that validates his geographic speculations. Columbus is not denying the existence of monstrous races here, but instead is refusing to commend these commonplaces simply on account of the affinities between *Can* and *Caniba*.

Thus linguistic expressions become one more sign to deci-pher: signs derived from cultural and natural phenomena are inscribed in the margins of an inherited fantastic geography. A series of associations of ideas, contagions of sounds, and in general an unbridled desire to forge phantasmata bearing resem-blances to a stock of symbols pertaining to the "Far East" offer the ingredients for a new discourse whose final texture is at variance with the structure of the prototypes.

With the adoption of an indigenous terminology (i.e., Caniba and Civao in play with Gran Can and Cipango), the new lands, even when they are identified in terms of medieval geography, attain a new semantic content in the process. The conjunction of stock knowledge with native information and nomenclatures produces a region differing from previous representations of Asia. The passages I have examined and the recurrent capture of "tongues," to be used as informants and interpreters, suggest *want* that Columbus explores the new territories with the "eyes" and *to* knowledge of the Amerindians. This dependence on indigenous *suggest!* discourse is, perhaps, nowhere more poignantly expressed than when he reminds future explorers in the course of the fourth voyage that "en la tierra es necessario que fíen sus personas de un salvaje" [in the mainland it is necessary that they entrust their persons to a savage] (*Racc.*, pt. I, 2:201). Evidently the indigenous conception of the territories undergoes a semantic transformation in the process. But the limits of the European code do not set the semantic boundaries for the borrowed names and spatial configurations, since a sense of the marvelous thrives precisely in the pursuit of a reality constantly eluding paradigmatic assimi- ? lations.

Columbus's invention of Cipango is more marvelous than *equally* the prototype. Legends and native information constitute the *fantastic* territories as texts to be read; Columbus, however, is not simply a reader but an inscriber.[31] Columbus's writings in fact contain little anthropological information. For the most part knowledge about Amerindian cultures either is limited to an incipient lexicon spread out over the *Diario* and his letters, or has undergone interpretations that in very crude terms anticipate ethnology as the science of oral cultures.[32] Take for example the passages quoted above where Columbus makes Amerindian terms such as *caniba* or *Civao* mean Gran Can and Cipango. However irritating these kinds of corrections might be to contemporary anthropology, like ethnology they assume the unconsciousness of orality and the power of writing to elucidate the true meaning of spoken words. Ultimately, Columbus's labor over Amerindian speech and culture forges an image that suggests the concept of "the natives" as a trope for "savages," which obviously may include the epithet "noble."

FROM LEGEND TO MARVEL

Let's take a passage from the *Diario* where a new syntax may be isolated: "dize aquí el almirante que oy y siempre, de allí adelante, hallaron ayres temperantissimos. . . . diz él: 'y era el tiempo como por abril en el Anda-"luzía" ' " [The admiral says here that today and always from then on, they found very temperate airs. . . . Says he: "and the weather was like April in Andalusia"] (Sunday, 16 September 1492).

Comparisons are the order of the day in this abbreviated passage. But the metaphorical language of resemblance gives place to contiguity and difference by means of a "synthetic" work over the known that produces a new sense—paradisiacal imagery from which New World motifs will eventually crystallize. April in Andalusia is a referent that allows Columbus to suggest a perpetual spring. Columbus himself never tires of speaking about the sweetness, *dulzura*, of the airs he first identifies in this passage. A slight variation of this comparison can be seen in the invocation of Castille for exalting the excellence of Hispaniola and his preference of this island over the others for the establishment of a colonial enclave. Comparisons to Andalusia or Castille fulfill the same metaphorical function for producing new significations.

The first images registered by Columbus are encoded as places for further elaboration within an ongoing concrescence of semantic values. What I may call the most "fortunate" metaphors from the point of view of an enthusiastic reception recur and attain a richer semantic value during the third voyage: ". . . en la tierra de Graçia hallé temperançia suavíssima, y las tierras y árboles muy verdes y tan hermoso como en abril en las guertas de Valençia. . . . entonçes era el sol en Virgen ençima de nuestras cabeças & suyas. ansí que todo esto proçede por la suavíssima temperançia que allí es, la qual proçede por estar más alto en el mundo, más çerca del ayre que cuento" [In the land of Gracia I found a very mild climate and the land and the trees very green and as lovely as the orchards of Valencia in April. . . . The sun was then in Virgo, above our heads and theirs. Thus all this must proceed from the very mild climate that is there, which proceeds from the fact that the land is highest in the world, nearest to the air that I speak about] (*Racc.*, pt. 1, 2:36). The

68

comparison of the new land to the April gardens of Valencia follows the same metaphorical logic of the Andalusia passage in the *Diario* by dating the season with the sign of Virgo.[33] For Columbus, who believed that the terrestrial paradise was on top of a pear-shaped world, this was indeed the highest region of the world. Columbus's worldview corresponds to Pierre d'Ailly's schema of the cosmos in the *Ymago mundi* where the sphere of the waters is higher than the sphere of the earth. It is a common conceptualization of the world in the fourteenth-century physiographical school of Paris, and it recurs with some alterations in Gregor Reich's *Margarita philosophica* (1503).[34] But more interestingly, a curious print by Honorius Philoponus in the *Nova typis transacta navigatio novi orbis Indiae Occidentalis* (1621) juxtaposes a floating Columbus signaling to the open horizon with a variant of d'Ailly's diagram containing a map of the New World in the higher regions once taken as uninhabitable (fig. 4). The chart in the lower right-hand corner suggests the inherited geographic backdrop where Columbus imagined his whereabouts. In the interstices of the diagram and the chart crystallized the errant significations first set in motion by Columbus; Philoponus's encyclopedic text is in itself a compendium of such items within a millenarian interpretation of the discovery.

D'Ailly's schema prefigures the location of the new world in an ontologically different region of the world; moreover, it constitutes the gestalt underlying Columbus's experience of geographic space. Columbus's location of the New World in the higher regions of the world is not an eccentric or aberrant form of envisioning the cosmos, but one consistent with other contemporary reinterpretations of d'Ailly. For Columbus it does not merely correspond to another climatic belt, but to an *other* world. By equating nature here with the gardens of Valencia, he takes the paradisiacal image of the land beyond a reference to climate into a depiction of the nature of the Indies in terms of a *locus amoenus* populated with idyllic natives.

Let us first observe the marvelous characteristics of the garden, and then proceed to the speculations on the location of Paradise informed by d'Ailly's schema of the cosmos.

In the *Diario*, Columbus has already expressed his sensitivity to nature: "andando por ella, fué cosa maravillosa ver las arboledas y frescuras, y el agua claríssima, y las aves, y amenidad,

Figure 4. A curious print juxtaposes a floating Columbus signaling to the open horizon with a diagram containing a map of the New World in the higher regions once taken as uninhabitable. *"Almirante de navios para las Indias." In Honorius Philoponus [Caspar Plautius]*. Nova typis transacta navigatio novi orbis Indiae Occidentalis *(Venice, 1621). Courtesy Benson Latin American Collection, General Libraries, University of Texas at Austin.*

que dize que pareçía que no quisiera salir de allí" [Wandering through it, it was such a marvelous thing to see the groves and luxuriant foliage, and the very clear water, and the birds and the pleasantness, that he says he did not wish to leave it] (Tuesday, 27 November 1492). Nothing like this personal immersion in nature can be observed in medieval travel literature. As in many other places in Columbus's *Diario*, this self-descriptive passage opens a sensitive point in the Western experience of exotic lands. The resonances up to our age are obvious in the so-called literature of going native, where a fascination with native ways also calls for an enchanting landscape. Columbus knows that surrendering forbids rendering the experience; only silence complies with going native. But nothing keeps Columbus from registering the interstices where such subjective abandonment begins. Despite this emotional retention, the *locus amoenus* of classical literature congeals into an empirical region in Columbus's experience and, accordingly, in his descriptions of the Indies as a natural garden. The invention of nature as a literary topic, so dear to the romantics, finds in Columbus one of its first expressions. As Claude Kappler has pointed out, the paradisiacal in medieval travel literature corresponds to artificial gardens: "In Marco Polo and Mandeville, one also finds gardens. But theirs are enclosed gardens, gardens organized by man, whereas Columbus's marvelous garden is a virginal space, vaste to the dimensions of the Creator more than of the creature."[35] In passing we should note that Kappler's observations on the passage from an enclosed garden to nature are correct, yet her notion of a "virginal space" operates within the ancient construct of a feminine Orient. Like the landscape, Columbus's Amerindians are virginal—without religion, hence not "tainted" by a sect.

For the most part, landscape is absent from Columbus's antecedents. When given, it is immersed in a symbolic field where deserts, the plains of Eurasia, or volcanos lack particularity, and function as scenarios for the inscription of the monstrous and the otherworldly. Individual items might be reminiscent of Paradise, but no elaborate description of a paradisiacal nature is given. Paradisiacal landscape is a legendary phantasm, but not an actual locus given for description.[36]

For instance, nowhere in the literature of the East do we find the eruption of color and immersion into nature that appears in Columbus's descriptions of Caribbean fish: "aquí son los peçes tan disformes de los nuestros, qu'es maravilla; ay algunos hechos como gallos, de la más finas colores del mundo, azules, amarillos, colorados, y de todas colores, y otros pintados de mill maneras; y las colores son tan finas, que no ay hombre que no se maraville y no tome gran descanso á verlos" [Here the fishes are so unlike ours that it is marvelous; they have some like roosters of the most exquisite colors in the world, blue, yellow, red, and of all colors, and others painted in a thousand ways; and the colors are so exquisite that there is no man who would not marvel and would not take great delight in seeing them] (Tuesday, 16 October 1492). *Disforme* (unlike) sets radical otherness in the tone of description, and at the end of the passage Columbus bursts into an aesthetic exclamation. A poetic vein in Columbus leads him to muse over the fish and avoid a facile comparison with European prototypes. As Columbus's thoughts leap to another species (roosters), he forges an unexpected simile. Shape is immediately displaced as the crystal waters of the Caribbean Sea become a pictorial canvas efflorescent with exquisite, subtle colors unprecedented in the literature of the exotic.[37] But the simile should not be seen as an example of pure poetry. As a sample of the marvelous it bears the possibility of an intertext for suggesting a legendary East, for substantiating the notion of a *new world*, and for speculating on the location of Paradise.

Since it is well known that Columbus names and charts the lands under survey with impeccable detail, it would be absurd to deny his onomastic powers. But one must distinguish these mnemonic devices from images that stimulate Western culture's long-term memory. The former guarantee the reiteration of the journey, while the latter continue to mediate our imagination of the exotic to this day. The name Española as well as the landscape Columbus depicts have vanished from our maps and field of experience, but the form of the description has not. Columbus must be credited for inaugurating the picturesque in travel literature, even though the passage below has come to us in the words of Las Casas: "aviendo andado media legua por la misma baýa, vido el almirante . . . unas tierras hermosas á maravilla, así como una vega montuosa dentro en estas montañas, y parecían grandes humos y grandes poblaçiones en ellas, y las tierras muy labradas" [Having gone half a league past the same bay, the admiral saw . . . some lands, as beautiful as to marvel, like a mountainous valley within these mountains, and within it were appearing many houses and big villages, and the lands very cultivated] (Tuesday, 27 November 1492).

The above description juxtaposes the two memories; it situates a marvelous location with utmost precision, and inserts a picturesque scenario. It also produces an effect of exploration, one that often recurs in the *Diario*, which characterizes the flow of daily entries as a penetration into a land of promise—the fertile, indeed, marvelous landscape of Hispaniola. The use of the imperfect *parecían* (were appearing) generates the tempo of the narrative as a slow nearing that produces a cinematic effect whereby the landscape gains resolution through description. Fertility guarantees foodstuffs and survival, but a magical landscape must surface to convey novelty and the mirage of the promised land. While light brushes sketch out large *humos* (literally "smokes"—a metonymy for "house" in Spanish) and large villages with cultivated fields to substantiate the adjective *hermoso* (beautiful), an oxymoron, *como una vega montuosa* (like a mountainous valley), justifies the supplement *á maravilla* (as to marvel). Thus a paradoxical landscape infuses the storehouse of the exotic with new dimensions and parcels of reality.

But this picturesque landscape, under an oxymoronic expression, also anticipates the staging of another paradox—the noble savage, whom Columbus depicts in no less picturesque terms. After one of the ships runs aground, a tableau describes the lord and his people lamenting the tragedy with the attributes we have come to recognize in the figure of the noble savage: "ellos aman á sus próximos como á sí mismo, y tienen una habla la más dulçe del mundo, y mansa y siempre con risa" [They love their neighbors as themselves, and have a talk that is the sweetest and gentlest in the world, and that always comes with a smile] (Tuesday, 25 December 1492). This transposition of the highest value to "savages" outside of civilization or Christianity, in itself, repeats an ironic use of the paradox that has been common at least since Tacitus.[38] But Columbus gives the motif an unexpected turn as he moves from an abstract ascription of virtue into a picturesque tableau: "el señor ya traýa camisa y guantes, qu'el almirante le avía dado, y por los guantes hizo mayor fiesta que por cosa que le dió. en su comer, con su honestidad y hermosa manera de limpieza, se mostrava bien ser de linaje" [The lord now wore a shirt and gloves that the admiral had given him, and for the gloves he made a greater show than for anything else. In his eating, by his decency and fine sort of cleanliness, he well showed that he was of good birth] (Wednesday, 26 December 1492). Here Columbus juxtaposes a festive adoption of gloves, a European mark of nobility, that accentuates the savage's natural disposition toward nobility, with clean table manners, which in turn confirm a noble descent. He thus inverts natural and cultural orders in the process: just as the adoption of European clothing, though in a comical if not bizarre manner, is a mark of nobility that reveals nature, clean and beautiful table manners reveal a blood line, a natural sign of the noble.

The constitution of the savage as noble mirrors Columbus's own transfiguration into a *don* upon his successful return. Columbus seems to anticipate the gallant display of the fineries as well as the deferential privileges of the admiralcy; for example, a meal like the one Las Casas describes in the company of the cardinal and archbishop of Toledo, D. Pero González, after which Columbus was to be always served like a *señor*, a lord: "Y aquella fué la primera vez que al dicho Almirante se le hizo salva y le servieron cubierto como a señor; y desde allí adelante se sirvío con la solemnidad y fausto que requería su digno título de Almirante" [And for the first time Columbus was served a full-course dinner with covered dishes and a food taster, and from then on everyone served him with the solemnity and pomp that his title of admiral commanded].[39] Such outward signs denoting the admiralcy motivate Columbus's particular version of the noble savage. If Columbus had sailed merely as a mariner or a merchant, the symbolic investments of the Amerindians might well have taken a different turn. In fact, however, the theme of the noble savage's natural virtue, which expands through most of the early accounts, is formulated with signs belonging to a particular European class—one that could be given only by someone from that class or by one preoccupied with analogous investments upon his own person.[40]

The two types of memory meet again. On the immediate record, the docility of the "native" guarantees a facile conversion within a civilizing mission and an overall project of colonization. In a long-term memory, the picturesqueness of the tableau bespeaks a travesty of indigenous peoples that long outlives Columbus's description of a proud but festive native lord half-clad in Western attire. Along with the stock noble savage incarnating the virtues of Christianity or civilization, we find a new version—the savages' willingness to adopt European customs and costumes, and thereby to submit their bodies to the inscriptions of power.

This last point takes us to the specific forms colonialism and exploration assumed in what we may call the age of writing. The writing of history and the formation of a New World encyclopedia are [no longer a] record *of* exemplary lives, or a compendium of the world, but a record *for* the imposition of an order on the world. Thus Columbus exemplifies writing in the mode of a master discourse—writing as a conquering and capitalistic enterprise. But more important than outlining such salient, colonialist features as the institution of slavery is the task of tracing less conspicuous forms of subjectivity still influential today. Whereas an emphasis on brutal forms of colonialism could serve to absolve our present by distancing it from Columbus's time, an examination of apparently benign sides of Columbus commonly found in his picturesque landscapes, his ethnographic descriptions, or his utopian dimensions would reveal a colonial legacy underlying our modern discourse.

PARADISE AND THE PROPHETIC PERSONA

It is evident in the preceding descriptions of an exotic landscape and a noble savage that Columbus's subjectivity must infuse marvel and paradox into his descriptions in order for a new reality to surface. By means of poetic expressions, he fabricates new realms of sense in the interstices of the familiar. In his own words Columbus prides himself for the production of a *new world*: ". . . cometí viage nuevo al nuevo çielo y mundo, que fasta entonçes estava oculto. . . . salió á pareçer de mi yndustria" [I entered upon a new voyage to a new heaven and a new earth, which up to then had lain hidden. . . . Through my industry it has appeared] (*Racc.*, pt. 1, 2:67). In the context of this "Letter to the Nurse," written after the third voyage, it is clear that Columbus refers not merely to the surfacing of new territories on the map but to an ontologically different region of the world with millenarian implications, "del nuevo çielo é tierra que hasía Nuestro Señor, escriviendo sant Juan el Apocalis . . . me hiso d'ello mensagero, y amostró á qual parte" [of the new heaven and earth, which Our Lord spoke of through Saint John in the Apocalypse . . . he made me the messenger and showed me where to go] (*Racc.*, pt. 1, 2:66). Within a millenarian theme Columbus builds his persona as a fulfillment of prophecy and as an illumination of the secret paths of Providence. The topics and themes of the exotic landscape and the noble savage conjoin and lend support to a millenarian interpretation of his discovery. In the process, Columbus elaborates and refurbishes these thematic blocks with new motifs and unheard-of fragments of reality to evoke the historical break he announces as being in the offing.

Thus during the third voyage Columbus bases his location of Paradise[41] on the mild climate and air that he carefully registered since the first voyage:

> yo no hallo ni jamás e hallado escriptura de Latinos ni de Griegos que çertificadamente diga ál, sino en este mundo, del paraýso terrenal; ni e visto en ningún mapamundo, salvo situado con autoridad de argumento, algunos le ponían allí donde son las fuentes del Nilo en Ethiopía; mas otros anduvieron todas estas tierras y no hallaron conformidad d'ello en la temperançia del çielo, en la altura hazia el çielo, porque se pudiese comprehender que él era allí. . . . algunos gentiles quisieron dezir por argumentos, que él era en las islas Fortunate, que son la Canarias, &c.
> [I do not find nor have I ever found any writing of the Romans or Greeks which give definitely the position in the world of the earthly paradise, nor have I seen it in any world map, save placed with authority by argument. Some placed it where are the sources of the Nile in Ethiopia; but others traversed all these lands and found no correspondance to it in the climate or in elevation toward the sky, to make it comprehensible that it was there. . . . Some Gentiles wished to show by arguments that it was in the Fortunate Islands, which are the Canaries, &c.] (*Racc.*, pt. 1, 2:37)

Columbus goes on to mention how Saint Isidore, Strabo, the Venerable Bede, Saint Ambrose, and Duns Scotus, and all sane theologians agree that Paradise is in the "Far East." What separates Columbus's account from mistaken locations depends on his having found a region in the world in conformity with the climate and height of the earth expected near Paradise.

Like most mariners and practical men of this time, he allows the empirical to override authority. What counts for empirical observation need not have anything to do with our own understanding of reality, as is evident in Columbus's experience of geographic space after crossing what he considers a "natural" line of demarcation between Spain and Portugal: "& para esto

allego todas las razones sobre escriptas de la raya que passa al
ocçidente de los Açores çient leguas de septentrion en austro,
que, en passando de allí al poniente, ya van los navíos alçándose
hazia el cielo suavemente, y entonçes se goza de más suave
temperançia" [And for this I give hereinafter all the arguments
about the line that passes from north to south one hundred
leagues west of the island of the Azores, that, in passing thence
to the westward, the ships went rising gently toward the sky and
then one enjoys a milder climate] (*Racc.*, pt. 1, 2:35). This
sensuous and dreamlike image of gliding to the top of the world
has the same pertinence to the real as the geographic location of
paradise Columbus is arguing for on the basis of experience.
According to Columbus, climate radically changes at the line of
demarcation set in the Second Bull, *Inter caetera* (1493), divid-
ing all future possessions of Portugal and Spain 100 leagues from
the Azores. Portugal contested this demarcation, and in the
Treaty of Tordecillas (1494) Spain consented to setting the line
360 leagues from the Azores. Such a concession diminished
Columbus's area of discovery and sovereignty, which in this
letter he seeks to correct by determining the appropriate geographic demarcation in terms of the unique climate of the regions
he discovered. For Columbus a natural vertical line 100 leagues
from the Azores separates two worlds. The day-by-day inscription of observations and metaphors in the course of the first
voyage not only constitutes a mnemonic device but also produces
the effect of random observations that allows Columbus to
transform his data into natural signs confirming an acknowl-
edged referent.

Along with the temperate climate and the experience of rising
to a higher region of the earth, the discovery of the mouth of the
Orinoco leads Columbus to believe himself in the vicinity of
Paradise. Legend and fact lend support to each other for the
invention of an austral land mass: "y digo que si no procede del
paraýso terrenal, que viene este río y proçede de tierra infinita,
pues al austro, de la cual fasta agora no se a avido notiçia. mas yo
muy assentado tengo [en] el ánima que allí, adonde dixe, es el
paraýso terrenal, y descanso sobre las razones y auctoridades
sobre escriptas" [I say that if it is not from earthly paradise that
this river comes, that this river comes from an infinite land,
toward the south, of which until now there had been no knowl-

edge, but I am very convinced in my own mind that there, where I have said, is the earthly paradise, and I rely upon the arguments and authorities given above] (*Racc.*, pt. 1, 2:39).

This passage echoes ancient and medieval projections of an austral fourth region of the earth, most notably in Pliny, Isidore, Bacon, and d'Ailly. Not only does Columbus's assertion follow this tradition, but Vespucci and Waldseemüller subscribe to it as well; the latter, as W. G. L. Randles has shown, almost repeats word for word a passage from Isidore's *Etymologies* when he proclaims Vespucci's discovery of a new continent in the *Cosmographiae introductio* (1507).[42] Novelty and fact, beyond the motivation of the authors, inscribe themselves on the margins of a textualized world. I do not want to deny the importance of Vespucci's observations, or the onomastic pun in the *Cosmographiae* that coined the name America,[43] or the crystallization of a notion of a new continent and a cluster of New World motifs associated with their name—but rather to assert the need of a pretextualization of the New World in order that the interplay between the imaginary and the real makes sense. Authoritative texts serve as a semiotic frame for the factual, while simultaneously providing elements and criteria for the production of new signs. With respect to Columbus, I have tried to show how a frame of reference surfaces in the transition from a metaphorical production of a climatic difference in the *Diario* to the naturalization of new significations as characteristic signs of the *new world*. In the above quote, authoritative texts lack the actual experience of the new lands—*fasta agora no se a avido noticia* (hitherto no knowledge has been obtained)—but both *razones y auctoridades* (arguments and authorities) ground Columbus's conviction. Whereas *razones y auctoridades* justify Columbus's beliefs, the mouth of the Orinoco provides empirical evidence.

Authorities favored by Columbus place Paradise at the end of the Orient, but vaguely outline the determinant traits of its location. As such, legend, without *noticia* (knowledge), serves as a prophetic paradigm when Columbus writes: "grandes indiçios son estos del Paraýso terrenal. . . . yo jamás leý ni oý que tanta cantidad de agua dulce fuese así adentro & vezina con la salada. y si de allí del Paraýso no sale, pareçe aun mayor maravilla, porque no creo que se sepa en el mundo de río tan grande y tan fondo" [These are great tokens of the earthly

78

paradise. . . . for I have never read nor heard of so great a
quantity of fresh water so far into the sea and near the salt water.
And if it does not come from there, from paradise, it seems to be
a still greater marvel, for I do not believe that there is known in
the world a river so great and so deep] (*Racc.*, pt. I, 2:35). Here
Columbus juxtaposes the mouth of the Orinoco as a great token
(signs correspond to what theologians say) with the experience
of an unprecedented phenomenon, *jamás leý ni oý* (never read
nor heard). A sense of the marvelous beyond legend surfaces in
both equations. Authoritative texts serve as a semiotic frame for
the factual while simultaneously providing elements and criteria
for the production of new signs. On the one hand, the site and
signs of Paradise are no longer things to be read about but to be
experienced; on the other hand, the mouth of the Orinoco, if it is
not a token of Paradise, would be an even greater marvel since it
has no legendary antecedent. Either way, Columbus's discovery
goes beyond the imagination of the poets and prophets.

   In Columbus's account of his fourth voyage, his persona as the
messenger and receptacle of prophecy gains even more precision
from an allusion to Joachim of Flora's prophecy concerning the
recovery of Jerusalem for Christendom: "El abbad Joachín dixo
que éste avía de salir de España" [Abbot Joachim said that this
one was to come from Spain] (*Racc.*, pt. I, 2:202). The eventu-
ality of the discovery has significance only in terms of a prophetic anticipation that entails the recovery of Jerusalem and the final
conversion of all the peoples. The event confirms the metahis-
torical, which, in turn, constitutes the event as the advent of a
new time. Elsewhere in a less "medieval framework" we find a
fine example of the "renascent imaginariness" at work in a slight
modification of a passage from Seneca's *Medea* in Columbus's
Libro de las profecías: "Vernán los tardos años del mundo ciertos tiempos en los quales el mar Ocçéano afloxerá los atamentos
de las cosas, y se abrirá una grande tierra, *y um nuebo marinero,
como aquél que fué guýa de Jasón, que hobo nombre Tiphi*,
descobrirá nuebo mundo, y entonces non será la ysla Tille la
postrera de las tierras" [An age will come after many years when
the Ocean will loose the chains of things, and a huge land lie
revealed; *and a new sailor, like the one who guided Jason, whose
name was Typhis*, will disclose a new world; then Thule will no
longer be the hindermost] (*Racc.*, pt. I, 2:141). I have empha-

79

sized Columbus's modification of Seneca's text, in which Typhis replaces Thetis, the nymph.[44] Columbus identifies himself with the pilot of the Argonauts and thus appropriates the prophecy. The allusion to Jason obviously is not intended to recall Horace's astonishment and anger at man's audacity to plow the seas, nor does it share the curse of the first builder of boats common to such Golden Age poets and playwrights as Tirso de Molina, Luis de Góngora, and Lope de Vega.[45] On the contrary, Columbus's reference to Jason certainly intends to celebrate technological innovation and suggest a wish-horizon where the Golden Fleece is now at hand within the mirage of Eldorado.[46] Once more the enterprise and its manufacturer become the master code for interpreting all possible prefigurations of the discovery. With the stereotypes of both the Middle Ages and the Renaissance, Columbus scrambles medieval canons of subordination to God by extolling his historical persona.

We have seen how new particulars surface and constitute a notion of a *new world* in Columbus's account of his exploration. Paradisiacal images generated by metaphor give place to a symbolic field of reference. Columbus appropriates the themes of noble savagery, exoticism, and millenarianism as he infuses them with new examples. Thus the beginning of a new legend, that of a New World, forms from the sediments of an empirical negation of legend. Facts more marvelous than the dreams of the poets and prophets must now be textually encoded, thereby acquiring a likeness to the very fables they refute. Columbus himself bemoans the inevitable suspension of belief with which readers will receive his accounts of the *new world*, thereby turning his empirical record into legend. Much will be lost in the transition from actually seeing to merely hearing about the marvels of the new land: "y finalmente dize que quando él que lo vee le es tan grande admiración, quando más será á quien lo oyere, y que nadie lo podrá creer si no lo viere" [And finally he says that if it fills one who sees it with such wonder, how much more will it be for one who hears it, and that nobody will be able to believe it without seeing] (Sunday, 25 November 1492).

Seeing and hearing establish a contrariety between the narrator and the addressee with respect to the given descriptions. The limits of the narrator are set by what cannot be said, whether because of a lack of denomination (that is, absence of a code) or because of an infinitude of particulars that must be sifted and organized in the descriptions. The meaning and force of the descriptions, however, lie outside the utterance itself, and in perceiving these parcels of reality readers are limited by the code significations available in their own stock of information. A map and a painting of the coastline would guarantee the reiteration of the voyage, but it would not evaluate the new lands' potential riches, generate desire, or inflame the imagination. A pictorial representation would require a caption. More than offering a mode for determining the meaning of the lands, then, the written text must elaborate the mirage and project desire. The conformity of the object of desire with legend sets the limits of the believable; but deviation from the familiar implies a lack of precedent and invites the imagination to receive semantic innovations. Indeed, a subtle alternation between tautological assimilations and novel metaphors makes Columbus an accomplished publicist. The above metadiscursive statement offers a glimpse of what Michel Beaujour calls in the quotation given at the beginning of this chapter the "mimesis of the visionary mind." Columbus's descriptions are embedded in a system where marvel and legend interplay with one another for the simultaneous production of a *new man* and a *new world*.

    Finally, we may relate Columbus's problematic writing of the new to an enigmatic inscription in the World Map of Hereford (c. 1290): "omnia plus legenda quam pingenda" (all things that must be read rather than painted). It is *legenda* (things to be read) and not *escribenda* (things to be written) that is set in contradistinction to painting. It is the reader's point of view that is asserted in this maxim, but the maxim also reduces the writer to an iteration of the readable. From all appearances, nothing is farther from Columbus and the scriptural economy of the Renaissance than this insistence on reading.[47] The wandering from one island to another in the pursuit of legend gives place to the errant, endless scriptural task of depicting the marvelous: ". . . para hazer relación á los Reyes de las cosas que vían no bastaran mill lenguas á referillo, ni su mano para lo escrevir, que le parecía qu'estava encantado" [To give an account to the sovereigns of the things that they saw a thousand tongues would not suffice, nor his hand to write, for it appeared that he was enchanted] (Tuesday, 27

November 1492). Enchantment, a paralyzed pen, seals this self-portrait. Indeed, a marvelous *new world* entails a marveled subject. And marvel implies a distance between the subject and the object, an opaque region that not only posits "nature" as a locus to be inscribed on a "blank page" but also marks a shift from finding topics to a reflection on writing the new.

Entrancement and marvel surface at the limits of productive discourse and define a horizon where the exotic, the noble savage, and the millennium betray ruptures in meaning. These discursive lapses inaugurate topics that in the course of history have come to define the specificity of the New World. Instead of identifying passages as pertaining to a medieval or a Renaissance corpus or mentality, we have seen how Columbus draws new significations from citations and references to medieval literature. Marvel, on the other hand, introduces a rift between the subject and the object where "nature" emerges as a locus of description—that is, as an amorphous surface that simultaneously prompts rapture and the project to exploit its riches. If I have privileged rapture over exploitation, it has not been to undermine the latter but to emphasize the legacy of colonial discourse in forms of sensibility and thought not readily associated with colonialism. The emergence of "nature" in the interstices of Columbus's discourse anticipates a particularly modern form of subjectivity generally identified with Descartes's *Metaphysical Meditations*.[48] Take as examples those passages from Columbus and other chroniclers of the Indies where a subject facing an unknown object is led to question language and the scope of a received tradition, and, a fortiori, to constitute a "blank page." The possibility in itself of posing a project leading to the discovery and colonization of America already presupposes the scriptural economy of the Renaissance. Indeed, Descartes is perhaps the most formalized expression of technological and epistemological transformations in effect since the mid-fifteenth century.

CHAPTER 3

Dialogue as Conquest in the Cortés–Charles V Correspondence

MULEY: *Valiente eres español*
y cortés como valiente
tan bien vences con la lengua,
como con la espada vences.
[Courageous you are, Spaniard,
and courteous as well as courageous;
As well you conquer with the tongue
as with the sword you conquer.]
    Pedro Calderón de la Barca, El príncipe constante, *1.11.703–6[1]*

Siempre publiqué y dije a todos los naturales de la tierra, así señores como
los que a mí venían, que vuestra majestad era servido que el dicho
Mutezuma se estuviese en su señorío, reconociendo el que vuestra alteza
sobre él tenía, y que servirían mucho a vuestra alteza en le obedecer y tener
por señor, como antes que yo a la tierra viniese le tenían.
[I always published and declared to the natives, both chiefs and those who
came to see me, that your majesty wished that Mutezuma should retain his
dominion, recognizing that which your majesty held over him, and that they
would be serving your highness by obeying him and considering him as their
lord as they had before I came to their land.]
    Hernán Cortés, Segunda carta a Carlos V[2]

CORTÉS AS PROTOANTHROPOLOGIST

The *Historia del Abencerraje y la hermosa Jarifa* (c. 1561) is generally credited for inaugurating a fashionable commonplace in Spanish literature of the Golden Age.[3] Following this novel, numerous ballads, histories, and plays tell of a Christian narrator who addresses and represents the image of a valiant Moor under defeat. What opens with an exaltation of the Moor's courage moves to a description of him sighing. Since captivity could not be the source of sorrow, the Spaniard presses the Moor to reveal the secret of his affliction: a love story lies at the core. In

Calderón's play *El principe constante*, Muley is a general in the Fès army who typically is first taken prisoner by the Christian prince Fernando and then reveals his secret and unhappy love affair with Fénix, the daughter of the King of Fès. In the above epigraph, however, Muley equates tongue with sword. This disperson of violence opens the Moorish genre not only to a new reading but also to the study of the representation of "alien" cultures.

The equation *discourse is violence*, obviously pertinent to the question of dialogue as conquest in Cortés's correspondence with Charles V, refines the commonplace *knowledge is power*; it displaces the formulation of the problem from misuse of information to an integral view of knowledge as a form of domination, of control. As Johannes Fabian has pointed out in *Time and the Other*, apropos of the uses of time by anthropology: "Anthropology's claim to power originated at its roots. It belongs to its essence and is not a matter of accidental misuse."[4] In the context of anthropology, dialogue with informants in fieldwork is the most prevalent form of acquiring information. Thus power relations can be traced, beyond the uses of time in the representation of alien cultures, to the initial production of "raw" data. In the case of Cortés we find an openly stated understanding of the uses of dialogue for conquest as well as a comprehension of the power of knowledge. In contrast, modern anthropology, despite the ambiguous roles functionalism played in the theorization of British indirect rule, resists the image of the anthropologists as conqueror.[5]

An apparent exception, from within a French tradition, would be Marcel Griaule's use of militaristic metaphors to convey the process of gaining access to another culture. The two main metaphoric structures of Griaule's ethnographic method are, as James Clifford sums them up, "a documentary system (governed by images of collection, observation, and interrogation) and an initiatory complex (where dialogical processes of education and exegesis come to the fore)."[6] Thus an ongoing, long-term penetration into the secrets of the culture complements a panoptic representation of the whole. But again, Griaule's metaphors of conquest pertain not to a direct filiation with a colonial power but to an unabashed acknowledgement of power and the manipulation of informants: "We'd make him smile, spit up the truth, and

we'd turn out of his pockets the last secret polished by the
centuries, a secret to make he who has spoken it blanch with
fear."[7] The quote speaks for itself. One cannot simply dismiss
this statement as a breach of objectivity (though to speak thus is
certainly a breach of the postcolonial ethic of fieldwork). It
expresses a will to sift biased information in the pursuit of a
neutral account.

By paying attention to the power dynamics of dialogue and
representation, I will attempt to gauge the distance separating the
interested conqueror from the *neutral* anthropologist. The point
is not to reduce these enterprises to a common project or
intentionality, but to understand how conquest displays forms of
colonial encounter and epistemological limits that haunt the
intended good faith of ethnography.

One readily grasps the image of the anthropologist as conqueror in the equation *knowledge is power*. But even before the
misuse of knowledge for imperialistic purposes, the production
of knowledge already entails conquest. In the spirit of Nietzsche's
assertion that the concept of "liberty is an invention of the ruling
classes,"[8] this chapter shows how ethnographic dialogue was an
invention of the conquistadores. It aims to elaborate an experimental, perhaps perverse, genealogy of the conventional anthropological enterprise and of recent dialogical experiments as well.

In the first part of this chapter I briefly outline some of the
most outstanding features of conventional anthropology and its
critique by dialogical alternatives. This exposition is geared
around the question of Cortés as a protoanthropologist, indeed,
as an inventor of dialogue. The second part analyzes Cortés's
objectification of Mexican civilization and the place of knowledge and dialogue in the Conquest of Mexico. A third examines
the dialogue between Moctezuma and Cortés in light of a passage
from Hegel's *Phenomenology of Mind* on the Master/Slave relation. And beyond Cortés's recorded speech of the Mexican ruler,
Book 12 of the *Florentine Codex* (c. 1579) exemplifies the
indigenous narrative of the conquest. A fourth part traces how
from the start Cortés's letters evince a narrative transformation of
Mesoamerica into an ideal New Spain. In the concluding remarks I return to the question of anthropology's descent.

I must point out that the overall project attempts to dismantle
the "Europe and its others" complex overhanging the master

85

discourses of conquest and modern anthropology. In Gilles Deleuze and Félix Guattari's terms, this chapter aims to deterritorialize the latter by opening up margins, interstices in the master narratives (as it were, to constitute a context) where minor discourses may emerge.[9] Thus it will contribute to what James Clifford has defined as the necessity "to imagine a world of generalized ethnography," where a dispersion of authority and a mishmash of idioms would make it increasingly difficult to formulate dichotomous Self/Other definitions of independent cultures.[10]

The epigraph drawn from Cortés's Second Letter to Charles V (1520) purveys an ideal sense of conquest in which Moctezuma (or better, Motecuhzoma) would remain a master while serving Charles V. This formulation seeks to retain the ancient order intact. But it is plagued with a paradox, since Tenochtitlan had become accessible through the formation of hostile collaborators, which already implied the dissolution of the political structure of Moctezuma's dominions. It can be read as an early expression of what the British would call indirect rule. Before discussing functionalism in the context of indirect rule, a description of Cortés's writings will help us visualize his range of topics and the multiple facets of his personality, and thus to assess their proximities and distances to the modern anthropological enterprise.

In what has been called the *Corpus cortesianum* (1519–26), commonly known to English-speaking audiences as the *Five Letters of Cortés to the Emperor* in the 1928 abridged translation by J. Bayard Morris, the Second Letter stands out with its vivid descriptions of the cultures encountered in the ascent to Tenochtitlan from the Gulf of Mexico, the topography of central Mexico, and the urban complexity of Tenochtitlan. In addition, we can mention two lasting motifs in the literature of colonial encounters that first crystallized in this letter. The first is the destruction of the ships, which, despite the falsification of the event, gave rise to the image of "burning the ships behind him." The second motif is the identification of Cortés with the god Quetzalcoatl in the dialogue with Moctezuma (according to native history this semidivine figure, banished in a distant time and place, had prophesied his return in the form of a conqueror). First printed in Seville in 1522, the Second Letter underwent several printings and translations in the sixteenth century. The most notable of these is the Latin version printed in Nuremberg in 1524, which is important not only because of its broad circulation but also because it included a map attributed to Cortés, known in English as the Map of Mexico City and the Gulf.[11]

This edition also included the Third Letter (1522). As it has often been remarked, Cortés's love and admiration for Mexico in the Second Letter is replaced by hatred, terror, and the display of military strategies that led to the capture and destruction of Tenochtitlan.[12] But the tone is epic, and Cortés praises the courage, intelligence, and greatness of the enemy. One might argue that the appearance of Cortés as a conquistador depends on the image he fabricates of the conquered—the enemy must be a worthy contender in order to infuse a chivalric tone into his narration. Indeed, a long tradition in Spanish letters that alternates between "vilified" and "idealized" Moors mediates Cortés's representation of his Mexican opponents.[13]

The Fourth Letter was first printed in Toledo in 1525 and underwent a second edition in Zaragoza in 1526. It did not have the diffusion in Latin of the Second and Third Letters and was not printed outside Spain until 1779, in a German edition. This letter dwells mostly on the organization of the new colony as well as on the reconstruction of Mexico City. Cortés appears at the peak of his political and military career.

Though the First Letter was written by the cabildo (the judiciary and council) of Vera Cruz, it forms part of the five major letters. This letter was discovered in the Imperial Archives of Vienna during the last century by William Robertson while he was searching for the lost "first letter" of Cortés and was never printed in Spain until 1844. This letter gives an account of the earlier explorations of the Gulf of Mexico by Francisco Hernández de Córdova and Juan de Grijalva. But more importantly, this letter justifies the disobedience of the trade-oriented instructions of Diego Velázquez, the governor of Cuba. It argues that the continuation of trade, specifically of slaves, would be detrimental to the interest of the empire. Access to what is described as a vast, highly sophisticated civilization ruling from the hinterland would be curtailed by following Velázquez's policies.

In the Fifth Letter (1526), also discovered during the above-mentioned search for the lost letter and never published until the nineteenth century, Cortés narrates the main events of his expedition to Honduras and informs Charles V how he followed an indigenous map of the territories. Thus the letter is highly revealing of how Cortés appropriated native texts.

In addition to these major letters (of approximately 40,000 words each, with the exception of the First and Third, with 10,000 and 20,000 respectively), Cortés wrote other shorter letters, ordinances, and instructions. One may further complement the corpus with the letters of Charles V to Cortés.[14] This chapter is mainly concerned with the policies expressed in those documents written between 1519 and 1526. As Marcel Bataillon has pointed out, Cortés became a forbidden author in 1527.[15] The "honeymoon" with Charles V ended, Cortés's power was undermined, and the correspondence increasingly pleaded for the value of his former deeds. It was indeed during these years that a concept of conquest, centered on dialogue, was jointly elaborated in their exchange of letters.

From the correspondence we can derive an image of Cortés that combines the functions of soldier, administrator, jurist, and, more important for the purpose of this chapter, of a protoethnographer. Cortés's early elaboration of indirect rule allots a place to the native elite that closely parallels the one given them later within the structure of the British Empire, and more poignantly, parallels the contributions made by functionalist anthropology to an efficient administration. But functionalism should not be reduced to a handmaiden of colonial authority. In keeping with its specialization as a discipline during the first half of the twentieth century, the scientific observation by academic anthropology of alien cultures was defined as objective and neutral (value-free). Such scientist claims set the ethnographer apart from the missionaries, administrators, and other practical types. And it was precisely on account of these claims that anthropologists were able to appeal to the Colonial Office, without this fact necessarily jeopardizing the autonomy of the discipline. After World War II, mainly as a consequence of changes in the colonial world, there was a rearrangement of the cadre and, perhaps, a reformulation of the ethics of the discipline. We may note that the claims of objectivity and neutrality were further reinforced. In a recent article George Marcus and Dick Cushman have pointed out how the American and British traditions, despite their different theoretical orientations (cultural versus social structural), consolidated ethnographic realism as "*the* 'literary institution' serving positivistic scientific goals."[16] Ethnographic realism sets the backdrop for recent experiments in ethnographic writing. Among the most notable changes are the inclusion of the encounter in the fieldwork and the substitution of dialogue for the us/them implicit in an omniscient point of view. The above schema of twentieth-century anthropology is far from complete, and I might add that it is subordinate to my purpose: to read Cortés as a protoethnographer whose writings manifest the determining historical structure of the "Europe and its others" complex that haunts the anthropological project.[17]

The same criteria of objectivity and neutrality, and the formulation of universal laws to explain social life that have defined anthropology as a positive science, have constituted the basis for the traditional histories of the discipline. Thus genealogies are set in motion where premodern figures state "felicitous" phrasings that anticipate the more rigorous propositions of modern anthropology. Within this perspective there is no room for Cortés or even for Bernardino de Sahagún among the other missionaries.[18] Their accounts are either bypassed or dismissed as aberrant forms of knowledge. Historians proceed as if to exorcise the discipline from demons of colonialism by excluding forms of inquest candidly posed as modes of gaining dominion.

Muley's unmasking of Don Fernando's conquering language in *El príncipe constante* may serve as an epigram to illuminate a blindness in the formation of anthropology as a scientific discipline—that is, the hiatus between colonialism and the claims of objectivity and neutrality. One could also fictionally transpose the setting to a dialogue between Moctezuma and Cortés. On the one hand, the use of language for conquest is indeed a constant in documents expressing Spain's imperial policies toward both the Moors and the Amerindians. On the other hand, anthropology constitutes itself as a scientific discipline by dissociating its task of knowing alien cultures from colonialism. The metaphorical use of the term *conquest*, however, recurs here and there in the literature to mean the art of seducing informants to reveal the truth of their culture. But certainly there is no room for Muley's unmasking of the power of discourse. Such a response would at least undermine the patronizing adoption as "my people," but more radically, it would breach the scientific claims of ethnography. As Jeanne Favret-Saada has pointed out, objectivity demands a transformation of the "I" and "you" in the fieldwork to an impersonal "we" (author/reader) and "s/he" (the other) in the written text.[19]

Muley's words furnish a motif that testifies to the "yoking of force and discourse."[20] They also suggest a clearing in the power of representation that Edward Said's *Orientalism* analyzes in terms of the concomitant production of a Western omniscient self and a silent other. Calderón's other not only speaks but deconstructs the textual violence effected on the Moor by an "abencerraje-inspired tradition of romantic and noble Moors."[21] As a self-deconstructive passage, it unmasks the violence of representation; moreover, the motif also conveys an intratextual reference where communication itself corresponds to a mode of conquest. Thus we may associate the two primordial elements of ethnography—fieldwork and writing—with domination.

Kevin Dwyer and Vincent Crapanzano, among others, have pointed out a need to include the confrontation with informants in the written text.[22] Against a monological approach that construes the reality of the other out of field notes or experiences, they propose a dialogical model where the voices of the interlocutors would reveal the joint construction of a shared reality. I cannot do justice here to the complexity and sophistication of Dwyer's and Crapanzano's proposals. It is not a question of writing them off, but of pointing out some shortcomings in what one may call the "becoming minor" of anthropology's master discourse. Dialogue is but one mode among others of ethnographic authority. As James Clifford has pointed out, Dwyer's and Crapanzano's texts "remain *representations* of dialogue," where the possibility of escaping typifications "depends on their ability fictionally to maintain the strangeness of the other voice and to hold in view the specific contingencies of the exchange."[23] Given the present discussion, the overriding control of the writer in the textualization of the encounter does not come as a surprise, but my point is to trace it back to the exchanges in the field.

"As Tuhami's interlocutor," writes Crapanzano, "I became an active participant in his life history, even though I rarely appear directly in his recitation." Crapanzano goes on to mention how "my presence and questions not only prepared him for the text he was to produce, but they produced what I read as a change of consciousness in him. They produced a change of consciousness in me, too."[24] Both persons change, and accordingly the text implies a critique of timeless, ahistorical ethnographies that silence the other. But who is the master puppeteer in the interview? Dwyer reflects on the virtues of his own text, a "direct" record of a taped dialogue. "I reject the Faqir's attempts to provide initial formulations of otherness." Only on the basis of such guided interrogatories can the project achieve the following results: "What emerges for the Faqir is a greater potential for self-realization, for me of self-transcendence; for one the development of self, for the other its mutation."[25] Even though there is a potential dialogical questioning of authority in the self-transcendence and mutation expressed in this passage, the ethnographer, once more, retains the stronger role in the communication as he fashions himself as a vehicle for the self-realization of the Faqir. Indeed, Dwyer defines what is real in his rejection of the Faqir's answers. This perhaps explains the Faqir's falling asleep during the last interview that closes Dwyer's book. It certainly testifies to Dwyer's honesty by displaying the limits of his enterprise.[26] The ethnographer aims (as a practitioner of an academic discipline) to produce a specific type of knowledge that delimits the nature of the questions as well as the answers of the informant. In fact, ethnographic dialogue pertains to a speech genre that molds the active response of the listener. Dialogical ethnography can only aspire, in its present form as a colonial/colonized discipline, to represent the power dynamics of fieldwork.[27]

A theoretical point will help us further understand the shortcomings of dialogical ethnography. Insofar as communication requires that an addresser and an addressee recognize a referent in the interior of a message, dialogue corresponds to a form of "worlding," of constituting unmotivated signs.[28] The becoming unmotivated of signs, however, implies a stronger discourse that ultimately defines a sense of reality. Moreover, the above definition of communication is specifically a Western invention. Roy Wagner has drawn the following distinction: "We should not be surprised to discover that urban Westerners stress the use of language as control, whereas tribal, peasant, and lower-class peoples control language through expressive formulations (through their use of the world, we might say)."[29]

Whenever these two modes of relating to language are dominant, it necessarily implies a breakdown in communication.
Referents can never be recognized as long as two different
contexts or discourses mediate their significance. As such,
dialogue with an other is an illusion. There is only dialogue
among the same, and indeed, it is power-ridden. Since going
native forecloses the possibility of representing the other, con-
— trol by means of translation seems to be the other alternative.
– Logical as well as rhetorical constructs, however, thwart the
project of translation. But perhaps the same forms of inquiry
from which ethnography dissociated itself might suggest another
alternative. Whereas the university-trained ethnographer posits
resistance at the limits of the enterprise, the missionary and the
colonial administrator reveal the spaces of counterdiscourse.
The former sublates the confrontation by straightening out the
informants' misapprehensions; the latter open the text to mock-
ery, parody, and hybridization whereby the colonized question
authority.[30] Paradoxically, domination provides a keener display of invention by the colonial subject.

The figure of Cortés and the event of the Conquest of Mexico
are well known and do not need a recapitulation here. I will not be
concerned with cataloguing further the cruelties, ideological
manipulations, and negative attitudes toward Mesoamerican
civilization that the partisans of the so-called Black Legend have
been busily composing from Las Casas and de Bry up to W. Arens
and Tzvetan Todorov.[31] Inevitably, they succumb to a totalizing
interpretation of the event. It seems to me that the apologists of
the conquest, and Cortés in particular, pose a more complex
question to examine: "Ya sus contemporáneos comenzaron la
enumeración de sus defectos, tarea que se ha proseguido hasta
hoy; pero que no se olvide un factor esencialísimo en la valoria-
ción de Cortés. El amor y la estimación de que gozaba entre los
indios" [Already his contemporaries began the enumeration of
his defects, a task that has been continued until today; but an
essential factor for the appraisal of Cortés must not be forgotten:
the love and esteem he had among the Indians].[32] Ramón
Iglesias's brilliant observation obviously implies Cortés's love for
Mexico. But why do I call this move by Iglesias brilliant? Simply
because I take the "love of Cortés" as a crucial aspect of the
conquest. A number of approaches can be derived from Iglesias's

point. On the one hand, one could accentuate the desire of a conqueror by the Indians, while on the other, one could also insist on the motif of the conquered conquistador. I have chosen instead to observe how "love" has a strategic place in the program of conquest. In brief, dialogue and communication constitute an integral component of the conquest, and not an extrinsic factor for evaluation. In what follows we will examine the terrain where the ordinary definition of discourse as dialogue emerges as a rule within the discursive formation that frames the performance of the conquistador and the production of Mexico. My purpose is to highlight how the figure and the actions of Cortés constitute paradigmatic motifs in New World literature that will also recur in other representations of colonial encounters, and certainly not to privilege Cortés, or any other individual for that matter, to interpret the entire social, political, and historical process.[33]

THE GARDEN IN THE IDEAL CITY OF THE CONQUISTADOR

Hernán Cortés's Map of Mexico City and the Gulf (fig. 5) juxtaposes an outline of the Gulf Coast to a plan of Tenochtitlan. From this map one can derive the basic elements that differentiate a discourse of explanation from one of conquest. The map provides as well a point of entry for a more elaborate analysis of the discourse of conquest in Cortés's correspondence with Charles V.

In a nutshell, the New World of the explorer corresponds to an idyllic garden whose contours need to be mapped and its specimens described and named; on the other hand, the New World city of the conquistador contains the secrets of the land, and thus learning the native text undermines the value of direct description.

In the discourse of exploration as represented by Columbus, we have found a territorialization of amorphous space. In its extreme form, it approximates a utopian Adamic state where names are given to things. Akin to this Adamic state of linguistic invention, the explorers define the particularities of the region by equating garden and nature. Not only Columbus, but Vespucci as well, describes the New World in paradisiacal terms and speculates on the location of the terrestrial paradise. Alongside description of unprecedented phenomena and the inscription of names on a map, the process of territorialization depends on

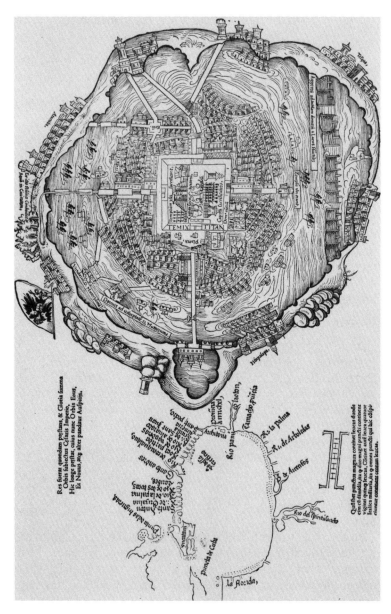

Figure 5. From this map one can derive the basic elements that differentiate a discourse of exploration from one of conquest. *Map of Mexico City and the Gulf Coast (1524), attributed to Hernán Cortés. Courtesy Benson Latin American Collection, General Libraries, University of Texas at Austin.*

lenguas (trained captives) who provide information on the land. Rules for the exchange of goods, political structures, and other cultural forms do not have visible expressions in the writings of the explorer (isolated ethnographic descriptions lack the representation of a cultural totality); but the indigenous text is certainly seen as a thesaurus that contains the things of the garden and their whereabouts. This same lack of indigenous cultural visibility (that is, a lack of readily identifiable cultural artifacts bearing the inscriptions of a native stock of knowledge) defines the proper program of the explorer as one of colonization—the enclave as a colony of settlers, which constitutes an appendage for further explorations. An exploitation of a labor force certainly exists, but not a material base in the form of farms, kilns, orchards, and so on which could be guerdoned—the prizes of war are problematic.[34]

Since a policy for settlement and the construction of new cities in the Americas represents a preamble to the discovery of vast urban complexes in Peru and Mexico, it is worthwhile to take a look at the crown's instructions given to Pedro Arias Dávila for building cities in the New World:

> Vistas las cosas que para los asientos de los lugares son necesarias, y escogido el sitio más provechoso y en el que incurren más de las cosas que para el pueblo son menester, habréis de repartir los solares del lugar para facer las casas, y éstos han de ser segund la calidad de las personas, e sean de comienzo dados por orden; por manera que, hechos los solares, el pueblo parezca ordenando, así en el lugar en que se dejare para plaza, como en el lugar en que hobiere la iglesia, como en la orden que tovieren las calles, porque en los lugares que de nuevo se hacen dando la orden en el comienzo sin ningud trabajo ni costa quedan ordenados e los otros jamás se ordenan.
>
> [Having considered the things that are necessary for the settlement of places, and having chosen the most beneficial site and where one runs into most of the things needed for the town, you must distribute the plots of land to build the houses, and these according to the quality of the persons, and from the beginning must be given with order; so that, having allotted the plots, the town appears ordered, as much in the place left for the market, as in the place for the church, as in the order of the streets; because when new places are built from the beginning with order, they remain ordered without toil or cost; otherwise they are never ordered.][35]

One may trace in the repetitive insistence on an initial order as means of preventing future disorder the basic characteristics of what Lewis Mumford, in *The City in History*, calls the Baroque City.[36] In its emphasis on hierarchy, geometry, surveillance, and discipline, this document anticipates the parallel corrective measures for patching up the "disorder" of the medieval city. The theoretical antecedents, specific politico-economic motivations, or the military exigencies that define the program for a new order in Europe need not concern us here; the theme is too vast and exceeds the particularities I seek to define with respect to the cities in the New World. We must note that the above instructions are not concerned with imposing an order on the Indians but with establishing one for the Spaniards. They seek to project a utopian structure into an "amorphous" political space. Indeed, it is a utopian order designed to avoid the vicissitudes of history. Moreover, the sequence of towns must be strategically arranged for future discoveries (in this particular case the Pacific Ocean), as another section of the document specifies: "Habéis de procurar con todo cuidado de tener fin en los de los pueblos adentro, que los fagáis en parte e asientos que os podáis aprovechar dellos para por tierra descubrir la otra costa de la mar" [You must endeavor with all the possible care to have a finality in the towns inland, that you build places and sites so that you can derive an advantage from them to discover the other coast of the sea].[37] Settlement remains an appendage to exploration, despite the promises of gold in Castilla del Oro. The above document defines a fundamental aspect of the invention of America, but it still lacks the specifics of a discourse of conquest.

In its effects on reality, the building of a colonial entrepôt may be likened to a palimpsest in the mode of an icon superimposed on a parchment bearing no textual connection with the image (fig. 6).[38] As the land is conceived as virginal, as a tabula rasa, the explorer proceeds according to the classical definition of colonialism—the building of colonies in unclaimed territories. It is not so much a question of imposing a foreign cultural model as of failing to perceive, recognize, decipher, and exploit Amerindian knowledge. The cultivated field with European produce, the introduction of cattle, and the buildings in the city cannot be differentiated from the space they constitute in the colonizing process. This geographic parallelism with a palimpsest has a corresponding form in the text written by the explorer. The explorer not only follows a native textualization of the land but

Figure 6. Colonization may be likened to a palimpsest in the mode of an icon superimposed on a parchment bearing no textual connection with the image. *A palimpsest. Personal collection.*

inscribes upon it the signs of the places and objects he expects to find. At the same time, the available map and stock of information are altered with new terms, pathways, and descriptions of unknown phenomena. Accordingly, the building of a colonial entrepôt is located in a *new* India. As a result of Waldseemüller's publication of Vespucci's letters, the term *New World* takes the status of a proper name—it defines a new continent to be called America. Although the silhouette of the landmass remains to be charted, the concept *New World* organizes the collecting of representative items and cultures.

The discourse of exploration provides the conquistador with two memories. One memory constitutes a geographic image of the territories for the objectification of new points in space; the other is a legal framework for the guidance of the historical actors. Next to these explicit codes, tentative formations of a thesaurus begin to appear in, for example, Martin Fernández de Enciso's *Suma de geografía* (1518) and the ongoing project of Peter Martyr's *Decades of the New World* (1494–1525). An implicit codification of New World things is also evident in the speech of the explorers, settlers, and future conquerors. In spite of the growing regulations set out by the crown, novel projects such as the exploration of the Gulf of Mexico crystallized in the speech of the Spaniards in the New World. Nevertheless, their relations to the crown must reflect the two memories pertaining to objectivity and legality so that the new territories make sense and the explorers' deeds are justifiable.

The early explorations of Juan de Grijalva and Francisco Hernández de Córdova antecede Cortés. They establish a register of Mesoamerican civilization with mostly offshore descriptions of stone buildings, massive populations, and tentative exchanges of quality goods; but the systematic collection of information for conquest, as well as the mirage of a fabulous city in the hinterland, does not surface until the First Letter drafted by the cabildo of Vera Cruz.

This letter announces the establishment of an autonomous government, separate from Velázquez's Cuba, under the authority of Cortés and furnishes the legal basis for justifying the rebellion against Velázquez. The rationale for disregarding the authority of Velázquez consists in replacing the trade-oriented instructions with a policy of settlement based on the prospect of

claiming additional territories in the future. Such a shift of
orientation depends at once on denunciation of the greed and
self-centeredness of Velázquez, and on a portrayal of this territory's difference from previous discoveries. Trade, *rescate*, in the
argument of the cabildo, implies wasting the land and arousing
distrust on the part of the Indians. The cabildo summons Cortés
to end trade: "Le requerimos que luego cesase de hacer rescates
de la manera que los venía a hacer, porque sería destruir la tierra
en mucha manera, y vuestras majestades serían en ello muy
deservidos" [We summoned him to immediately stop trading in
the way that he had come to do, because in many ways it would
greatly destroy the land, and your majesties would be greatly
disserved].[39] All the gifts are sent to Charles V as indices of the
wealthy civilization Cortés and his followers have encountered.
The above passage foregrounds the wealth and glory the emperor
will derive from their immediate subordination, which bypasses
all the intermediate authorities in the Indies.

Years later, Juan Ginés de Sepúlveda, the controversial jurist
and adversary of Las Casas in the debates at Valladolid, praises
Cortés's legal trappings for developing a subtle rationale, "dis-
curriendo una razón sutil, por la que hacía saber que desem-
peñaba el mando de la flota y los compañeros por un derecho
nuevo" [discoursing a subtle reason, by means of which he made
it known that he carried out the command of the fleet and his
comrades by a new legal right]. The legal grounds, according to
the speech of Cortés recorded by Sepúlveda, consist in declaring
an extraterritoriality of New Spain from all previous discoveries:
"Que hasta ahora él había desempeñado el cargo de capitán en
virtud del derecho y facultad que le había sido conferido por los
monjes, quienes tenían el supremo poder y gobierno en las islas
conquistadas, cuyo derecho de presidir y mandar abarca los
límites de las islas y el océano. Ahora, cuando se había llegado a
un nuevo Mundo y a otra tierra continental, juzgaba que había
que tratar de buscar una nueva base y usar un nuevo fundamento
jurídico" [Until now he had carried out the post of captain given
the right and faculty of the monks, who held supreme power and
government in the conquered islands, and whose right of presid-
ing and ruling included the limits of the islands and the ocean.
Now, upon arriving at a new World and another mainland, he
judged it necessary to search for a new ground and use a new

99

juridical foundation].[40] Whether Cortés spoke in those terms, or whether it is a fabrication of Sepúlveda's cannot be ascertained since the first letter to Charles V remains at large.

The reliability of Sepúlveda's recorded speech, moreover, is inconsequential with respect to the displacement of the garden by the city as an emblem of the New World. Nonetheless it is interesting to note some elements of this argument, the *razón sutil* of Cortés, in the legend on the upper left-hand corner of the Map of Mexico City and the Gulf (fig. 5). The legend speaks in terms of a new *Orbis*. It announces a world in itself, and provides a mirror for Charles V: the *Gloria summa* highlights the deeds of the conquistadores with a divine apportionment and qualifies the momentous increase this *novus Orbis* represents for the empire, *Orbis subxiectus Cesaris Imperio*. The standard of the Habsburgs on the plan of Tenochtitlan leaves little doubt about who is the Caesar, as it marks the *novus Orbis* of the conquistador with the city. Beyond the cartographic determination of the territories, the plan of the city infuses newness into what otherwise would be solely the contours of a coastline without a semantic difference.

The circular form of the plan of Tenochtitlan, its location on a lagoon on a par with Venice, and the broad avenues and open spaces reveal the projection of an ideal city onto the fabric of a real one. The idealization follows Cortés's verbal descriptions, not on a one-to-one basis, but as an imaginary representation of the different indigenous codes contained within the city. Little is to be gained by denouncing the distortion when the import of the plan is symbolic.

For the conquistador, the city constitutes not only an object of discourse in need of codification but a new mode of discursivity as well. The plan of Tenochtitlan is a duplicitous representation. On the surface both maps (the plan of Tenochtitlan and the chart of the coast) would seem to fulfill an analogous informative function about two distinct geographic objects requiring different forms of representation. The two maps can also be seen as clarifying each other; while the map of the coastline locates particular features in a broader geographic context, the plan of the city defines the novelty of the region. But under closer inspection, the plan of the city does not denote a real object; the plan is an ideal reconstruction of a city by then in ruins. The

pluperfect *fuerat* (had been) in the legend establishes the plan as
an imaginary projection that fulfills a purpose other than cartographical accuracy. As an imaginary reconstruction, the plan is a
sine qua non for the *Gloria summa* expressed in the legend. It
provides a mirror for the emperor wherein the effigy of the
conquistador surfaces as a faithful and bold servant pushing
further the bounds of the empire. The codification of the exotic
city of the New World depends on a metaphorical transposition of
the known for its depiction, but the city is also equivalent to an
indigenous encyclopedia and a power structure that reduces the
world beyond its confines to a spatial text. For instance, in the
Second Letter Cortés mentions *pinturas* (paintings, indigenous
maps) of the political structure of the Mexican dominions, and a
pintura of the gulf that provides the initial data for the chart of
the coast: "Otro día me trajeron figurada en un paño toda la
costa" [The next day they brought me a cloth with a figuration of
the whole coast] (65). Quite literally the city contains all the
secrets.

But the plan of Tenochtitlan bears the imprint of the historical
momentum of the conquistador; it portrays the strategic benefits
of the site and an urban structure whose avenues, open spaces,
and unrepresented debris of the city in ruins provide a material
substratum for imagining a new city. The plan bespeaks a
spatialization of native history and the infusion of a new historical temporality. On the ruins of the ancient city, Mexico City
arises and retains indelible traces of the ancient order for the
present. This transformation of reality may be likened to a
palimpsest where the text of the conquered furnishes and retains
its formal structure in the text of the conqueror. It is not the
explorer's accidental and fortuitous mushrooming of colonial
entrepôts on a landscape that murmurs an extraneous language.
The *fuerat*, the had-been of Tenochtitlan, retains a ghostlike
presence in a mnemonic deposit of information about the land
despite the city's destruction.

Thus the city is not opposed to the garden of explorers since it
contains the forms of the zoo and the botanical garden. The
market in the city and the indigenous library further complement
the mimicry of nature (the artificial garden) with a native code
that registers economic, political, historical, nutritional, and
medicinal secrets. The destruction of the city obviously does not

imply the disappearance of Mesoamerican civilization. Rather, the codes registered within the plan continue to exist, though in a dismembered form. And it is precisely in the interstices of this objectification of the city that a whole array of the oppositional practices of everyday life proliferates in an invisible mode.[41]

The force of the plan of Tenochtitlan is obviously strategic in the sense defined by Michel de Certeau as the mastery of places by vision: "The look transforms strange forces into objects which one can observe and measure, therefore controlling and 'including' them in one's vision."[42] In addition, the proper place of strategy implies a mastery of time as well as the transformation of the uncertainties of history into readable spaces. On the other hand, tactics belongs to oppositional practices. For de Certeau, tactics is defined by the absence of a proper place; it is wily and creates surprises. It operates in time and scrambles the proper places of mastery by changing the very organization of space. Sahagún's *Historia general de la cosas de la Nueva España*, the Spanish title of what is commonly known as the *Florentine Codex*, further elaborates Cortés's strategic program with an encyclopedic compendium of the various codes registered in the plan. But it also provides a space where the informants inscribe their ethnicity. Thus Sahagún's text serves as a place for tracing oppositional practices.

As an encyclopedic work, the *Historia general* seeks to build a linguistic thesaurus: "Es esta obra como una red barredera para sacar a luz todos los vocablos desta lengua con sus propias y metaphoricas significaciones y todas sus maneras de hablar y las mas de sus antiguallas buenas y malas" [This work is like a dragnet to bring to light all the words of this language with their exact metaphorical meanings, and all their ways of speaking, and most of their ancient practices, the good and evil].[43] Sahagún specifies that "por mj industria, se an escripto doze libros: de lenguaje proprio y natural, desta lengua mexicana . . . tambien authorizados, y ciertos: como lo que escribjo Vergilio, Ciceron, y los demas authores, de la lengua latina" [through my efforts twelve Books have been written in an idiom characteristic and typical of this Mexican language . . . as well verified and certain as that which Virgil, Cicero, and other authors wrote in the Latin language] (13:50). Thus the *Historia general* is not just a thesaurus but will constitute a corpus of Nahuatl literature from which a dictionary, a *calepino*, could be prepared.

Sahagún undertakes his *Historia general* to reconstruct Nahuatl language before the conquest in order to preserve what he considers valuable, but also to provide a semiotic repertoire for identifying superstitious practices and idolatry to enable priests to preach against them: "Para predicar contra estas cosas y aun para sauer si las ay: menester es, de saber como las vsauã en tiempo de su ydolatria: que por falta, de no saber esto en nr̃a presencia hazen muchas cosas ydolatricas: sin que lo entendamos" [To preach against these matters, and even to know if they exist, it is needful to know how they practiced them in the times of their idolatry, for through [our] lack of knowledge of this, they perform many idolatrous things in our presence without our understanding them] (13:45).

I must add that the informants themselves, with more or less editing from Sahagún and the trilingual Nahua collegians, produced the original Nahuatl versions of the *Historia general*.[44] Here we will be mainly concerned with how the indigenous version of the conquest contained in Book 12 suggests a subversion of the semiotic-linguistic purposes of the *Historia general*. As we will see shortly, Book 12 is an invaluable document for tracing the other side of the dialogue and its tactical interventions.

THE DIALOGUE WITH MOCTEZUMA

As a panoptic overview, the plan of Tenochtitlan entails a dialogical process that sought to retain Moctezuma as a master in servitude, and in the long run to preserve the native order. Dialogue is at once both a mode of controlling the Spaniards and a means of gaining knowledge; it is also an imperceptible mode of conquering. Dialogue indeed establishes what is proper, and obviously mediates Moctezuma's recognition of Charles V. Take for instance the insistence on dialogue in the following passages from Charles V and Cortés:

Charles V on avoiding cynical uses of legal warfare against Indians:

[H]abéis de estar sobre el aviso de una cosa que todos los cristianos . . . ternán mucha gana que sean de guerra y que no sean de paz. . . . E porque no os podáis excusar de platicar con ellos, es bien estar avisado desto para

dar el crédito que en esto se les debe dar, y para remediar que de ninguna manera se haga.
[[Y]ou must be warned that all the Christians . . . will want them to be of war and not of peace. . . . And so that you do not excuse yourself from talking to them, you must be forwarned about this so that they receive due credit, and thus prevent that it ever happens.] (589)

Cortés on assessing legal slavery and precontact practices of slavery:

[D]areis las dichas licencias, con aditamento, que todos los esclavos que ansi rescatasen, los traigan ante vos e ante vuestro escribano, y en presencia del Señor o persona que les rescatare, e les fareis preguntar que orden es la que ellos tienen antiguamente de facer esclavos, entre si; o sabreis de los dichos esclavos, apartadamente, sin que esté el Señor delante, de que manera o porque son fechos esclavos, e pareciendo serlos, segun su horden e costumbre, adxudicallos eys a la persona a quien obieredes dado la tal licencia para rrescatar.
[[Y]ou shall grant licenses to trade, with a condition, that all slaves traded are brought before you and your actuary, and in the presence of the lord or person who traded them, you shall question them about the order they formerly had of making slaves among themselves; you shall learn from the slaves, separately, without the presence of the lord, how and why they are enslaved, and if it seems to be according to their order and custom, you shall adjudicate them to the person to whom you had given the license to trade.] (458)

Charles V on fairness and love as ways to the recognition of his mastery:

Y porque una de las principales causas por donde los indios naturales de esa dicha tierra y provincias della han de venir en conocimiento de lo susodicho, es tomando ejemplo en los christianos españoles que a esa dicha tierra fueren, y con su conversación y texto ha de ser tratando y rescatando y conversando los unos con los otros, habéis de ordenar y mandar de nuestra parte.
[And because one of the main ways the Indians native to that land and provinces shall learn about the above [the mastery of Charles V], is by having the example of the Christian Spaniards who go to this land, and you must instruct and order from our part that it must be carried out with their conversation and text through treating and trading and conversing.] (587)

These instances of dialogue do not include a dialogical pro-cess in which a dominant culture would come to question its forms of life. But even then, the figure of the conquered conquistador suggests a mutation of the Spanish self—transformations that make up the stock of creolized languages and cultures. As in the case of dialogical ethnography, however, the will to knowledge of the conquistador establishes what are significant questions as well as informative answers. It is beyond the scope of this chapter to comment in full on the context of the above passages and others that exemplify dialogue. Let it suffice to point out that one can open the Cortés–Charles V correspondence at random and find numerous passages that insist on love and elaborate on what they call *conversación* (conversation in the sense of social intercourse) and *plática* (talk in the context of inquiries) as modalities of conquest. For the present purposes, then, I will delineate some general characteristics of dialogue as defined in the correspondence.

The process of learning about the other not only produces data but also introduces dialogue into a web of practices ranging roughly from the exchange of goods to conversion. For Charles V and Cortés, fairness and love are the ways to conversion and the recognition of lordship. Though with metaphors opposite to Marcel Griaule's, Cortés complements the panoptic with dialogue. Cortés's letters elaborate a clear understanding of cultural differences and the need to establish a common ground of discourse, a third order that would not dissolve the specific cultures. Inquiries into the kinds of tributes the Indians paid in the past, trade equivalences, forms of slavery, and so on, conjoin the dialogical paths, as recommended above by Charles V, of "treating and trading and conversing" as modes of gaining a deeper understanding of the codes contained within the city. Among the codes to inquire about are the "tributo o servicio ordinario que daban a los dichos sus teules" [tribute and ordinary service they gave to their *teules*] (587). The conquistador becomes a mediator for introducing the new order and making effective (through the payment of tribute to the new *teules* [gods?]) what Charles V calls the "reconocimiento del vasallaje que nos deben" [the recognition of the vasallage they owe us] (587). Moreover, Charles V constantly prohibits war and any other form of unfair treatment "porque de miedo no se alboroten ni se levanten" [so that out of fear they do not riot or rebel] (588).

Conversation suggests an imperceptible mode of conquering; it would transform the consciousness of the Indians by immersing them in a new sociopolitical order that includes the conquis-tador as well. It implies at once a fair dealing and a relegation of the old order to the past. The pluperfect *fuerat* (had been) in the legend of the map refers not merely to a time that has passed but also to the stoppage of native history, imposed by the momentum of the conquest from the beginning.[45] This stoppage operates under two paradoxes: On the one hand, it seeks to retain the ancient order intact, but ignores the inevitable transformation of the object in the process of gaining power. On the other, it ignores an ongoing historical consciousness in the subjectivity of the Indians requisite for a recognition of Charles V. We can trace a glimpse of the latter illusion in the concerns the emperor expresses in the previous quote about the precariousness of domination. Revolt remains a possibility.

A series of precautions and detailed instructions to Indians as well as Spaniards in the Cortés–Charles V correspondence manifests a long-term conquest and an elaborate process through which Charles V would be recognized as the supreme lord. Most of the letters were written after the fall of Tenochtitlan—under truce, as it were. They can be seen as immersed in a contradiction deftly posited by Hegel in a famous passage on the Master/Slave relation in *The Phenomenology of Mind*: "But for recognition proper there is needed the moment that what the master does to the other he should also do to himself, and what the bondsman does to himself, he should do to the other also. On that account a form of recognition has arisen that is one sided and unequal." Hegel goes on to mention how the master depends on the slave. But in the end, Hegel dismisses the independence of the slave "as a piece of cleverness which has mastery within a certain range, but not over the universal power nor over the entire objective reality."[46]

Hegel, of course, announces here the coming of Reason as the next stage in the development of *mind*. We need not discuss the "magical solution" of the contradiction, nor what elsewhere Hegel calls the *cunning of reason*—the belief in progress beyond the surface of historical events.[47] Let us observe, instead, how the contradiction and incomplete recognition arise from the initial proposition about self-consciousness wherein the truth of each adversary depends on the other: "Self-consciousness has before it another self-consciousness; it has come outside itself.

This has a double significance. First it has lost its own self, since it finds itself as an *other* being; secondly, it has thereby sublated that other, for it does not regard the other as essentially real, but sees its own self in the other."[48] The relationship partakes of two illusions, that of the master and that of the slave; hence the truth of the relationship reveals itself as a precarious truce where a future resurgence of strife is inherent to the unfolding of the illusions. The unfolding of the subjectivities implies a mutual process of translation and appropriation. Not only must the slave speak the language of the master, but he also must speak from the representation the master renders of the adversary's language.[49]

Let us examine in this light some instances of the representation of the initial encounter between the two cultures and observe how the textual production of the conquistador is indissolubly bound to that of the conquered. Our concern will reside in the representation and not with straightening out the actual events. Since the purpose is not to retell the story but to analyze the discursive exchange, I do not follow the sequence of events.

Under the ideal conceptualization of the conquest given in the epigraph to this chapter from the Second Letter, a temporal stoppage of native discourse seeks to retain Moctezuma as a master in servitude. Charles V figures as a master over both Cortés and Moctezuma. But mastery depends solely on the role Charles V might play as Quetzalcoatl in the historical narrative of Moctezuma. The primal dialogue of the two cultures, represented in the Second Letter by the meeting of Cortés and Moctezuma at the gates of Tenochtitlan, reveals an appropriation of native history that precludes an assimilation of the slave into the language of the master. In other words, the illusion of Moctezuma is indispensable for the representation of the master and mastery in the truce: "Yo le respondí a todo lo que me dijo, satisfaciendo a aquello que me pareció que convenía, en especial en hacerle creer que vuestra majestad era a quien ellos esperaban" [I replied to all that he said, satisfying him in those things I thought most fitting, especially in making him believe that your majesty was he whom they were expecting] (60). In the speech of Moctezuma, Cortés exposes justifications for the conquest and for Moctezuma's belief that Charles V is the *subject* of a narrative that prefigures the conquest in native history. The representation of the dialogue with Moctezuma is in itself a mode

of communicating with Charles V; it legitimates Cortés's proceedings and, ultimately, conquest. But it also reveals the frailty
of the discursive exchange.

First, in the reported dialogue Moctezuma establishes the
history of the Nahuas as conquerors, late intruders in the Valley
of Mexico: "Muchos días ha que por nuestras escripturas tenemos de nuestros antepasados noticia que yo ni todos los que en
esta tierra habitamos no somos naturales de ella sino extranjeros,
y venidos a ella de partes muy extrañas" [For a long time we have
known from the writings of our ancestors that neither I nor any of
those who dwell in this land are natives of it, but strangers who
came from very foreign parts] (59). In legal terms, this amounts
to a self-denial of a natural right to power; hence the conquest of
a conqueror under the banner of Christianity is more than
justifiable.

Second, Cortés's stratagem, leading Moctezuma to see the
intruders as the protagonists of a narrative, sorely decries the
belief that the truce will last the span of an illusion. Moctezuma's
identification of the Spaniards with Quetzalcoatl can not be
sustained for long, since it contradicts the missionary character
of the conquest. "Siempre hemos tenido que los que de él
descendiesen habían de venir a sojuzgar esta tierra y a nosotros
como a sus vasallos; y según de la parte que vos decís que venís,
que es a do sale el sol, y las cosas que decís de ese gran señor o
rey que acá os envió, creemos y tenemos por cierto, él sea nuestro
señor natural, en especial que nos decís que él ha muchos días
que tenía noticia de nosotros" [We have always held that those
who descended from him would come and subjugate this land
and make us their vassals; and according to the place from which
you claim to come, that is, from where the sun rises, and the
things you tell us about that great lord or king who sent you here,
we believe and are certain that he is our natural lord, especially
since you tell us that he has known about us for some time] (59).
Yet Cortés's appropriation of the narrative provides a vehicle for
representing "natural" servitude and the illusion of the slave qua
his own language.

But Moctezuma's voice quivers, and he previews his own death
as well as the imminent end of the truce when he pleads with
Cortés not to believe the collaborators about the wealth of
Tenochtitlan; moreover, Moctezuma feels obligated to raise his

clothes in order to prove to Cortés that he is not a god, "A mí véisme aquí que soy de carne y hueso como vos y como cada uno, y que soy mortal y palpable" [See that I am of flesh and blood like you and all other men, and I am mortal and substantial] (59). The raising of the clothes could be seen as emblematic of an absolute submission—providing one's body for the inscription of the new order.[50] A deep sigh, which echoes the chivalric effect of Boabdil's sigh after the fall of Granada, must be heard in Cortés's representation of Moctezuma's submission to Charles V. Moctezuma expresses a stoic resignation in contemplating the tragic unfolding of events. In the abdication of power Moctezuma assumes the likeness of a noble savage condemned to die as a consequence of an ideality Cortés fabricates. Moctezuma is noble because of rank and spirit; but at the same time, he is a savage because he ignores the ideality of what he says beyond the confines of his own language.

Cortés's representation of Moctezuma infuses an ethos derived from chivalry into the theme of the noble savage. Chivalry certainly provides a paradigm for staging and representing battles, or for displaying military strategy. But the code of chivalry exceeds those elements of representation in the provision of ritualism and mannerism that antecede the battle and are ultimately more important for generating a chivalric effect. One may have battles without chivalry, but never chivalry without ritual. Chivalry demands two worthy contenders for its representation and enactment. Honor and courage convey an ethos and a formalization of risk. For instance, Cortés's destruction of the ships leaves the Spaniards without choice (it aims to prevent mutiny by those left on the coast and leaves no alternative but death or victory to those who march with him), but it also constitutes a self-referential statement where the assumption of absolute risk (one without alternative) posits him as a conqueror for Moctezuma.[51] The truce between Moctezuma and Cortés comes as a result of a symbolic duel. Even the battles on the way to Tenochtitlan display cultural forms of life and messages for Moctezuma, who matches the risk of Cortés with watchful waiting, dissuasion, and magical incantations. Both Cortés and Moctezuma know that struggle to the death corresponds to a confrontation of two forms of life; the eventual slaughter is but a conclusion, awaited with resignation, of this ceremonial duel.

Moctezuma seals defeat in the limits of a language incapable of translation and appropriation. Recognition is nothing but a tenuous truce that ultimately depends on a stoppage of native history. Mesoamerican civilization is reduced to the significance it has in the time of the empire—it is a *thing* without subjectivity.

Historical records tell us about the Indians and a taciturn Moctezuma who see the intruders as *teules*. The meaning of this term remains far from clear (what for instance is a "god" in the Nahua pantheon?).[52] From all appearance Charles V thinks of himself as an equivalent when he calls, in the passage cited above, for an inquiry into the amount of tribute that was payed to their *teules*. An amusing passage from Bernal Díaz del Castillo, where he describes Cortés and Moctezuma's chuckling and "elbowing each other" about their common attribute *teule*, should have cautioned historians about drawing far-fetched and comprehensive explanations of the conquest on this misnomer. Delusion after all does not preclude knowledge, nor can myth and religion be reduced to ideologies.

Let us observe from the other side of the dialogue how minor knowledges concur with misnomers and misrepresentations in delusion. In Book 12 of the *Florentine Codex* one finds the Spaniards characterized in terms of an absence and inversion of culture. This is the *visión de los vencidos* (vision of the vanquished) in Miguel León-Portilla's words; it is also a subversion and appropriation of Spanish forms of culture.[53] The conquistadores exist on account of the illusion of the conquered, where the Indians' insistence on calling the Spaniards *teules* implies retaining an indigenous narrative of the event. The end of the *teule* interpretation would entail an end of the Nahua understanding of history and the world. Book 12 forges a memory of an atrocious event that intends to prevent its dissipating into forgetfulness. It constitutes a register that perpetuates a form of memorizing in the process of inventing the Spaniard. In the process, as Sahagún's informants adopt alphabetical writing and three-dimensional perspective they transform those Western technologies by incorporating them to a native understanding of language and the world. Beyond a version of mestizo culture, where the two cultures mingle into a new one, we should take it as a form of hybridization and adopt Homi Bhabha's phrase—"less than one and double." As Bhabha defines it: "hybridity intervenes in the exercise of authority not merely to indicate the impossibility of its identity, but to represent the unpredictability of its presence."[54] This ambivalent space certainly troubled Sahagún.

Passages and vignettes reveal the adaptation of alphabetic writing, of "hispanic" forms of life, and moral criteria for constructing a nefarious Spaniard: "And when they have given them these [golden banners, precious feather streamers, and golden necklaces], they appeared to smile; they were greatly contented, gladdened. As if they were monkeys they seized upon the gold. It was as if there their hearts were satisfied, brightened, calmed. For in truth they thirsted mightily for gold; they stuffed themselves with it; they starved for it; they lusted for it like pigs" (12:31). From all appearances the syntactical doublings of metaphors is a characteristic trait of prehispanic poetry.[55] Whereas the Franciscans would comply with the moral outrage expressed in this passage, they would not express it as such. The fixation on gold, as revealed in its monotonous repetition in the text, implies a native view wherein the Europeans are mocked ("like monkeys," "like pigs") and wherein gold is seen as a lowly object of desire. I am not qualified to evaluate the accuracy of Anderson and Dibble's translation of the Nahuatl. Nor does it matter if we simply observe the surface of the text. The translation certainly captures the intensity of the passage; its doubling of metaphors actually upturns and makes redundant any pursuit of a figurative meaning as it marks an insistence on expression over content. Paraphrasing Deleuze and Guattari, we might add that just as the Spaniards become pigs and monkeys, so the pigs and monkeys become Spaniards.[56] *and in mesoamerica?*

Pigs, of course, have a long tradition connoting lust in European letters since Circe's island, and regarding monkeys, it is not only with lust that they have been associated, but also with satyrs and monstrous races usually located in Africa and Asia; so these animals do not just connote lust, but — at least for a European reader — identify lust and pigs, and the ever-present apes among the fabulous, semihuman races in remote parts of the world, with Spaniards.[57] Thus the characterization of the Spaniards as savages, *popolcas* (those who cannot speak Nahuatl), gains intensity with their animal behavior and the suggestion that they eat gold. The attributes *teule* and *popolca* do not contradict but reinforce each other, with the image of an uncouth god that brings about the destruction of culture; after all, the Spaniards melt down artifacts in order to devour gold.

On the other hand, the pictorial version of the conquest in the *Florentine Codex* (fig. 7) is not an illustration of the text but a mode of writing the event. The pictorial version antecedes the written both in terms of the order of research followed by Sahagún and with respect to the innumerable oral stories that could be told about the events depicted in frame 25, which tells about the gifts Moctezuma sent to Cortés on his way to Tenochtitlan. Indeed, the written portion illustrates the pictorial with intensive images. It all suggests that the transformation of the Spaniards into animals does not imply a reterritorialization but a deterritorialization of alphabetic writing and its privileged domain of the signified. As a form of counterdiscourse the language in the quoted passage from Book 12 produces effects rather than objects of description by altering the Spanish system of representation.

Likewise, the dominant three-dimensional space represented in the vignettes is deterritorialized. The fanciful mountain in the right-hand corner is not merely a background scenario but a glyph denoting the location of the event near Popocatepetl, "smoking mountain." Thus, stylized prehispanic pictographs furnish captions to a version of the conquest expressed by means of a clash of forms of life and pictorial conventions: beyond the depiction of particular battles, the juxtaposition of European and indigenous modes of representation convey an understanding of conquest and resistance as a long-term cultural struggle.[58] Indeed landscape (a European trait) becomes an element for writing glyphs. In a less obvious place we find this practice recurring in frame 105 (fig. 8), where the toponym of the town Citlatepetl, "star mountain," remains invisible to all but the trained eye. Other frames, on the right-hand column, further exemplify the use of glyphs to caption events and the clash of forms of life. Frames 89 to 92 (fig. 9) vividly portray the confrontation of pictorial conventions in a movement that concludes with the amorphous depiction of the battle in the bottom vignette. This sequence of frames seems to mock the representation of war itself. The opposing forms reemerge in frame 93, which depicts the Indians in pursuit of the Spaniards and allies.

Figure 7. Landscape (a European trait) becomes an element for writing glyphs. *Scenes of the Conquest of Mexico. In* Florentine Codex *(1579), after Francisco del Paso y Troncoso. Courtesy Benson Latin American Collection, General Libraries, University of Texas at Austin.*

Figure 8. The toponym of the town Citlatepetl, "star mountain," remains invisible to all but the trained eye. *Scenes of the Conquest of Mexico. In* Florentine Codex *(1579), after Francisco del Paso y Troncoso. Courtesy Benson Latin American Collection, General Libraries, University of Texas at Austin.*

Figure 9. This sequence of frames seems to mock the representation of war itself. *Scenes of the Conquest of Mexico.* In Florentine Codex *(1579), after Francisco del Paso y Troncoso. Courtesy Benson Latin American Collection, General Libraries, University of Texas at Austin.*

Again three-dimensional space becomes a place for inscribing signs from the old order; notice the floating headdress and insignia. In the words of de Certeau, we may sum up the above observations by stating that "memory does its work in a locus which is not its own."[59]

In the interstices of alphabetic writing and three-dimensional space one may trace a casual insertion of pictorial details and forms of storytelling that metonymically transforms the plot of the conquest from a military defeat of the Nahuas to an endless discursive struggle. As I have pointed out above, Sahagún's project had two purposes: to build, on the one hand, a classic repertoire of Nahuatl texts that would eventually give place to a dictionary for arresting what he viewed as a deterioration of Nahuatl language, and to reconstruct, on the other, the ancient order for the identification of superstitious beliefs in everyday practices. But this dual intent of Sahagún also opens a space for tactical interventions by the informants. The so-called spiritual conquest reiterates Cortés's stoppage of native history. Cultural innovations cannot be anticipated, nor enclosed in a proper place—strategy finds its match in the surprises of tactics.

THE NARRATIVE THREAD OF NEW SPAIN

The historical stoppage that the discourse of conquest seeks to introduce by superimposing the temporality of a new master creates a paradox: conquest demands a native representation of the conquistador, but ignores the extraneous historical and symbolic matrix that produces such an image outside a European system of representation. The discourse of conquest partakes of another paradox: it seeks to retain the ancient order intact, but Tenochtitlan becomes accessible only by debunking the Mexican power structure in alliances with native collaborators. In contrast to the city as a topos containing the garden, penetration into the land reduces natural and cultural phenomena into strategic arrangements for gaining power. Moreover, as the information is written down, it already functions within a narrative thread of what Cortés eventually calls New Spain.

On his march to Tenochtitlan Cortés describes the different topographical regions, determined by altitude, in terms of a correspondence to degrees of civilization among those who populate the areas. Lowlands are equated with sodomy and decadence, the mountainous regions with indomitable savagery. Moreover, Cortés draws a political map as he identifies potential enemies and allies. Mountain people tend to represent those who had resisted Tenochtitlan and supported the independent confederation led by Tlaxcala. Tlaxcala's urban sophistication is, in turn, considered inferior to that of the towns subordinated to the Mexican dominion. The initial allies from the coast guide Cortés about the politically unstable territories ruled from Tenochtitlan. Yet Cortés equates Tenochtitlan with the cusp of Mesoamerican civilization and compares the climate of the Valley of Mexico with that of Spain—making the site of Tenochtitlan an ideal location, in terms of both climate and culture, for his "new capital" of the New World. Hence Cortés at the end of the Second Letter gives the rationale for the name New Spain: "Por lo que yo he visto y comprendido cerca de la similitud que toda esta tierra tiene a España, así en la fertilidad como en la grandeza y frios que en ella hace, y en otras muchas cosas que la equiparan a ella, me pareció que el más conveniente nombre para esta dicha tierra era llamarse la Nueva España del mar Océano" [From what I have seen and understood about the similarity between this whole land and that of Spain, in the fertility as well as in the size and the cold climate, and in many other things, it seemed to me that the most convenient name for this land was New Spain of the Ocean Sea] (114).

It is the first occasion, aside from the use of the overarching term New World, when *new* conjoins a European toponym. The choice of Spain over a more particular region such as his native Extremadura, Castile, or Andalusia seems hardly coincidental. It all suggests the political importance given to the regions, as well as the preeminence of Spain as a nation state. A complete study of Cortés's choice of this name lies outside the scope of this chapter, but I will explore some of the cultural traits within Cortés's historical projections that reinforce the title New Spain.

Next to an inventory of material resources (sulfur, mines, agriculture, and labor are included), Cortés draws a tentative cultural anthropology (degrees of civilization) and a political diagnosis of the power structure supporting the Mexican dominions. But these attributes of Mexico do not fully justify the title of New Spain. The transmutation of the urban areas as well as the religiosity and talents of the Indians are the fundamental base for

Cortés's ideal (new) Spain in America. That is, Cortés has in mind a prospective transformation of Mexican urban centers into European-style cities with the program of converting the Indians to Catholicism and turning their talents to productive labor for the European market.

Although the letter of the cabildo speaks of idolatry and rituals invested with demonic symbolism, a politics of conversion is defined on the basis of the religiosity of the Indians. Thus Cortés tells Charles that "Dios Nuestro Señor [sería] muy servido, si por mano de vuestras altezas estas gentes fuesen introducidas e instruídas en nuestra santa fe católica y conmutada la devoción, fe y esperanza que en estos ídolos tienen, en la divina potencia de Dios" [Our Lord God would be greatly served if by the hand of Your Majesties these people were initiated and instructed in our holy Catholic faith and their devotion, faith, and hope in their idols were commuted in the divine potency of God] (25). A good portion of the so-called spiritual conquest and its theological disputes is contained in this proposition. On the one hand, the transference of theological virtues from idolatry to Christianity conveys an imaginary conversion as it implies a continuous set of habits and a homogenous subject who simply chooses to accept a new religion; on the other hand, not all the participants in the spiritual conquest shared the belief that the Indians' religiosity manifested theological virtues only lacking the perfectivity that comes through commutation in the divine potency of God.[60] As for Cortés, conversion lacks complexity: "Los más principales de estos ídolos . . . derroqué de sus sillas y los hice hechar por las escaleras abajo e hice limpiar aquellas capillas donde los tenían, porque todas estaban llenas de sangre que sacrifican, y puse en ellas imágenes de Nuestra Señora y de otros santos" [The main of their idols . . . I threw off their pedestals and had them thrown down the stairs and had the chapels where they kept them cleaned up, because they were full of the blood they sacrifice, and I put in them images of Our Lady and other saints] (74).

Conversion is merely a question of investing faith in the right image. With a blink of the eyes the temple has been exorcised and sanctified; it is ready for Mass. But this passage also provides an index of Cortés's admiration for the buildings and urban structure of Tenochtitlan as it was intended to remain and be transfigured into his imaginary New Spain. The same intentions recur when, in the midst of being besieged within Tenochtitlan, Cortés is forced to destroy the main temple to recapture the Christian images. Cortés writes, "Yo les respondí que no pensasen que les rogaba con la paz por temor que les tenía, sino porque me pesaba del daño que les hacía y del que había de hacer, y no por destruir tan buena ciudad como aquella era" [I replied that they should not think that I was pleading for peace out of fear of them, but because it grieved me the damage I was inflicting upon them, and that which I would have to cause them, and moreover to avoid destroying such a fine city as that one was] (93). In Cortés's initial project the city was to remain intact. Temples and religiosity were to be transmuted to Christianity. A parallel formulation reappears when he assesses the Indians' talents by making them sculpt crucifixes and other European ornaments:

> Y no les paresca a vuestra majestad fabuloso lo que digo, pues es verdad que todas las cosas criadas así en la tierra como en la mar . . . tenían contrahechas muy al natural, así de oro como de plata, como de pedrería y de plumas, en tanta perfección, que casi ellas mismas parecían; de las cuales todas me dió para vuestra alteza mucha parte, sin otras que yo le di figuradas, y él las mandó hacer de oro, así como imágenes, crucifijos, medallas, joyeles y collares. . . . Hice labrar a los naturales . . . platos grandes y pequeños y escudillas y tazas y cucharas, y lo labraron tan perfecto como se lo podíamos dar a entender.
> [And let not what I say seem fabulous to Your Majesty, since it is true that all things that breed in the land as well as in the sea . . . they had them made in a very lifelike form, in gold as in silver, as in precious stones and feathers, with such perfection that they almost seemed the thing itself; of these [Moctezuma] gave me a great quantity for Your Majesty, without counting others, such as images, crucifixes, medallions, carved jewels and necklaces, for which I provided models to imitate, and he ordered them made out of gold. . . . I had the natives . . . carve large and small dishes and bowls and cups and spoons, and they carved them as perfectly as our instructions could be understood.] (70)

Cortés highlights the realism of the sculptors and complements the inventory of culture with an inventory of talent. The list moves from religious paraphernalia to eating utensils. Thus the possibility of fabricating European objects, of recreating Spanish ways of life, further reinforces the project of a New Spain.

Ultimately, the city is destroyed, but the site of Tenochtitlan remains as the capital of New Spain and, in Cortés's fantasies, a possible center of all future imperial dominions abroad. Such a dream is manifest in his intense search for a passage to the Pacific Ocean, which would give Mexico a privileged position to shorten potential traffic to the East.[61] The dream of Columbus seems at hand. And equally great are Cortés's plans in the Fourth Letter for the new city to arise from the ruins of Tenochtitlan. Cortés anticipates a fast reconstruction "porque hay mucho aparejo de piedra, cal y madera, y de mucho ladrillo, que los naturales labran, que hacen todos tan buenas y grandes casas, que puede creer vuestra sacra majestad que de hoy en cinco años será la más noble y populosa ciudad que haya en lo poblado del mundo, y de mejores edificios" [because there is such abundance of stone, lime, and wood, and lots of brick that the natives make, and they build such comely and large houses, that Your Majesty may be certain that five years from now it will be the noblest and most populous city in the inhabited world, and with the best buildings] (231). Cortés's fantasies run high in the midst of the destroyed Tenochtitlan. The Indians constitute a talented labor force behind his project. In this same letter Cortés introduces the *cihuacoatl* (second position after the *tlatoani*) into the political and material reconstruction of what he now already calls Mexico City, though still signs Tenochtitlan. Thus the native elite takes a secondary, nevertheless important position (eventually dissolved) within the new order of things.

All these elements, however, retain only a shadow of the original utopia. The Mexican grandeur is gone forever, and by the time the first missionaries arrive they will encounter, in Georges Baudot's terms, a civilization *demi-effondrée*. Hence the missionaries will face the task of reconstructing the foregone Tenochtitlan in their ethnographic histories, and of building the new church that Cortés calls forth with millenarian undertones toward the end of the Fifth Letter. Cortés envisions "una nueva iglesia, donde más que en todas las del mundo Dios Nuestro Señor será servido y honrado" [a new church will arise, in which Our Lord will be served and honored more than in any other part of the world] (318). Thus New Spain emerges as the site for the greatest and most devout city of the world.

Implicit in what I have called the narrative thread of New Spain are the historico-anthropological stages of savagery, barbarism, and civilization. European culture remains the embodiment and model of civilization in spite of Cortés's admiration for

Tenochtitlan. Mexican culture is great because it resembles Spain, hence forming a potential substratum for a New Spain. Indeed, the humanity of the Indians is measured against their capacity and willingness to duplicate Spanish culture, accept its religion, and recognize the authority of Charles V—that is, to engage in the nefarious terms of a dialogue called the *requerimiento*. This narrative undercurrent, however, requires the ethnographic task of knowing cultures and appropriating their knowledge. But such a narrative reduces indigenous cultures to imperfect moments within a linear progression. As a result of this very European teleology the destruction of Tenochtitlan was all but inevitable.

Despite the destruction of Tenochtitlan, in the Fifth Letter Cortés seeks to universalize his style of appropriation when he proposes to Charles V a conquest of the "Far East" in contradistinction to the practice of the Portuguese: "Yo me ofresco a descubrir por aquí toda la Especiería y otras islas, si hubiere arca de Maluco y Malaca y la China, y aun de dar tal orden, que vuestra majestad no haya la Especiería por vía de rescate, como la ha el rey de Portugal, sino que la tenga por cosa propia, y los naturales de aquellas islas le reconozcan y sirvan como a su rey y señor natural" [I will undertake to discover a route to the Spice Islands and many others, so that there shall be a coffer of Maluco, Malaca, and China, and even to arrange matters so that Your Majesty will no longer possess the Spice Islands by trade, as the king of Portugal has them now, but as your property, and the natives of those islands recognize and serve you as their king and natural lord] (320).

But again, what kind of conquest does Cortés have in mind in the "Spice Islands"? From a letter addressed to King of Tidore in the so-called Moluccas, we find that a pattern recurs in Cortés's generous offer to provide him with European goods: "Si de alguna cosa de que hay en esta tierra, como en todos los otros reinos e señorios de Su Majestad os quisieredes aprovechar, que haciendomelo saber so hará con vos como con verdadero servidor y amigo suyo" [If there is anything in this land, or in any other kingdom of Your Majesty's that you would want, let me know and it will be done as with a true servant and friend of his] (475). Under the appearance of friendliness and liberality the *Su Majestad* (Your Majesty) surreptitiously encapsulates the King of Tidore under the authority of Charles V with *como verdadero servidor y amigo suyo* (like a true servant and friend of his). Cortés thus reiterates the rules of representation and the play of recognition that I have sketched out in this chapter. It also evidences the crystallization of the specific discursive mode of conquest. It could, perhaps, also be read as one more variant of what eventually constitutes British indirect rule and its international division of labor—the exchange of natural resources for European manufactured goods.

On the basis of Cortés's Map of Mexico City and the Gulf, we have seen how the definition of the New World as an ideal garden was replaced in the discourse of the conquistador by the city that contained the secrets of the land. From there we have observed how Cortés's use of dialogue entailed an overcoding of the native text. The formation of a palimpsest imposes a stoppage of indigenous history as well as the introduction of a new narrative time. Beyond a question of representation, the superimposition of a new historical temporality on the indigenous structure brings forth a material transformation of Mesoamerican civilization despite the intention to keep the old order intact. The conquistador was thus caught up in two paradoxes: one ignored the continuity of an indigenous discourse outside the conquistador's representation of indigenous discourse; the other disregarded the transformation of the objects in the process of gaining knowledge. A blatant example of the latter would be the fact that the city became accessible only by the formation of hostile collaborators. Furthermore, this implies that the appearance of the conquistador and the notion of a *conquista* by a handful of men are nothing but a textual illusion.[62]

Cortés's letters seem to encapsulate the limits as well as the possible variation of colonial discourse. They thus constitute a sort of ur-dialogue of encounters between Europeans and alien cultures. Our focus has been not Cortés's genius, nor the origin of colonialism, but the emergence of a particularly modern form of colonial power and corresponding forms of resistance. This chapter has attempted to elaborate an experimental genealogy. In Foucault's words, our concern with descent has sought "to identify the accidents, minute deviations—or conversely, the complete reversals—the errors, the false appraisals, and the faulty calculations that gave birth to those things that continue to exist and have value for us."[63]

As we have read Cortés, we have traced passages that indicate a will to objectivity and neutrality. Knowledge introduces a closure of native history, but this transformation of the other into a *thing* is not an exclusive practice of conquest. We find it prescribed by the best intended anthropologists. Remember Lévi-Strauss's famous proposal, "I believe the ultimate goal of the human sciences to be not to constitute, but to dissolve man."[64] Dialogical ethnography attempts to respond to this proposition; nevertheless, it cannot elude the shortcomings of dialogue. Ideal communication requires mutual recognition, but the representation of the encounter (already a form of power) must exclude the violence of the dialogical process. Muley's words cannot be represented without serious consequences for professional ethics.

Since I am not an ethnographer in the strict sense of the term, I need not be concerned with the ethics of the discipline. But I do have a positive proposal—one that has inspired this chapter—to contribute to the conceptualization of a world of generalized ethnography. Perhaps something is to be gained by dispersing the confrontation beyond crass, culturally defined dichotomies of Self-Other (which reproduce ad nauseam the "Europe and its others" complex), and by starting to wonder about the inner Other—that all too Eurocentric Self that haunts the ethnographer's most venerable intentions. Evidently, Eurocentrism is not an "out there" that we can identify, but the locus where minor discourses intervene.

Cortés's discourse of conquest exemplifies the discursive possibilities of the second moment of the invention of America. It presupposes a New World as distinct from Asia for the inscription of a new territory that enables him to claim legal rights. The differences between Cortés and Columbus have less to do with attitudes toward "the Other" than with the constitution of a code and the emergence of the New World city as a new discursive topos. In the intervening years, the map of the world was redrawn, but the intent to find a western route to Asia remained in both discourses. Cortés's plans for a colonization of Asia now places Tenochtitlan and New Spain, and no longer Hispaniola, as an intermediate region between the two ends of the Old World.

But does Rabasa actually do this?

The economic potential of New Spain is certainly much greater than Hispaniola's, as it is the power of the discourse that informs the production of wealth. And yet these transformations are principally due to the indigenous stock of knowledge and the political infrastructure that Cortés finds in Tenochtitlan.

So? need more here

CHAPTER 4

The Time of the Encyclopedia

No se entienden estos misterios sino con solo advertir el cumplimiento de la profecia que dixo el bendito padre Fray Domingo de Betanzos, de que antes de muchas edades se acabarian de tal manera los indios, que los que viniesen a esta tierra, preguntansen de que color avian sido. A otro pestilencia como esta no fuera menester esperar mas, para que este dicho se hubiera cumplido del todo, como ya lo esta en la mayor parte. . . . Intentaron varios modos para que los Españoles enfermasen. Echavan los cuerpos de los difuntos en el caño de agua que entra en Mexico, con casi un buey della. Indios huvo que cogian la sangre de los enfermos, y la rebolvian en el pan que vendian en la plaza, pensando dar la muerte a bocados, como ella se los comia.

[One does not understand these mysteries unless one acknowledges the realization of what was prophecized by the blessed father Fray Domingo de Betanzos, that before many ages the Indians would disappear, that those who would come to this land would ask what color they were. There is another pest and it will be realized as it has been for the most part. . . . Many Indians tried ways of making the Spaniards ill. They threw corpses into the large volume of water that the canal brings into Mexico. There were Indians who collected the blood of the sick and mixed it with the bread sold at the market, intending to give bites of death, since death was eating them away.]

Augustín Dávila Padilla, Historia de la fundación . . .
de Santiago de México *(1595)*[1]

A TRISTE TABLEAU

By Augustín Dávila Padilla's estimate, the plague that ravaged the Valley of Mexico from 1576 to 1580 killed 80 percent of the population.[2] His grotesque tableau suggests that the Indians responded with a form of caste warfare: since the plague hardly affected the Spaniards, the Indians attempted all forms imaginable to infect the invaders. Dávila Padilla's reference to Fray Domingo de Betanzos harks back to the early period of evangelization, when the friar predicted for the natives of Mexico a destiny parallel to that of the island Indians: complete extermination. The gravity of the situation is expressed by imagining

125

Inventing America

newcomers wondering about the complexion of the ancient inhabitants.

In the face of this tragic unfolding of events, one finds a series of tentative definitions of the New World made by Gonzalo Fernández de Oviedo, the Franciscan ethnographers, and Fray Bartolomé de Las Casas in an attempt to reconstruct an originary state. Before examining the encyclopedic compendia of those authors, a brief exposition of a context (here reduced to Mexico as exemplum) will illustrate the evanescent New World that Dávila Padilla deplores. This historical backdrop discloses how the temporal reconstitution of the New World by the encyclopedias operates in the tense of a "past present." The encyclopedias at once fabricate a timeless image of the New World and describe the transformations (beyond the destruction of the ancient orders) the colonization imposed on specific cultural and natural New World things. They generate a past present in a dual sense. On the one hand, they forge concepts of a New World that, though it no longer exists, retains a full, legendary (i.e., readable) presence and essence. On the other hand, they provide a repertoire of images, lores, and vocabularies—in brief, a collection of information about a past that continues, often imperceptibly, under the plan of what by the mid-seventeenth century constitutes Mexico City as a baroque metropolis—Nova Mexico (fig. 10).

The writing of the particular histories draws from a virtual encyclopedia of American phenomena (information that has been deposited in letters, *relaciones*, oral accounts), and establishes a thesaurus beyond the specific compendia. This sense of a storage of information beyond the ordinary sense of an encyclopedic text can be clarified with Umberto Eco's semiotic definition of the term encyclopedia: "What he [Barthes] calls here code is the whole of the encyclopedic competence as the storage of that which is already known and already organized by a culture."[3] The production of an encyclopedia (code) entails an emergent semiological context. Particular histories not only draw from this virtual encyclopedia but depend upon it for their comprehension as well. Thus they contribute to the formation of a timeless storehouse of motifs for endless representations of America. Less concerned with constructing a context for a critique of the ideologies in the texts, I am interested here in

126

Figure 10. A colonial metropolis with exuberant gardens and magnificent buildings has definitely taken the place of the fantastic Tenochtitlan described by Cortés. "*Nova Mexico.*" In John Ogilby, America (London, 1671). Courtesy Benson Latin American Collection, General Libraries, University of Texas at Austin.

outlining a disjuncture between what is available for observation and the particular inventions of an ever-present New World.

By the late sixteenth century (1595), when Dávila Padilla writes, there was little left to observe of the Tenochtitlan of the Nahuas. Tenochtitlan has become a site for reading the past in the present. One can document this becoming legend of Tenochtitlan with passages from Fray Diego de Durán's *Historia de las Indias de Nueva España e islas de Tierra Firme* (1582).[4] Since Durán's history actually comprises two different texts, I will refer to it as the *Historias*. One is ethnographic in spirit and documents the ancient rites and calendar as well as the continuation and invention of new "superstitions"; the other corresponds to a history of Mexico-Tenochtitlan up to the Spanish conquest. Whereas the extirpation of superstitions and beliefs furnishes the leading motif of the former, the resurrection of the ancient grandeur is the motif of the latter. The following passage illustrates extirpation:

La segunda piedra era una que agora tornaron a desenterrar en el sitio donde se edifica la Iglesia Mayor. . . . La cual deseo de ver quitada de allí, y aun también de ver desbaratada la Iglesia Mayor y hecha la nueva: es porque se quiten aquellas culebras de piedra que eran por basas de los pilares, las cuales eran cerca del patio de Huitxilopochtli y donde sé yo que han ido a llorar algunos viejos y viejas la destrucción de su templo, viendo allí las reliquias, y plega a la divina bondad que no hayan ido allí algunos a adorar aquellas piedras y no a Dios.

[The second stone has recently been unearthed where the main church is built. . . . I would like to see it taken away from there, and likewise to see the main church torn down and a new one built: the reason being to take away those snakes made of stones which served as bases of pillars and used to be near the patio of Huitxilopochtli. And I know that elders have gone there to cry over the destruction of their temple, seeing the relics there. God willing, no one has gone there to worship those stones instead of God.] (1:100)

Durán calls for a total erasure of all signs from the ancient religion. A mirage of a city in ruins surfaces in this passage alongside a church that must be torn down and rebuilt without traces of the old order. It is an appropriate metaphor for the need to extirpate old beliefs in order to build a *new church* without syncretism. For Durán, signs of the old must be registered and identified so they can be recognized in everyday life. This ethnographic task of identification for extirpation exemplifies the past present I mentioned above in the mode of a continuation of the old under a new order. Another sacrificial stone lying around the city becomes a motif for introducing African slaves into the new city: "Donde perpetuamente se recogían cantidad de negros a jugar y a cometer otros atroces delitos, matándose unos a otros" [Where constantly many blacks used to get together to gamble and to commit other crimes, killing each other] (1:100). Sacrifice merges with homicidal blacks, as if the stones carried a malefic influence.

Needless to say, Durán's ethnographic text is itself encyclopedic. I cite it to provide a (con)text, a series of scenes of Tenochtitlan from the second half of the sixteenth century, and not to set an exemplary attitude toward otherness or some sort of historiographic model. Indeed, the dyad extirpation/resurrection expresses with unequal pathos the contrarieties and contradictions the missionaries faced in their assessment of and writing about a civilization whose destruction they simultaneously lamented and abetted. Duran's *Historias* are particularly useful for constituting a historical backdrop because, in the process of reconstructing ancient rites and the calendar, and of rewriting the history of Mexico-Tenochtitlan, they include vivid observations of Indian life and attitudes toward the new Spanish/Christian order. *accurate ?*

In the section of the *Historias* dedicated to the native history of Tenochtitlan we can observe the production of a timeless presence of the bygone Mexican grandeur:

> Pero los historiadores y pintores pintaban con historias vivas y matices, con el pincel de su curiosidad, con vivos colores, las vidas y hazañas de estos valerosos caballeros y señores, para que su fama volase, con la claridad del sol, por todas las naciones. Cuya fama y memoria quise yo referir en esta mi historia, para que, conservada aquí, dure todo el tiempo que ella durare, para que los amadores de la virtud se aficionen a la seguir. *?!*
> [But the Mexican historians and painters painted with vivid histories and tints, with the brush of their curiosity, with vivid colors, the lives and feats of these courageous knights and lords, so that their fame would fly, with the clarity of the sun, over all nations. To their fame and memory I wish to allude in this my history, so that, conserved here, it will last for the time it may last, that the lovers of virtue may take fancy to follow it.] (2:99) *not forever ?*

Durán not only calls for a promotion of new paradigmatic leaders but hyperbolically praises Mexican historians for their political

encyclopedia
what is it? function?

and rhetorical genius as well. He seeks both to emulate their style in the *Historias* and to revive their political virtue in the present: *para que los amadores de la virtud se aficionen a la seguir.*

Extirpation is paradoxically reconciled with the resurrection of the ancient Mexican grandeur in the *Historias*: "Ha sido mi deseo de darle vida y resucitarle de la muerte y olvido en que estaba, a cabo de tanto tiempo." [My desire has been to give it life and resuscitate it from the death and oblivion in which it has rested for such a long time] (2:27–28). Resurrection, however, does not exclude the juncture of past and present in Durán's recasting of the indigenous narrative: "Oída la voz, acudió toda esta nación a hacer la calzada, que hoy en día se anda de la cuidad de México a Xuchimilco" [Upon hearing the call, the entire nation began to build the highway on which today one walks from Mexico to Xochimilco] (2:112). An archeology of a material past ultimately enhances nostalgia and admiration for the old political order. On the other hand, this sort of historical zigzag also produces mnemonic devices for understanding modifications of landscape and geographic demarcations, as well as routes of communication between towns that continued after the conquest and thus determined the material and cultural power structure of colonial Mexico.

These passages from Durán convey semantic and material transformations, quite literally layers of stones and words that have accumulated on and around New World phenomena. Paradoxically, the notion of a New World cannot be apprehended without these supplements, notwithstanding the intent to recapture and represent a timeless image of American nature, languages, and cultures. New ethnic groups, moreover, will form a part of descriptions both in regard to their functions as social actors as well as to the meanings they have invested on things by naming plants and animals, by adopting medicinal practices, or by building business enterprises.

Both Durán and Dávila Padilla provide glimpses of the indigenous and African social tissue inhabiting the Nova Mexico depicted in figure 10. The baroqueness of the city gains specificity as Durán tells us about the old stones used for the new buildings, and it reminds us of the highways built in ancient times. However, the exotic gardens and orderliness of Nova Mexico also harbors a new elite—the criollo, the Spaniard born in the New World.

A few years later Bernardo de Balbuena writes his long poem *La grandeza mexicana* (1604) in praise of Mexico City. But a colonial metropolis with exuberant gardens and magnificent buildings, without trace of an indigenous nobility, has definitely taken the place of the fantastic Tenochtitlan described by Cortés. Durán's notion of Mexican grandeur is totally absent from Balbuena's. Instead, Balbuena's exotic natural description becomes an allegory for the opulence of the white (criollo) population. Irving Leonard has assessed the documentary value of the poem as follows: "It would be idle, of course, to seek realism in this mellifluous description, yet it does give an impression of what life was like in the Mexican capital which, in its own way, could rival the interest and charm of many cities of Old Spain."[5] One can add that descriptions of Nova Mexico reveal the emergence of a new subject: the New Spaniard or, why not, the New Mexican—it would all depend on whether we want to underline the European or the American elements of the new culture.

The poem accentuates the transmutation of the New World into a European prototype:

> Jonio, corintio, dórico compuesto
> mosaico antiguo, áspero toscano,
> y lo que falta aquí si más hay que esto
>
> Oh ciudad bella, pueblo cortesano,
> primor del mundo, traza peregrina,
> grandeza ilustre, lustre soberano:
>
> fénix de galas, de riquezas mina,
> museo de ciencias y de ingenios fuente,
> jardín de Venus, dulce golosina . . .
> [Ionian, Corinthian, Doric compound
> Ancient mosaic, knotty Tuscan,
> and what lacks here since there is more
>
> O beautiful city, courtly people
> beauty of the world, peregrine outline,
> illustrious grandeur, sovereign luster:
>
> phoenix of gala, of riches mine,
> museum of science and of talent source
> garden of Venus, sweet delicacy . . .][6]

Far from Balbuena's concerns are the monsters isolated in the New World. The phoenix, a run-of-the-mill symbol for renewal, becomes an emblem for the "monstrous" transfiguration of the ashes of Tenochtitlan into the most grandiose metropolis of the New World, if not of the world itself. Mexico, accordingly, assumes a privileged position for the renewal of Old World knowledge and artistic forms. Balbuena nourishes the pride of the criollos throughout every turn of phrase. Next to architectural jewels, political wisdom, and linguistic finesse, the poem highlights the gallantry of the criollo:

> Pues la destreza, gala y bizarría,
> del medido jinete y su acicate,
> en seda envuelto y varia plumería,
>
> qué lengua habrá o pincel que le retrate
> en aquel aire y gallardía ligera,
> que a Marte imita en un feroz combate?
>
> Si el gran Faetón estos caballos viera
> nunca los de su padre cudiciara,
> que por menos gallardos los tuviera.
> [Because the dexterity, spirit, and bravery
> of the disciplined horseman and his spur,
> in silk enveloped and varied plumage
>
> what language is there or brush to portray it
> in such gait and swift gallantry,
> that in a ferocious combat imitates Mars?
>
> If the great Phaeton saw these great horses
> never would he covet his father's,
> for he would esteem them less gallant.] (75)

While ancient mythological figures seem to fall short for characterizing the criollo, Balbuena seeks a renewal of classical commonplaces in his praise of Mexico City. The deeds of the Spanish conquest do not concern him, and the natives disappear from Balbuena's tableaux with the exception of the incidental but highly revealing "indio feo" at the end of the poem. Traces of ancient Mexico are left to rest among the ruins buried under the new edifices that strings of hyperboles exalt:

Dejo también el áspero concurso,
y oscuro origen de naciones fieras,
que la hallaron con bárbaro discurso;

el prolijo viaje, las quimeras
del principio del águila y la tuna
que trae por armas hoy en sus banderas;

los varios altibajos de fortuna,
por donde su potencia creció tanto,
que pudo hacer de mil coronas una.
[I also leave aside the rough concourse
and dark origin of fierce nations
that founded her with barbarous discourse;

the prolix journey, the chimera
about the beginning of the eagle and the prickly pear
that bears for arms today in its banners;

the various vicissitudes of fortune
whereby its power grew so much
that it could make a thousand crowns one.] (69)

Even if Balbuena abstains from incorporating the glories of ancient Mexico into his poem, it is significant that in the course of a few lines he can, by combining a few motifs, evoke a voluminous historiography designed to unearth Mexican history prior to the conquest. The criollo embodies the New Mexican that Durán had envisioned in terms of a resurrection of the ancient virtues. The greatness of Balbuena's criollos, however, consists in their capacity to create unique forms of civilization. Although Balbuena shuns the pre-Hispanic grandeur, a long line of criollos building on sixteenth-century historiography will reinvent ancient Mesoamerica as the antiquity of Mexico. The disparity between the historical grandeur of the ancient Nahuas and the often depicted decrepitude of the surviving indigenous communities grows as the opulence of the criollo increases.[7]

Balbuena's poem, in particular his laconic allusion to ancient Mexico, exemplifies the fourth moment in the invention of America. The data collected in the histories of Tenochtitlan can now be invoked not to define the nature of the New World but precisely to replace pre-Hispanic motifs (strategically reduced to an "indio feo" without redemption) with those belonging to the grandeur of Nova Mexico (the criollo of "pure" Spanish stock). There is a streak of hope in Durán's admiration and emulation of ancient Mexican historians, indeed, a vocation to resurrect the ancient grandeur. Duran's will to bring to life the history of Mexico Tenochtitlan suggests that in spite of the decay of the Indian communities, he still perceives a native elite powerful enough to resume an influential, if not a dominant position (obviously as Christians) in New Spain. By the time Balbuena writes *La grandeza*, only a couple of decades later, the civilized Nahuas of Cortés have been reduced to ignorant Indians plagued by what religious authorities viewed as superstition and opportunistic sorcerers.

Three socioeconmic phases underlie the marginalization of indigenous communities and the formation of the criollo elite that Balbuena praises in his poem. The following historical excursus seeks to define further the historical backdrop I have elaborated from fragments of Durán and Balbuena.

By the 1620s the colonial economy had become independent from the depressed and bankrupt Spain,[8] and by the 1640s the criollos had bought most of the colonial government positions that the crown had sold to help finance an armada to defend its American territories. Practically speaking, the *gañán*, or free laborer, was the most economic and common form of labor within a dominant capitalist structure.[9] The socioeconomic processes giving shape to the *gañán* are too complex to deal with here, but one can say that the *gañán* slowly became dominant (before its official institution in 1632) and formed a labor pool consisting mostly of culturally or racially defined mestizos. On the other hand, the indigenous communities, whose members were accorded the status of perpetual minors,[10] were increasingly impoverished and marginalized from mainstream cultural life. Another important change in the early seventeenth century was the sale of title deeds permitting the formation of the great estates.[11] One has the feeling that when Balbuena speaks of the "indio feo" he means both the mestizos as well as members from the marginalized Indian communities that provided the labor force to the great haciendas. The formation of haciendas closed the process, initiated with the conquest, of transfiguring Mexico into New Spain. The consequences, however, are far from the first dreams envisioned in Cortés's political projections.

Two earlier forms of organization preceded the *gañán*. The *encomienda*, a system of private labor and tribute jurisdiction, along with slavery, predominated from the conquest to about 1544;[12] the *encomienda* was succeeded by the *repartimiento*, which consisted of a labor draft and thus favored a much larger group of employers, who in turn were obliged to pay salaries. If slavery and personal services persisted, as they did indeed, they were masked and legally displaced by the *repartimiento*.[13] Although individual *encomiendas* lasted until the end of the colony, the *encomienda* as a socioeconomic system became obsolete by the mid-sixteenth century, since an economy founded on tribute and personal services contradicted the incipient agricultural developments and, especially, the mining enterprise beginning to boom in Zacatecas during the late 1540s.[14]

The enforcement of antislavery laws, first promulgated in 1542, was immediately followed by one of the most devastating plagues of the sixteenth century. A first plague occurred in 1520, during the conquest, while the most devastating one corresponds to Dávila Padilla's tableau of the late 1570s. The plague from 1544 to 1546 greatly diminished the number of tributaries and, as a consequence, left large spaces of land untended. It thus gave momentum to an appropriation of land by Spaniards and to what eventually became the latifundia of the seventeenth century.

Along with the new economy introduced by the *repartimiento*, the midcentury points toward a hispanicization of political structures. Already during the *encomienda* and the *corregimiento* (the civil administration of the crown's lands and subjects), a tendency toward hispanicization was implicit in the modification of traditional patterns of life and areas of tributaries. A new Spanish mapping redefined the political geography of the Valley of Mexico.[15] The early congregations (mainly a Franciscan effort) of natives dispersed into towns patterned on Castilian communities, or utopian models, are also an instance of social modeling outside the large concentration of people in the valley.[16] Notably, in the *encomienda* system, the power of the indigenous elite was fragmented and limited to municipal centers (*cabeceras*) without the old political interrelation among them; the new map gives political power over several *cabeceras* to the *encomendero* or the *corregidor*.[17] This initial disfiguration of the geography was soon accompanied by endless litigations over land and social status. Such litigations implied both the "evils" of hispanicization and the need to carry out extensive research into pre-Hispanic tributary patterns, systems of heredity, land demarcations, and religious beliefs in order to formulate a just and preservative policy.

By midcentury a second face of hispanicization came about with the introduction of elections for indigenous posts within town offices patterned after the cabildo, the Spanish municipal government. Until then, Mexico City had been the only area with a white population sufficient to demand a Spanish structure. Even if the caciques remained strong, the introduction of elected posts represented a hard blow to the native nobility, since the power of hereditary posts was reduced. Initially, this program of hispanicization was received with an enthusiasm parallel to that which greeted the early missionary efforts. But this political change also promoted the decay of community pride. The original enthusiasm soon disappeared, and few aspired to the new offices. As Charles Gibson has pointed out, however, the new posts nevertheless penetrated into the heart of the communities: "Occasional references in the historical literature to informal bodies of elders (*viejos* and *ancianos*) suggest a residual community power that survived all colonial pressures. This influence appears not in the cabildo tasks of tribute collection or labor regulations but in those areas of life where a covert Indian symbolism was called into question or where community traditions were at stake."[18] In the long run, the new posts became obligatory, and so they overtly furthered Spanish ends to the detriment of the indigenous communities.

I have concentrated on two dates corresponding to the plagues in the 1540s and 1570s. Not only is the midcentury important because of the decimation of the indigenous population, but this period also corresponds to radical economic, social, and political transformations. The 1570s also represent a period when the crown carried out an exhaustive inquest on its domains and confiscated the major ethnographic works of the century.[19]

One more preliminary methodological indication is necessary before embarking on the analyses of the particular encyclopedias. Those initiated in Spanish New World historiography know that the corpus that comprises Oviedo, the Franciscans, and Las Casas encompasses tens of volumes, not including the secondary

[handwritten annotation: idea of apocalypse — revelation in — revolution]

literature. My reading of this mass of texts tries to define characteristic traits with a minimal use of representative examples. I believe my observations may be generalized to other parts of the corpus, but this remains a future task to be verified in detailed studies. Clearly the intent of this chapter is not to exhaust those monumental texts, but to illustrate and analyze the third moment in the invention of America: the formation of a corpus of encyclopedias. Since the conflicts between the different authors in the political arena have already been subjected to a number of studies as well as to heated debates, those conflicts will be incidental to us.[20] Moreover, since these authors write against each other, it has been easy to highlight or diminish the figure of one in favor of another, based on what they said about each other. The order of exposition should not be taken as an evaluation of the various writers' positions and the topics they prefer, but as an exigency for an independent analysis of how the exotic, the millennium, and the noble savage crystallize as dominant themes in the encyclopedic ensembles.

Needless to say, nothing in these encyclopedic compendia resembles the notion of the New World as a "blank page." On the contrary, they display a full awareness of a native text that must be known and appropriated. In fact, the production of New World knowledge in these texts further reinforces and divests the epistemic mutation and the new forms in the will to truth that we have observed in Columbus's need to register new phenomena as a consequence of the breakdown in the European stock of knowledge — clearly not a mere assimilation of the new under the old — and in Cortés's appropriation of the code registered in Tenochtitlan in the form of the book, the market, the botanical garden, the zoo, and the system of tributaries — the New World city as a deposit of information.

GONZALO FERNÁNDEZ DE OVIEDO: AN ENCYCLOPEDIC AMERICANA

Oviedo first began his career in the New World in 1514, when he was appointed supervisor to the smelting of gold in Tierra Firme, and remained in America for the rest of his life, with the exception of a few short trips to Spain. He became the crown's official chronicler of the Indies in 1532. We can assume that from the start, Oviedo began collecting data for his monumental

Historia general y natural de las Indias (1535–49).[21] From the title (*general*) we can infer his encyclopedic intent. The *Historia* is simultaneously a book of prodigies, a bestiary, an account of discoveries and conquests, a book of shipwrecks, an ethnography, and a tenacious attempt to describe the exquisiteness of American flora and fauna. Within this immensely broad spectrum of topics, I would like to isolate Oviedo's concept of the New World and his laborious descriptions of nature as keys for reading the other books of the *Historia*.

By the time he arrives, Oviedo feels that the New World has been for the most part disfigured by metaphorical nomenclatures and conquest. In a moment of frustration, he compares New World maps with a disordered religious calendar, "Mirando una destas cartas de marear, paresce que va hombre leyendo por estas costas un calendario o catálogo de sanctos, no bien ordenado" [Seeing one of these sea charts, one has the impression of reading in these coasts a calendar or a catalogue of saints, not well ordered] (2:334). Not without a comic touch, Oviedo excuses this practice on the grounds of the religiosity of the discoverers, and adds that as far as the participants were concerned "a su propósito bien lo ordenasen" [it was well ordered for their purpose] (ibid). The duplication of saints' names was unavoidable, so Oviedo recommends that "nombres propios donde saberse pudieran, se conserven" [wherever the proper names are known, they should be kept] (ibid). This statement best exemplifies Oviedo's historiography as a general attempt to recuperate indigenous nomenclatures and correct disfigurations. His anticlerical comment "me parece de verdad que estas tierras manan o que llueven frailes" [it truly seems to me that these lands ooze or rain friars] (4:264) well satirizes not only the reformist policies of Bartolomé de Las Casas but also Franciscan millenarian versions of the New World as well as the priority of building a new church. Oviedo's position is primarily that of a businessman and a settler.

The attitude of conquerors, bureaucrats, and clergy led him, early in his career, to a pessimistic view of human history. Natural history became an escape from an empire increasingly ruled by absurd and grotesque policies. As Antonello Gerbi has underlined: "The sovereign himself, so grandiosely allegorized at the outset, ends up being accused of petty greed and almost of deceit."[22] If human history appears tragic beyond redemption in the *Historia* (often told in the mode of a comic satire), the natural world moves him to a quasipantheistic praise of creation.

When studying American phenomena, Oviedo alternates between, on the one hand, the use of metaphor to incorporate the new for survival purposes and, on the other, inquiries into the "mysteries" of American nature. He tends to move from what resembles the old to meticulous depictions of what is unique. A vital logic underlies his approach, since a survey of natural resources for survival must begin with the identification of the same and move on toward constant experimentation. Oviedo praises his work above those written in Europe and gives it authority by remarking that "el experimentar de las aguas e manjares fuese a costa de nuestras vidas" [our lives depended on experimentation with water and food] (1:10). Not only historians are undermined, but all latecomers who "agora gozan de muchos sudores ajenos" [now enjoy the sweat of others] (ibid). Likewise, Oviedo can now afford to take delight in describing the marvels of the Indies, and a sensuous authority punctuates the *Historia*. The delicacies of taste displace the initial vital experiments for exploiting one of his favorite topics: food. There is hardly a dish or a drink that Oviedo does not taste and elaborate at length on its flavors, odors, and textures. He constantly undoes ready-made assimilations of New World phenomena to Old World prototypes with metonymic sensual exaltations of particularities and marvels: whenever Oviedo finds metaphorical expressions based on associations of resemblance, he dissolves and replaces them with a chain of juxtaposed partial comparisons with Old World things in a pursuit of sensual details.

But as such his task becomes infinite and, ultimately, it demands a shared experience of the items for a possible communication. Oviedo thus magnifies his enterprise and hands it down to all future generations: "Aquesto [no es] relatar la vida de un principe, ni muchos, ni de un reino o provincias, sino una relación de Nuevo Mundo e un *mare magno*, en que no puede bastar la pluma ni estilo de uno, ni dos ni muchos historiales, sino de todos aquellos que hobiere e los supieren hacer y escrebir en todos los tiempos e siglos venidores hasta el final juicio e fin de los humanos" [This is not the narration of the life of a prince, nor of many, nor of a kingdom or provinces, but the relation of a

New World and a *mare magno*, for which does not suffice the pen and style of one, nor two, nor many historians, but of all those existent and capable of doing it and writing in all times and centuries to come until the last judgment and end of the humans] (5:417).

Oviedo self-consciously proves the limits of attaining and communicating knowledge of the New World, as well as pursuing criteria for establishing taxonomies. The tasks of naming and describing flora, fauna, cultures, and landscapes are, however, haunted by the disfiguration of previous metaphors, which Oviedo's history attempts to rectify in order to promote marvel and a "fresh" representation of the new phenomena. Exoticism serves both to identify the New World with the infinite power of nature and to direct an endless pursuit of detail in the description of particulars. Oviedo lacks an adequate grid for drawing an abstract and coherent view of the whole; moreover, his fascination with diversity seems to preclude a reduction of difference into a table of classifications that would annul the experience of sensual qualities. Throughout the *Historia* he delights in exploring the limits of representation; a perpetual displacement of linguistic approximations, within a maze of sensual associations, attempts to communicate an experience of things. We may like Oviedo's obsession for particularities with Dutch paintings where unity and harmony were lost in the aggregations of details, as Michelangelo pointed out.[23]

The structure of the *Historia* reflects this aggregation of detail and lack of unity. It is, however, a generic characteristic of chronicles. As a *cronista*, Oviedo is charged with collecting accounts of particular events and gathering information on natural and cultural phenomena from all parts of the New World. Oviedo interpolates moral commentaries on the irresponsible behavior of such conquistadors as Hernando de Soto, who not only roamed the land enslaving Indians and tearing up fields of maize but also led an armada into the interior of Florida (all the way to Tennessee and Arkansas) without knowledge of the land: "El gobernador propuso, como siempre había seído, que era lo mejor ir adelante, sin saber él ni ellos en qué acertaban ni en qué lo erraban" [The governor proposed, as usual, that it was best to go on, without him nor them knowing when they guessed right and when they erred] (2:166). He also comments at length on the

"savagery," *la salvajez*, of Amerindian cultures, without excluding "sympathetic" comparisons of *areitos*—feasts where
histories were sang—to the romances and other orally transmit-
ted histories in Europe, "No le parezca al lector que esto que es
dicho [*areitos*] es mucha salvajez, pues que en España e Italia se
usa lo mismo" [The reader should not be surprised and consider
these [*areitos*] excessively savage, since in Spain and Italy it is
similarly done] (1:114).

His prologues lend unity to the *Historia* by connecting different accounts, providing methodological observations, and explaining the expository order of the different books. It is ultimately the overall "story" that the collected accounts reveal,
however, that makes of Oviedo's text a *Historia*. The larger
narrative lies beyond the power of the chronicler, since it would
convey the secrets of nature and the paths of Divine Providence.
That the *Historia* breaks off with the announcement of a forth-
coming fourth part further underscores a chronicle effect. But
perhaps this is also due to an encyclopedic intent. After all, the
task of writing about a New World, as Oviedo himself remarks,
demands more than one writer and style. Furthermore, it is a
New World with regard not only to nature and Amerindian
cultures but also to the behavior of Spaniards. In Oviedo's vision
of the New World exoticism colors natural, cultural and historical phenomena.

An examination of Oviedo's entry on pineapples illustrates the
labyrinthine quandaries Oviedo faces when trying to depict a
reality that becomes more slippery at every turn of phrase. A
close reading of this entry reveals the power of objectification of
Oviedo's taxonomy, but also conveys a sensual excess that over-
burdens the will to classify. Thus, it constitutes an allegory of the
invention of the exotic as America.

Pineapples assume a wondrous silhouette in Oviedo's description; they are among the principal regalia of exotic Americana.
The section dedicated to pineapples also typifies his method of
moving from the metaphorical to the particular. Hence, Oviedo
opens the chapter with a taxonomical observation: "Hay en esta
isla Española unos cardos, que cada uno dellos lleva una piña (o,
mejor diciendo, alcarchofa), puesto que, porque paresce piña, las
llaman los cristianos piñas, sin lo ser" [There are in this island of
Hispaniola some thistles, which carry each a pineapple (or,

better said, artichoke); insofar as they look like pines, Christians called them pineapples without their being so] (1:239). The total overlapping of *piña* with *pine cone* is obscured in English through the addition of "apple"; however, this latter fruit also retains a highly abstract or "quintessential" comparison. Although Oviedo seems to attribute the name to a vox populi, the juxtaposition of *piña* (pine cone) and *alcarchofa* (artichoke) also evokes one of the first descriptions of pineapples. Michele di Cuneo, a companion of Columbus during the second voyage, compares the fruit with a pine cone and the plant with an artichoke.[24] Oviedo here ignores this distinction between the fruit and the plant when he favors artichokes.

The drawing of the pineapple in the *Historia* depicts both parts of the fruit with no resemblance whatsoever to an artichoke or a pine cone (fig. 11). When he finally discusses this distinction later in the entry, he focuses on the appropriateness of the terms and not on the similitude with the other plants. The names remain as fossils of a first comparison. Oviedo's proposal of "artichoke" hardly improves the initial similes, and, if his argument for the latter term gains anything, it prevents an association of *piña* with pine cones as well as *alcarchofas*. He eventually dissolves the comparisons as he insists on the taxonomical value of *alcarchofas* by pointing out that in "verdad . . . no se parte *totaliter* de ser alcarchofa, ni de las espinas, porque en la coronilla, encima de la piña, nace e tiene esta fructa un cogollo áspero, e adórnala mucho en la vista" [truth . . . it does not part *totaliter* from being an artichoke, nor from the thorns, because on the crown on top of the pineapple, it has a rough shoot and is the part from which it is born, which embellishes it greatly] (1:241–42).

In the etymological sense of *discurrere*, Oviedo's discourse on pineapples moves "back and forth" from *piña* to *alcarchofa* without finding a final taxonomical anchoring point. To paraphrase Hayden White, Oviedo alternates between these two ways of encoding the fruit.[25] But also following White, we may comment that Oviedo's discourse moves to and fro between a received code and the clutter of phenomena that refuse to be incorporated into conventionalized notions of "reality," "truth," or "possibility."

Oviedo considers using an indigenous term, but he encounters several words from different linguistic areas, along with an equal

Figure 11. Other stages in the naturing process elude his graphic depiction. *A Pineapple. In Gonzalo Fernández de Oviedo*, Historia general y natural de las Indias *(Seville, 1535). Courtesy Newberry Library*.

variety of pineapples. Because he wants to avoid generalizing a particular type, he decides to retain the term in common usage. Despite this particular case, the *Historia* generally promotes the use of indigenous terms, and careful recordings of proper phonetics abound. An extreme case at issue is the heading of chapter 4 in book 8: "Del árbol llamado *higüero*. El acento de la letra *u*

143

had de ser luengo, o de espacio dicho, de manera que no se pronuncien breve, ni juntamente estas tres letras *gue*, sino que se detenga poquita cosa entre la *u* y la *e*, e diga hi . . gü . . ero. Digo esto, porque el lector no entienda higuero, o higuera de higos" [On the tree called *higüero*. The accent on the letter *u* must be long or with a space, so that it is not pronounced briefly, nor these three letters *gue* together; instead one must stop briefly between the *u* and the *e*, and say hi . . gü . . ero. I say this, so the reader does not understand *higuero*, or fig tree] (1:251). Oviedo did not use the diaeresis in the 1535 and 1547 editions, and the rationale for the diphthongal distinction *güe* from the silent *u* in *gue* must be one of the earliest in Spanish. Other elementary forms of phonetic descriptions are used throughout the *Historia*. If Oviedo refrains from generalizing a type of pineapple, his attempt to retain an indigenous vocabulary is plagued by analogous linguistic reductions and impositions over other languages in the continent. Notable cases are Arawak words in use since Columbus's *Diario*, such as *hamaca*, *cacique*, *maíz*, and so on.

These linguistic problems notwithstanding, his chapter on pineapples exemplifies Oviedo's attempt to avoid metaphorical distortions—that is, wrong associations with what he considers the most delightful fruit in the world. But how does he avoid, or even better, manipulate the ever-slippery metaphoricity of language? Let us look at his theoretical gaiety and at the inevitable "punchy" associations with other fruits.

As a sensualist, Oviedo disregards or gives second place to universals. We see him open the chapter with *cardos* (thistle) as a taxon, but again, it follows more the need to open a topic with a general concept than a conviction about the value of abstractions. Under the general category of *cardos* Oviedo includes *tunas*, *pitayas*, and other specimens. In the *Historia* a tentative taxonomy of flora according to shapes of leaves and thickness of branches or of bark allows him to draw comparisons with European plants. The formal categories for the organization of the *Historia* are inherited from Pliny: "Yo entiendo seguir o imitar al mismo Plinio (no en decir lo que él dijo, puesto que en algunos lugares sean alegadas sus auctoridades como cosa deste jaez universal de Historia Natural, pero en el distinguir de mis libros y géneros dellos, como él lo hizo)" [I intend to follow and

144

to imitate Pliny himself (not in repeating what he said, although I appeal to his authority as a thing from the harness of Natural History, but in distinguishing my books and genres as he did)] (1:11).

Invention (the distinct books and genres) and the universal harness of natural history (*jaez universal de Historial Natural*), borrowed from Pliny, help Oviedo organize his materials. Beyond classificatory purposes, Pliny serves as well to authorize phenomena that may seem fabulous. As Gerbi puts it, for Oviedo, "Two contemporary witnesses and one ancient make up a winning hand."[26] Hence in Oviedo's book we can trace an open acknowledgement of the validity of eyewitnessing as well as an epistemological matrix where monsters and marvels described in ancient histories and those circulating in New World accounts constitute a realm of reality. On the other hand, if Pliny is a rhetorical model, Oviedo makes clear that he differs from Pliny inasmuch as the ancient naturalist drew all his materials from written sources, whereas the *Historia* builds on observation and experimentation: "No he sacado de dos mil millares de volúmines que haya leído, como en el lugar suso alegado Plinio escribe, en lo cual paresce que él dijo lo que leyó" [I have not drawn from two million volumes that I might have read, as in the aforementioned place Pliny writes, and as a result it seems that he said what he read] (1:11). As a consequence of not borrowing topics and anecdotes from an established corpus, his descriptions emphasize sensuous depictions of experienced particularities.

Three main senses form the bulk of Oviedo's description of pineapples, "hermosura de vista, suavidad de olor, gusto de excelente sabor" [beauty of sight, mildness of smell, taste of excellent flavor] (1:240). Oviedo adds that touch might also convey qualities. But in the discussion he attributes, with a droll pretence of naïveté, these senses to fruits. Oviedo moves on to deny hearing to pineapples and corrects the conceptual catachresis: "El quinto sentido, que es el oír, la fructa no puede oír ni escuchar; pero podrá el lector, en su lugar, atender con atención lo que desta fructa yo escribo, y tenga por cierto que no me engaño, ni me alargo en lo que dijere della" [The fifth sense, which is hearing, the fruit cannot hear or listen; but the reader, in his place, may follow attentively what I write about it, and be certain that I am not deceiving myself nor exaggerating what I say about it] (1:240). With this slip into the absurd, Oviedo introduces an ironic dimension to his own enterprise by reminding the reader that there is nothing farther from the delights to be derived from pineapples than "listening" to a written description of sensations derived from smell, taste, or sight.

Oviedo had received training in painting as a child, and was acquainted with both Flemish and Italian painting.[27] Throughout the *Historia* he uses visual representations as a historical ancilla, and he may well be the first to provide Europeans with direct drawings of American phenomena. About the use of painting, Oviedo writes: "Mas, porque yo deseo mucho la pintura en las cosas de historia semejantes, e que en nuestra España no son tan usadas, quiero aprovecharme della para ser mejor entendido, porque, sin dubda, los ojos son mucha parte de la información destas cosas, e ya que las mismas no se pueden ver ni palpar, mucha ayuda es a la pluma la imagen dellas" [Indeed, because I much desire likeness in the painting of things in history, which in our Spain is not practiced that much, I want to take advantage of it to be better understood, because undoubtedly, the eyes play a great part in the information of these things, and since the same cannot be seen or touched, of great aid to the pen are their images] (1:268). But as Oviedo includes a painting of a pineapple, he encounters another difficulty: he can only draw a particular form of *natura naturata*, while the other stages in the naturing process elude his graphic depiction. The readers must excuse him, pleads Oviedo, if the descriptions lack the particularities of their actual experience.

As in a passage quoted earlier, the historical task takes on an infinite dimension requiring the work of all mankind, for all ages to come. If universals are poor in content, the depiction of particularities becomes a labyrinthine and illusory attempt to avoid metaphor. For instance, when Oviedo compares the smell of pineapples to a combination of peach, quince, fine melons, "y demás excelencias que todas esas fructas juntas y separadas" [and other excellencies of all these fruits together and separate] (1:240), we conclude with a "punch" of aromas that ever eludes the specific fragrance of pineapples. On the other hand, the expression of visual delight ends up with a hyperbolic comparison of the care *la natura* has taken in dressing a peacock and the composition and beauty of his favorite fruit.

146

Hugh Honour has traced what became a proverbial impossibility of describing the taste of pineapples in a philosophical point made by Locke, "If a child were kept where he never saw but black and white, he would have no more idea of scarlet, than he that never tasted a pineapple has of that peculiar relish."[28] The trajectory of the pineapple finds a resting place as a descriptive motif in philosophy. An echo of this philosopheme recurs in Wittgenstein, "Describe the aroma of coffee. — Why can't it be done . . . ?"[29] The answer, certainly, is not because coffee is exotic. But why coffee and not bread?

The descriptiveness of Americana certainly cuts deeper than the playful remembrance of the pineapple I have elaborated here. For instance, toward the end of the sixteenth century the English refer to the Scots and the Irish as the "Indians at home," and Pierre de Lancre speaks of a displacement of Satan's abode from America to the Basque countries on account of the missionary activity outside of Europe;[30] elements from the constitution of savagery and witchcraft on the other side of the ocean become operative for isolating otherness back home. In philosophy, primitivism provides a fulcrum in the tradition that goes from Hobbes to Rousseau. And let me briefly evoke that "chance encounter" of the old and the new within the soul of nineteenth-century Europeans. Our universality, today, bears the imprint of an imperceptible other in the projection of modernity as the historical destiny of all mankind. A bare reminder of our expurgated memory remains in the saturation of the world market with, say, canned pineapples still tokened as an exotic produce.

Oviedo's entry lucidly debunks his own representation of the New World. The entry, I believe, allegorizes the first three of the four moments outlined in the Introduction, and furnishes the European storehouse of images with a descriptive motif. Despite this brilliant moment, an ideology of exoticism harbors the indescribable in Oviedo. His exoticism, in turn, furnishes a key for reading his depictions of "savagery," the historical books, and other sections making up a zoology in the *Historia*.

If a surreal juxtaposition of fragrance is limited to a sensual musing on the part of the readers, a similar approach in zoology concludes with fantastic entities, especially when the account is based on hearsay. Oviedo corroborates monsters and prodigies with ancient sources but, vice versa, American phenomena also

147

why exoticism?

lend authority to ancient descriptions. The case of the *gatico monillo* (little cat, little monkey) offers an extreme instance where Oviedo's realism merges with "social" evidence and produces a fantastic entity within a conception of the New World where everything is possible. Let us take the description of the *gatico monillo*:

> La cual cuentan que, en la tierra austral del Perú, se ha visto un gatico monillo, destos de las colas luengas, el cual, desde la mitad del cuerpo, con los brazos e cabeza, era todo aquello cubierto de pluma de color parda, e otras mixturas de color; e la mitad deste gato para atrás, todo él, e las piernas e cola, era cubierto de pelo rasito e llano de color bermejo, como leonado claro. Este gato era muy mansito e doméstico, e poco mayor que un palmo.
> [It is told that, in the austral lands of Peru, a *gatico monillo* has been seen, of the kind with long tails; this one had half of its body, including arms and head, all covered with brown feathers, and other color mixtures; and the other half of this monkey, the whole of it, and the legs and tail, were covered with short and straight red hair, somewhat tawny. This monkey was very tame and domestic, and a bit larger than a hand.] (1:223)

To this description of a miniature feathered monkey, Oviedo adds that it sang "como ruiseñor o una calandria," like a nightingale or a lark, and specifies that it had teeth. It is impossible to translate the diminutives *pelo rasito*, *mansito*, *gatico*, *monillo*, which reveal Oviedo's enthusiasm and care in the description. We could speak of tenderness, though he does not hesitate to add that if he had seen it he would have preserved it in salt. Nor does he avoid speculation over its species: "Tal animal no nació de tal adulterio, sino que es especie sobre sí e natural, como lo son por sí los grifos; pues que el maestro de la Natura ha hecho mayores obras e maravillas, el cual sea loado e alabado para siempre jamás" [Such an animal was not born out of adultery, but is a species in itself, and natural, such as the griffin; since the master of Nature has created greater works and marvels; be he praised and extolled forevermore] (1:223–24).

The parallelism between the ancient griffin and the *gatico monillo* opens a taxonomical category for the inclusion of juxtaposed species as a species in itself, and not a monstrous hybrid resulting from "adultery" (as Oviedo puts it, an impossibility because the generative organs of birds and cats are incompatible).[31] Ancient and American phenomena corroborate each other in an image of nature full of wonders and a New World where the unexpected constantly erupts. It is important to note that earlier projections of European beasts or monsters open, with Oviedo, into a scenario of American nature where new and marvelous entities thrive within the domain of legend. Beyond God, Oviedo seems to praise nature for its prodigality. Whereas the chapters on human history suggest an unredeemable tragedy, those dedicated to nature celebrate its marvels and an uncommitted glorification of American nature. The New World in Oviedo's *Historia* takes on a symbolic value in terms of its exoticism, which leads Oviedo to affirm the contiguity of the Indies: "La Tierra Firme destas Indias es una otra mitad del mundo, tan grande o por ventura mayor que Asia, Africa y Europa; . . . toda la tierra del universo está dividida en dos partes, y . . . la una es aquella tierra que los antiguos llamaron Asia e Africa y Europa . . . y, la otra parte o mitad del mundo es aquesta de nuestras Indias" [The mainland of these Indies is another half of the world, as big as or perhaps bigger than Asia, Africa, and Europe: and . . . all the land of the Universe is divided into two parts, and . . . one is the one the ancients called Asia and Africa and Europe . . . and the other part or half of the world is this one of our Indies].[32]

As Oviedo places the New World outside the Old World, he reveals the primacy of the exotic in the invention of America. The millenarian, the signs of a new time, can be found at home, in the midst of the cooking pot, as Saint Teresa of Avila would put it. Likewise, the noble savage can be read as a chapter from the scriptures as it testifies to a possible immanence of innocence in a second birth. In order for the millenarian and the noble savage to assume New World forms, exoticism must underline their newness and difference. Topics pertaining to the millenarian and noble savagery barely occur in Oviedo, if at all. Like all historians of his time, he appeals to a providential design to explain the eventfulness of the discovery. But his narrative of the events is all too human; he abstains from tracing the hand of the Lord. Oviedo's exoticism, however, carries a force that weighs down the centuries.

We will close Oviedo by examining how nineteenth-century editors of the *Historia* transformed a drawing of a hammock and a woman in Oviedo's unpublished manuscripts. An annotation,

"Por hazer," next to the drawing indicates that Oviedo intended this more realistic representation—which illustrates how the hammock molds to one's body—to replace an earlier flat, diagrammatical version. Nineteenth-century editors incorporated the image into a representation of an exotic landscape, ostensibly to gain scientific accuracy (fig. 12).[33] With a scientific agenda in mind they proceeded to correct the austere aesthetic of Oviedo's woodcuts (as can be perceived in the pineapple illustration). In José Amador de los Ríos's illustration for the edition of 1851–55, we find a dreamy Amerindian lying in a hammock with his head reclined on one hand. The illustration of the hammock is surrounded by realistic and detailed drawings of New World plants, with a house barely perceptible in the right-hand side of the background. The original woman, however, has become an androgyne. The facial features suggest a man, but the posture is "feminine." Notice for instance the tightly pressed thighs facing frontward as the waist curls up toward the chest. Beyond the androgynous, it suggests a feminization of otherness among the integral components of exotic man. The drawing also bears a striking similarity in its composition with Stradanus's allegory. Undoubtedly, Stradanus never saw Oviedo's drawings of the hammock, anteater (although this too bears a striking similarity with his own), sloth, and so on, which at that time remained unpublished. But he probably was familiar with Giovanni Ramusio's edition of the *Sumario* and the *Historia general* in his *Terzo volume della navigationi et viaggi* (Venice, 1556). Ramusio's version of the hammock slightly breaks the flatness of Oviedo's woodcut by giving it some depth. It is most likely that Stradanus had Ramusio's image in mind when he made his drawing. After all, Oviedo is but one compendium in the encyclopedic competence that Stradanus presumes and draws from.

The sensual Amerindian in the hammock would seem to ratify Oviedo's view that the Indians were a "nación muy desviada de querer entender la fe católica" [it is a nation very unfit to understand the catholic faith], and that their skulls (hence understanding) were different from other peoples: "Y así como tienen el casco grueso, así tienen el entendimiento bestial y mal inclinado" [And as they have a thick skull, they have beastly and badly inclined understanding] (1:111). Oviedo held that Hespero, the twelfth king of Spain, had conquered the Indies 161 years

Figure 12. The facial features suggest a man, but the posture is "feminine." *A Hammock. In Gonzalo Fernández de Oviedo*, Historia general y natural de las Indias *(Madrid, 1851–54). Courtesy Benson Latin American Collection, General Libraries, University of Texas at Austin.*

before Troy was founded (1:18–19), and believed that the gospel had already been preached all over the world before Columbus sailed to America (1:111). Thus he explained Amerindian culture as a degeneration from antiquity and accountable for its sins. As twice fallen, Amerindians could be legitimately punished and subjected to Spanish rule.[34]

FRANCISCAN ETHNOGRAPHY: UTOPIA AND THE DEVIL'S DWELLING PLACE

In this section I present a series of topics first introduced by the Franciscans. I do not pretend that the themes or perspectives outlined were shared by all Franciscans, nor that they are constant throughout the sixteenth century. Following the general trend in this essay, they constitute one more complex of topics investing the concept of the New World with significant motifs and tropes.

The Franciscan chroniclers follow a mystical vein for interpreting the New World. Many of the insights, mystical flights, and possible historical exegeses in Columbus, and less radically so in Cortés, recur with the Franciscans. The letters of Cortés prompted among the Friars Minor, especially those from the province of San Gabriel,[35] an enthusiastic reception and a dominant millenarian interpretation of the Indies. Cortés's description of Mesoamerican civilization and the immense population of the Valley of Mexico gave place to unprecedented topics: Satan's stronghold is identified with the New World, and a church militant is organized for a spiritual conquest. Their agenda merges the end of time with the building of a new church. "Ethnography" becomes an evangelical and political ancilla for preparing for the coming of the millennium.

As early as 1523, in the instructions given to the first twelve missionaries, Fray Francisco de los Angeles, better known as Quiñones, draws the following diagnostic, "Y porque en esta tierra de la Nueva España ya dicha, siendo por el demonio y carne vendimiada, Cristo no goza de las ánimas que con su sangre compró . . ." [And because in this forementioned land of New Spain, being unlawfully reaped by the devil and the flesh, Christ does not enjoy the souls that he bought with his blood . . .].[36] Quiñones moves on to equate their mission with that of the twelve apostles and the twelve disciples of Saint Francis; the original apostleship is an emblem for accentuating the Franciscan historical mission.[37] In an "Obedience" of the same year, Quiñones fully characterizes the Franciscans' mission with that of a church militant in the spirit of St. Francis:

A imitacion de varón apostólico y seráfico padre nuestro S. Francisco, procure yo con toda ternura de mis entrañas y sollozos de mi corazon librar de la cabeza del dragón infernal las ánimas redemidas con la preciosísima sangre de Nuestro Señor Jesucristo, y que engañadas con la astucia de Santanás viven en la sombra de la muerte, detenidas en la vanidad de los ídolos, y hacerlas que militen debajo de la bandera de la Cruz, y que abajen y metan el cuello so el dulce yugo de Cristo.
[In imitation of the apostolic man and seraphic father our St. Francis, I shall endeavor with all the tenderness of my bowels and sobs from my heart to free from the head of the infernal dragon the souls that were redeemed with the very precious blood of Our Lord Jesus Christ, and that, being deceived by the cunning of Satan, live in the shadow of death, captive to the vanity of idols, and shall make them militate underneath the banner of the Cross, so that they lower and place their neck under the sweet yoke of Christ.] (203)

As a result of this identification of New Spain with Satan's dwelling place, Quiñones interprets the formation of the new church with an exegesis of the eleventh hour in the parable of the vineyard in Matthew 20, "acercandóse ya el último fin del siglo" [already approaching the last end of the century] (204). This apocalyptic statement is further reinforced by the explication of the origins of the Amerindians as descendants from the ten lost tribes of Israel. As John Phelan points out, "According to Apocalypse 7:4–9, the lost tribes were to reappear on the day of the Last Judgment."[38] Quiñones's eschatology includes the belief that the Parousia of Christ will be prepared by a rapid evangelization of the last gentiles; this belief is in full accordance with the prophetic writings attributed to Joachim of Flora, the evangelical spirit of Saint Francis, and the fertile terrain in sixteenth-century Spain for apocalyptic exegeses of historical events.[39]

One of the first twelve missionaries, Fray Toribio de Benavente, commonly known as Motolinía ("poverty" in Nahuatl), follows this same mystical vein in a letter to Charles V where he interprets the statue in Daniel 2. For Motolinía the Conquest of Mexico corresponds to the fifth kingdom that concludes four earlier militarily defined stages in world history (those of Cyrus, Darius, Alexander the Great, and Caesar): "Lo que yo a vuestra majestad suplico es el quinto reino de Jesucristo, significado en la piedra cortada del monte sin manos, que ha de henchir y ocupar toda la tierra, del cual reino vuestra majestad es el caudillo y capitán, que mande vuestra majestad poner toda diligencia que sea posible para que este reino se cumpla" [What I plead to your majesty for is the fifth kingdom of Jesus Christ, which is signified by the stone cut from the mountain without hands; it will fill and occupy the whole earth; of this kingdom your majesty is the leader and captain; let your majesty order to place all possible diligence so that this kingdom is fulfilled].[40] In this letter from 1555, bitterly written against Las Casas's condemnation of the Spanish enterprise in the Indies, Motolinía not only repeats the theme of preparing for the Parousia of Christ but defined it as Spain's imperial destiny. Thus Motolinía fully justifies the conquest within a historical paradigm. Ethical questions take a subservient position to the evangelical significance of the conquest. Quoting Daniel, Motolinía puts forth the schemes of God beyond moral law: "Dios muda los tiempos y edades, y pasa los reinos de un señorio en otro" [God changes the time and the ages, and moves kingdoms from one lordship to another] (ibid). In such relativism we can trace the influence of Ockham, and even Duns Scotus, insofar as these major Franciscan thinkers asserted the primacy of the will and revelation in ethical questions as well as the exegeses of God's designs.

In itself, calling Charles V to be the emperor of the end of time conveys nothing specific about the New World. The category of the exotic must underlie the uniqueness of the land as brooding millenarian signs. It is not, however, the exotic of the naturalist Oviedo, who takes delight in a pursuit of sensual particularities, but a mystico-marvelous sense of difference. Motolinía's commentary on the hibernation of hummingbirds can serve as an example:

> Si Dios ansí conserva unos pajaritos y después los resuscita, y cada año en esta tierra se ven estas maravillas, quién dudará sino que los cuerpos humanos, que son sepultados corruptibles, que no los resucitará Dios incorruptibles por Jesucristo, y los vestirá y adornará de los cuatros dotes, y manterná de la suavidad de su divina fruición y visión, pues a estos pájaros tan chiquitos ansí sustenta del rocío y miel de las flores, y viste de tan graciosa pluma, que ni Salomón en toda su gloria ansí fue vestido como uno de éstos.
>
> [If God thus preserves some small birds and afterward resurrects them, and year by year one sees these marvels in this land, who would doubt of human bodies, which are buried corruptible, that God shall not resurrect them incorruptible by Jesus Christ, and that he will dress and adorn them with the four gifts, and sustain them with the tenderness of his divine fruition and vision, since he sustains these so small birds with the dew and honey of flowers, and dresses them with such gracious feathers, that even Solomon in all his glory was not arrayed like one of these.] (377)

By implication, the hummingbird is a sign of the care God has taken in dressing the New World landscape with metaphors that prove an article of faith.

Generally Motolinía finds tedious the description of natural phenomena; at the opposite end of the spectrum with respect to Oviedo, he finds relief in apocalyptic excursus when treating natural history, "Por aliviar el fastidio de lo historial, algunas veces converná salir a lo moral o espiritual o figurativo" [In order to alleviate the fastidiousness of the historical, at times it will be fitting to digress to the moral or spiritual or figurative]

(220). Moral, spiritual, and figurative commentaries invest landscapes with mystical qualities. This note on style refers to a digression from the description of the Mexican highlands to a characterization of the region as "muy propia tierra para ermitaños e contemplativos, y aun creo que los vivientes antes de mucho tiempo han de ver . . . como esta tierra fue otra Egipto en idolatrías e tinieblas de pecados e después floreció en gran santidad" [very proper for hermits and contemplatives, and I even believe that the living before long shall see . . . how this land was another Egypt in idolatries and darkness of sins and afterward flourished in great holiness] (219). Like Egypt, in the course of time, Mexico will move from idolatry and sin to the flourishing of saintliness; but the reference to Egypt also prepares the ground for a historical statement. The growth of the church announces the end of times within the geographic movement of history from East to West: "Y como floreció en el principio la iglesia en oriente, que es principio del mundo, bien ansí agora en el fin de los siglos ha de florecer en occidente, que es fin del mundo" [And as in the beginning the church flourished in the Orient, which is the beginning of the world, likewise now at the end of the centuries it must flourish in the West, which is the end of the world] (220). Although the flocks of natives seeking baptism in the thousands are among the imminent signs of the Apocalypse, Motolinía includes the Spaniards in his millenarian speculations.

Thus the plan of Puebla de los Angeles is envisioned as an ideal city where Spaniards would build the new Jerusalem: "Cibdad de los Angeles no hay quien crea haber otra sino la del cielo. Aquélla está edificada como ciudad en las alturas, que es madre nuestra. . . . Qué tal sea esta ciudad, ya está escrito, porque la vio y la contempló San Juan Evangelista en los capítulos 21 e 22 del *Apocalipsi*" [No one believes that there is another City of the Angels but the heavenly one. That one is built as city in the heavens, which is our mother. . . . That so shall be this city, it is already written, because Saint John the Evangelist saw it and contemplated it in chapters 21 and 22 of the *Apocalipsis*] (262). Motolinía tells us that the city was built under the auspices of Sebastián Ramírez de Fuenleal (who also ordered the first ethnographic inquests in the 1530s), to correct the destruction that vagrant Spaniards were imposing on indigenous communities.[41] In Ramírez's agenda poor Spaniards were to be given land so they could develop an agricultural infrastructure, provide good examples to the natives, and enamor themselves with the fatherland.

Later on in the *Memoriales*, Motolinía substantiates the *ya esta escrito* (it is already written) in Saint John's *Apocalypse*. As he highlights the fertility of the terrain and benevolent climate, Motolinía reinforces the claim that this is an ideal site by comparing it to the terrestrial paradise: "Ansí este valle por tiempo ha de ser un paradiso terrenal, porque tiene mucho aparejo para lo ser, ca ciertamente paraíso quiere decir huerto o jardín gracioso a do hay abundancia de aguas, rosas y frutales, como los hay aquí, y por eso se llama Val de Cristo" [In the course of time this valley will thus be a terrestrial paradise, because it is naturally disposed; paradise certainly means orchard or gracious garden where there is an abundance of waters, roses, and fruit trees, as there are here, and so it is called the Valley of Christ] (271). The building of paradise and its natural disposition also matches phenomena described in Genesis 3:8: "Siempre a medio día viene por aquella vega un viento muy gracioso y templado, que . . . yo le llamo *auram post meridiem*, que ansí dizque se llamaba un viento gracioso que corría en el paraíso terrenal" [Always at noon a very gracious and temperate breeze comes through that valley, which . . . I call *auram post meridiem*, since thus was called a gracious breeze that ran through terrestrial paradise] (ibid).

For Motolinía, paradise does not correspond to nature, as it did for Columbus, but to a garden recreated by industry. Moreover, as Motolinía places it in the past (*se llamaba, corría*), he shuns the question of a permanent geographic location. Thus the building of the New Jerusalem is equated with paradise: "Y no me aparto mucho de decir los bienes de la Cibdad de los Angeles, pues le doy por villa un paraíso terrenal, que ya que los hombres lo perdieron, si algunos lo podían mejor hallar, era los ángeles para su cibdad" [And I do not restrain myself from telling the goods of the City of the Angels, because I am giving you a terrestrial paradise for hamlet; and since it was man who lost it, if there was someone better fit to find it, it was the angels for their city] (ibid).

Well in accord with millenarian expectations, the coming of the new time is historical in the sense that it must be the product of labor; paradise as the New Jerusalem must be built, not found.[42] A land of promise provides the disposition for angelic men and women (the new Spaniards) to build the ideal city. The locus and the subject of world history is thus displaced to the New World. At one point, indeed, Motolinía hastens to recommend the autonomy of New Spain as an independent kingdom in the context of the empire: "Una tierra tan grande y tan remota no se puede bien gobernar de tan lejos, ni una cosa tan divisa de Castilla, ni tan apartada no puede perseverar sin padecer gran desolación e ir cada día de caída por no tener consigo a su rey y cabeza" [Such a large and remote land cannot be well governed from so far away, nor can a thing as different from Castile, and as distant, persevere without suffering great desolation and falling day by day owing to not having its king and leader with it] (222). Motolinía goes on to state that in the spirit of Alexander the Great, who divided his empire among his friends, the king should send one of his children. But the question of *tan divisa de Castilla* (so different from Castile) taints the *su Rey* (its king) with the possibility, and speculations at the time, of returning political power to one of Moctezuma's heirs.[43] These statements from the 1560s belong to a peak in the millenarian aspirations of the Franciscans. As the secular clergy gained ascendance and the Jesuits entered Mexico in 1572, the Mendicant orders lost power. Moreover, millenarian fantasies and undertones became subject to surveillance.[44]

For our purposes, it is interesting to note how the predominance of the millennium transfigures the elements collected in the encyclopedia into mystical data bespeaking the place where prophecy will be fulfilled. Before moving on to observe the function ethnography plays in millenarian expectations, let us briefly look at the interpretation of Cortés and Columbus, and the transposition from extrinsic explanations of the apocalyptic significance of the New World to intrinsic evidence based on the angelic nature of the Indians in Fray Gerónimo de Mendieta's *Historia eclesiástica indiana* (1596).

Cortés, in Mendieta's *Historia*, becomes a legendary figure. For Mendieta, Cortés is a Moses for the New World; God chose and guided Cortés throughout the conquest. Regardless of the atrocities, the liberation and incorporation of innumerable souls into the Church exculpates him from all evil. In general, the

Franciscans sympathized with Cortés and even cooperated in his revolt against the first *audiencia* in 1527, but Mendieta also indulges in a numerological interpretation of Cortés: wrongly, he equates the date of Cortés's birth with the occurrence of the most intense mass sacrifices in Mexico, and insofar as the conquest began the same day as Luther started to corrupt the Gospel, these calendrical correspondences are, for Mendieta, signs of the divine significance of Cortés's feat. A similar, if not more fabulous, mystical strain appears in Mendieta's explication of Columbus's discovery. Mendieta favors the version of an anonymous pilot who passed on information to Columbus; however, his interpretation takes on a fantastic tint as he pictures the pilot taken by angels: "Entendamos no haber sido negocio humano, ni caso fortuito, sino obrado por divino misterio, y que aquel piloto y marineros pudieron ser llevados y regidos por algunos ángeles para el efecto que se siguió" [We must understand that it was not a human deed, nor a fortuitous feat, but worked out by divine mystery, and that such a pilot and mariners could have been taken and directed by some angels for the effect that followed].[45]

The antirational leaning toward a supernatural explication reinforces the transcendental and magico-religious destiny Mendieta reserves for the new church in New Spain. He takes the mystical leanings of Quiñones and Motolinía to their ultimate consequences and gives an ideological coherence to earlier eschatological views of the New World. For Mendieta, Amerindians take on an angelic aura inasmuch as they are incapable of sinning, partake of a childlike innocence, and "naturally" live in apostolic poverty. In a letter from 1562, Mendieta would even consider that Amerindians belong to another species if such a belief did not go against the faith, "Si no fuera porque tenemos por fe que todos descendemos de Adam y Eva, diríamos que es otra especie por sí" [If we did not believe that all of us descended from Adam and Eve, we would say that they are another species in themselves].[46] Under these attributes, the discovery of the New World represents for Mendieta the beginning of the millennium announcing the Parousia of Christ, whose signs according to Joachim of Flora would include the participation of man in an angelic nature.[47] Thus Mendieta reinforces millennial fantasies by moving from the extrinsic interpretation of the historical importance of the Conquest of Mexico espoused by Motolinía and Quiñones to an intrinsic evaluation of the Indies and the souls of the Indians.[48] Whereas Motolinía interprets history for Charles V, Mendieta accuses the Spaniards of a satanic influence on the indigenous population and condemns the policies of Philip II for furthering hispanicization.

Mendieta casts world history with God and Satan in strife until the end of time. Such a perpetual strife implies a providential scheme and romance as the mode of emplotment in the *Historia eclesiástica*; Mendieta recasts the chivalric paradigm to convey spiritual battles. Before beginning to narrate the formation, tribulations, and seraphic quality of the new church represented by the Franciscan mission, Mendieta writes:

> Porque si para escribir historias profanas y henchir sus libros los autores se aprovechan de mil menudencias y cosas impertinentes, pintándolas con mucho colores retóricos, monstrándose cronistas puntuales . . . con mas razón podré yo escribir estas menudencias (si así se sufre llamarlas), pues escribo historia verdadera y no forjada de mi cabeza, no profana sino eclesiástica, ni de capitanes del mundo sino celestiales y divinos que subjetaron con grandísima violencia al mundo, demonio y carne, y á los príncipes de las tinieblas y potestades infernales.
> [Because if in order to write profane stories and aggrandize their books authors use thousands of trifles and impertinent things, painting them with many rhetorical colors, showing themselves as punctilious chroniclers . . . with more reason will I write trifles (if they can be called as such), because I write true history and not forged from my head; not profane but ecclesiastic, not of captains of the world but of celestial and divine captains who subjected (with great violence) world, demon, flesh and the princes of the infernal darknesses and dominions.] (208–9)

Implicit in Mendieta's justification of the rhetorical colors is the metaphor of a spiritual conquest. By transposing the vehicle of chivalry to a spiritual domain he retains the tenor of conquest: for a spiritual conquest, the Franciscan ethnographers must learn how to identify the religious practices registered within the city of conquistador. But parallel to the politico-military conquest, the spiritual conquest partakes of a momentum that destroys the sources of information. It is not only the missionaries who are responsible for the burning of books and the effacement of images, but also the Indians who destroy information out of fear of punishment. The second form of destruction poses a more interesting problem: the spiritual conquest, the process of conversion, is aimed not only at the outward display of Christian mores but also at self-discipline—at producing a subject that polices itself.

In the above example, self-discipline destroys the code that would provide the key to understanding everyday practices and linguistic expressions betraying idolatrous or superstitious beliefs. It also precludes identifying benevolent forms of life that must be retained for building the new church. As Mendieta recalls it, the ethnographic project of the 1530s was precisely a response to these concerns: "Fue encargado el padre Fr. Andrés de Olmos de la dicha órden (por ser la mejor lengua mexicana que entonces había en esta tierra, y hombre docto y discreto), que sacase en un libro las antiguedades de estos naturales indios . . . para que de ello hubiese alguna memoria, y lo malo y fuera de tino se pudiese mejor refutar, y si algo bueno se hallase, se pudiese notar" [Father Fr. Andrés de Olmos from the forementioned order (because he was the best Mexican tongue that there was in this land, and a knowledgeable and discreet man) was entrusted to make a book about the ancient beliefs of these native Indians . . . so that there would be a memory, and thus be able to refute what was evil and outlandish, and if something good was found, that it could be noted] (75).

Fray Andrés de Olmos, before coming to Mexico, had participated with Fray Juan de Zumárraga, the archbishop of New Spain, in the late 1520s in an inquest on witchcraft in the Basque countries.[49] As a demonologist (implicit in *docto y discreto*, knowledgeable and prudent) and a linguist (*la mejor lengua*, the best tongue), he carried out the first inquests and trained a series of Franciscans, among them Fray Bernardino de Sahagún. From Olmos I will draw an example of self-discipline in the framework of a semiotic "warfare." Sahagún provides, on the other hand, the most elaborate formalization of the Franciscan encyclopedia.

As a linguist, Olmos writes the first grammar of Nahuatl, which is followed by a series of dictionaries and more refined grammars. As a demonologist, he carries with him a treatise written in Spain for the Basque witch-hunt. To this compilation of ways to identify superstitions, witchery, and fortune telling as well as their remedies, Olmos adds a list of specific forms the devil assumes in the New World in his Nahuatl version of the

Tratado de hechicerías y sortilegios (1553). Take as an instance the following apparition of the devil: "Muy de noche, al encender una vela encima de la casa, allá en un sitio desierto se me apareció el Diablo; como el rey se presento engalanado, así iban engalanados los señores en los tiempos antiguos cuando iban a bailar; yo tuve gran miedo" [Very late at night, when I was lighting a candle on top of the house, there in a deserted place the Devil appeared to me; dressed up as the king he presented himself, and thus the lords used to dress up in ancient times when they would go to dance; I had great fear].[50] The *Tratado*, written in the first person and addressed to the indigenous population, intercalates this direct testimony and description of the devil by a native from the region of Cuernavaca. On the surface of the Nahuatl text we can observe an initial semiotic operation with the introduction of the Spanish word *Diablo* (devil), "opoliu in Diablo" [the devil disappeared] (353). The preference for *Diablo* suggests a need to prevent syncretism with the specific signification of the devil in Christianity. What is most important in the passage from a semiotic point of view, however, is that the devil appears in the array of the ancient lords.[51] Here, beyond the obvious religious and ideological manipulations, lies a political dimension.

Erasing the signs of the old is not simply a matter of burning and tearing down, but also entails a self-induced semiotic extirpation of signs as they are attributed to the devil; whether the story of this apparition was told by an Indian or invented by Olmos, its effect on the listener establishes a correspondence between the devil and the semiotic repertoire of old. As Baudot reminds us in his study of the passage, "La guerra del Mixtón, la rebelion de los indígenas de Nueva Galicia es de 1541, y por tanto reciente, un recuerdo cosquilloso en 1553" [The war of the Mixton, the rebellion of the Indians of Nueva Galicia, is from 1541 and thus recent, a ticklish memory in 1553].[52] A fear of rebellion and a return to paganism lurks in the background. But another Spanish word in the Nahuatl text reveals a more clearly defined political arena fully interlocked in the long-term conquest inaugurated by Cortés, "yn teupan nemia yn casado" [a married man lived in a temple] (353). The inclusion of *casado* ("married" in Spanish) suggests a particular signification nonexistent in Nahuatl as well as a "normalized" political subject;

the informant's sense of indigenous family structures underwent a reorganization and sifting until it agreed with the Spanish order.[53] Monogamy had certainly something to do with it. But when they are applied retrospectively, the criteria for determining true marriage reduce the legitimacy not only of "wives" within the native system but also, and more importantly, of heirs. It is not our purpose to examine the consequences of such a rearrangement of the family cadre, but to underline that the spiritual conquest is not merely a metaphor; it constitutes an integral element of that policy of conversation and dialogue we have traced in the Cortés–Charles V correspondence.

Fray Bernardino de Sahagún's *Historia general de las cosas de la Nueva España* represents yet another facet of the Franciscan ethnographic work. As we have already observed in the context of Cortés's discourse of conquest, the *Historia* constitutes a monumental effort to reconstruct Nahuatl culture as it existed before the arrival of the Spaniards. Sahagún, like Oviedo, follows Pliny's organization but fills in the substance with data produced by native informants.[54] Leaving aside the "harness" of Pliny's natural history and its possible distortion of what might have been an original indigenous taxonomy,[55] let us instead emphasize that Sahagún conceives the project of writing an encyclopedia of Nahuatl language and culture in terms that remind us of the regime of similitude that characterizes the sixteenth-century episteme, according to Foucault in *The Order of Things*. Instead of evaluating Sahagún's attitude, then, we ought to see how he seeks to register the pre-Hispanic world as a regime of signs. Sahagún needs, for an accurate register of Nahuatl, a vocabulary that comprises literal as well as symbolic meanings. Accordingly, the semiology and hermeneutics of the ancient order must be reconstituted with its own original logic. Such a reconstitution must comprehend the identity of signs and their possible significations in Nahuatl culture. The language of old is thus invented as a code for interpreting daily life and unmasking the continuation of pagan beliefs. Ultimately, Sahagún's encyclopedia builds an arsenal for future battles against the devil: "Facil cosa le sera para entonces despertar todas las cosas, que se dizen estar olvjdadas, cerca de la ydolatría. Y para entonces bien es, que tengamos armas guardadas, para salirle al encuentro" [And it will then be an easy matter for him to awaken all the things pertaining to idolatry that are said to be forgotten. And for that time it is good that we have weapons on hand to meet him with].[56]

What is outstanding, however, is that an investigation of Nahua culture as grounded in the logic of similitude presupposes a modern epistemology where subject and object have been fully separated as discrete realms of inquiry. Moreover, Sahagún's ethnography implies an open book independent of a specific subject. Thus, in the admonition to "Al sincero lector" in Book 11, he first provides a description of a landscape: "Tienes, amigo lector, en el presente volumen vn bosque con grã diuersidad de mõntañas, mõtes, i riscos: donde hallaras, arboles siluestres, de todo genero: i bestias fieras, i serpientes" [Friend reader, thou hast in the present volume a forest with a great diversity of mountains, woodlands, and cliffs, where thou wilt find all kinds of native trees, wild beasts, and serpents]. But Sahagún moves on to assert that he will not follow this procedure, but rather will register information according to a taxonomy: "El primer capitulo, trata de los animales: contiene siete parraphos. El segundo, trata de las aves: contiene diez parraphos. El tercero de los animales de agua: como son peces" [The first chapter deals with the animals; it contains seven paragraphs. The second deals with birds; it contains ten paragraphs. The third chapter deals with the aquatic animals, like the fish]. This method, according to Sahagún, has the advantage that it enables the inscription of new information: "Queda la puerta abierta: para añadir, lo que paresca convejr" [The door remains open to add that which may seem proper] (*Florentine Codex* 13:88).

Thus a whole series of historiographic remarks (prologues, admonitions, observations on the course of history and the political circumstance that have surrounded his project) constitute a subjective plane where Sahagún defines his task, establishes a method, and generally reflects on his status as a subject of knowledge. On the other hand, in the books of the *Historia* there is a concerted effort to inscribe indigenous culture in its own terms. The modernity, "scientificity," of Sahagún's objectification of Nahua culture has less to do with an intention to be value-free than with the task of reconstructing a native text that would enable missionaries to decipher public behavior and trace symbolic references and associations in confession. The ancillary roles of ethnography, nevertheless, do not necessarily exclude an awareness of treading on new epistemic grounds.

Even a quick glance at specific portions of the ethnographic works of such Franciscan figures as Olmos and Sahagún would require a lengthy exposition for which I do not have space here. For my present purposes, I would merely like to underscore that as a result of the conquest, the ethnographic inquests could not proceed otherwise than by a metonymic treatment of the ancient civilization. The first Franciscans encountered a fragmented world where a "decapitated" culture lingered on. They thus faced the need to reconstruct a corpus of texts for understanding and interpreting a dispersion of discrete cultural manifestations. An agent-act relationship was established between the "absent" ideology and everyday practices. Cultural instances, according to such a scheme, manifest a foregone ideological agency. The reconstruction of the old order sought both to identify Satan's "ways" and to invent a pedagogy that would perpetuate those cultural forms that the missionaries wished to conserve.

The destruction of sources of information (manuscripts) and the syncretism ever growing out of the interiorization and appropriation of European symbols required an identification of pre-Hispanic beliefs and customs to guarantee a proper conversion. But the extirpation of beliefs had to be complemented with a preservation of language and cultural patterns that would lay the foundations of a new church. Thus ethnography became a political and evangelical ancilla for the realization of millenarian dreams. While millenarianism was rooted in an exegesis of history already encoded in the Bible, its transposition to the New World produced an interpretation that displaces the agents and the locus of world history. The New World concludes and concretizes the symbolic allusions announcing the last phase of history. This dominant Franciscan theme, like Oviedo's exoticism, forms a whole out of one of the predications inaugurated by Columbus.

LAS CASAS: A SYSTEM FOR IDEAL PRIMITIVISM

Bartolomé de Las Casas is, perhaps, the most monumental figure in the history of the Americas.[57] Here we will be concerned with his systematic attempt to formulate an ethnology of the New World in the mode of an ideal primitivism, which Las Casas attributes to the Amerindians. As such, his thought carries out one more reduction of the topics first inaugurated by Columbus. Las Casas does not concern himself with an exegesis of the historical rupture as the Franciscans do, nor with a meticulous depiction of exotic items as does Oviedo, but with the paradisiacal climate of Hispaniola and the cultural and physical differences of the Amerindians. Practically speaking, his ethnology lacks a philosophy of history: Las Casas equates humankind with a sum of potentialities defined and determined by climate and body structures. Because of physical determinants, American cultures surpass other pagans as well as the ancients.

Las Casas's disregard for the historical differences that result from the Conquest of Mexico, and his preference for a purely rational explanation of Columbus's discovery, are indicative of his ahistorical bent. By ahistorical, I do not mean that Las Casas does not realize the historical uniqueness of his time, but that he does not find, and even refuses to search out, a providential design. Indeed, Las Casas underscores that the atrocities committed in the New World lack historical precedent. Ironically, in the *Brevíssima relación de la destruyción de la Indias* (1552), Las Casas lists the massacres and destruction of innumerable peoples among the marvels of the "discovery": "Todas las cosas que han acaescido en las yndias desde su marauilloso descubrimiento . . . han sido tan admirables . . . que parece auer añublado y puesto silencio . . . a quantas por hazañosa que fuessen en los siglos pasados se vieron y oyeron en el mundo. Entre estas son las matanças y estragos de gentes inocentes" [All the things that have occurred in the Indies since its marvelous discovery . . . have been so admirable . . . that they seem to have obfuscated and silenced . . . all earlier deeds, however daring, that the world saw and heard about in past centuries. Among these are the massacres and desolation of innocent peoples].[58] The paths of God are for Las Casas an obscure mystery and one upon which the human understanding should not tread. Nonetheless, human reason can define a just policy within a Christian understanding of history.

A judgment on Cortés in the *Historia de las Indias* (1527–c. 1560) summarizes his view of the conquest and colonization of the New World. After presenting the episode leading to an alliance between Cortés and the peoples from Cempoala, before the march into Tenochtitlan, Las Casas adds that "de aquí se siga debérsele nombre de puro tirano y usurpador de reinos ajenos y matador y destruidor de innumerables naciones" [consequently he deserves the name of pure tyrant and robber of alien kingdoms and murderer and destroyer of innumerable nations].[59] The long list of adjectives that opens with *puro tirano* (pure tyrant) and moves on to *matador* (murderer) ends up with the dominant topic in Las Casas: *destruidor de inumerables naciones* (destroyer of innumerable nations), which indeed recalls the title of his already cited propagandistic pamphlet, the *Brevíssima relación de la destruyción de las Indias*. The *Brevissima* is credited for inaugurating the so-called Black Legend—a corpus of motifs and attacks on Spain with innumerable echoes up to our time.[60] The Moses-like image of Cortés among the Franciscans is gone in the reduction of the conquest to sheer destruction. In the *Historia* Las Casas draws comparisons between the conquest of the Indies and events from ancient history; for instance, the condemnatory statement of Cortés quoted above comes at the end of a commentary on Plutarch's justification of Titus's conquest of Greece as a liberating act. According to Las Casas, however, Cortés's alliance with Cempoala did not bring a liberation from Tenochtitlan; rather, it was a stratagem that led to the enslavement of Cortés's collaborators. The deeds of Cortés are condemnable, not only because of Machiavellian resonances one can trace in the accusations, but also because they lack all basis for a legal justification. In the judgment of Las Casas, "Duda ninguna hay en que pecase mortalmente Cortés y los suyos y fuesen obligados a restitución de todos los daños que rescibía la parte agraviada" [There is no doubt that Cortés and his followers commited mortal sin and should be forced to give a restitution for all the damages that the aggrieved party received] (3:250).

For Las Casas *conquistar* and *descubrir* are euphemisms for destruction. In the last analysis, destruction becomes an operative concept only on the basis of an exotic (outside) New World Las Casas invents: war against the Amerindians is unjustifiable because they never showed aggression toward "Christians" (there are no historical antecedents). Moreover, Las Casas postulates their ideal primitivism in such a way that conquest implies the destruction of meek souls and gentle bodies. Finally, his demographic numbers of Amerindians living in the New World before the conquest fulfill in the *Brevíssima* a rhetorical function rather than an accurate census; the dimensions of the destruction are what matters: "Era cosa verdaderamente de admiracion ver quan poblada [estaba] de pueblos que quasi durauan tres y quatro leguas de luengo" [It was truly wonderful to see how [it was] populated by villages of almost three or four leagues in length].[61] This invention of a New World for accentuating destruction, however, opens the terrain for utopian speculations as well.

As José Antonio Maravall has pointed out, primitivism in Las Casas plays upon a utopian project where "un mundo nuevo era la plataforma idónea para una sociedad nueva" [a new world was the suitable platform for a new society].[62] Maravall, furthermore, insists on the difference between utopian projects and eschatological millenarianism in that utopian thinking does not posit its ideal society outside of history. Utopia negates a particular historical configuration; indeed, it does not posit an extrinsic design that would explain, justify, and render events intelligible within a linear perspective that prefigures an end of history.[63] The poverty and disregard for wealth of the Amerindians augments their virtuousness and lends them a stoic tint in Las Casas's representations of ideal primitives victimized by the conquistadores. The Conquest of Mexico lacks the specific providential significance of the Franciscans; it neither alters the meaning of the discovery nor modifies the nature of the New World. Las Casas thus interprets the conquest as one more example of the sordid ideology responsible for a destruction of the Indies that his writings condemn. Las Casas evidently also seeks to elaborate a just policy to prevent destruction in other regions of the New World.

The only event with providential significance, for Las Casas, is Columbus's initial opening of a navigational route. Later enterprises lack any specific historical import beyond their destructive effects. Las Casas is definitely aware of the cultural complexities that differentiate the Mexicans from the Arawaks, and the climatic variations between the Caribbean tropics and the coolness of the Mexican highlands; but in the scholastic parlance of Las Casas, these are only accidents of an essentially different New World, which he reduces to a paradisiacal climate and ideal primitivism. Within a providential scheme, Las Casas places Columbus as the instrument, or material cause, of the discovery, but insists that Columbus acquired the necessary knowledge and technology by natural means.

For Las Casas, Columbus was a great mariner, and thus he fulfilled God's designs, but because of ignorance of natural and canonical law he planted the seeds of the destruction of the Indies:

> Yo no dudo que si el Almirante creyera que había de suceder tan perniciosa jactura como sucedió, y supiera tanto de las conclusiones primeras y segundas del derecho natural y divino, como supo de cosmografía y de otras doctrinas humanas, que nunca él osara introducir ni principiar cosa que había de acarrear tan calamitosos daños, porque nadie podrá negar él ser hombre bueno y cristiano; pero los juicios de Dios son profundísimos y ninguno de los hombres los puede ni debe querer penetrar.
> [If the admiral had believed that such a pernicious fracture would happen, and had he known as much of first and second conclusions in natural and canonical right as he knew cosmography and other human doctrines, he would have never introduced nor started a thing with such calamitous consequences, because no one would deny that he was a good Christian; but the judgments of God are very deep and no human being can, nor should, try to penetrate them.] (1:208)

This passage explicitly confirms Las Casas's hesitance to speculate on divine intentionality. Likewise, intentions in human affairs are outside his speculations. For instance, Columbus surfaces as a "victim" of the discursive practices circumscribing his voyage; the need to satisfy the crown's expectations and to outflank the "common opinion" that contradicted his ideas led Columbus to pursue gold and to capture Amerindians for display in Spain. These are the seeds Las Casas bitterly deplores. As far as Cortés is concerned, he condemns him not in terms of a "hidden" intentionality, but because of his blatant foolhardiness: "Oigan vuestros oídos lo que dice vuestra boca" [May your ears listen to what your mouth says] (3:227).[64]

One can follow two main tendencies in the *Historia de las Indias*. On the one hand, Columbus's writings give Las Casas the material for speculating on ideal primitivism and the paradisiacal climate of the West Indies. On the other, a picturesque depiction of American nature where the Amerindians live unburdened by toil sets an introductory motif that rhetorically serves the function of augmenting the violent intrusion of the Europeans, as well as the sordid ideology behind Spanish domination.

These paradisiacal and primitivistic topoi in the *Historia* function as ontological categories for praising as well as arguing the
physical and cultural excellencies of the Amerindians in the
Apologética historia sumaria (c. 1559), Las Casas's major ethnological treatise.[65]

Before analyzing some passages in the *Apologética* dwelling
on primitivism, I would like to point out that in his discussion of
Columbus's journey in the *Historia*, Las Casas displays a repertory of "all" the possible ancient and mythical references to the
New World. It is a summa of brief allusions dating back to
antiquity. He discards those theories stating, for example, the
uninhabitability of the Torrid Zone, but insofar as they suggest a
possible New World, they are recorded as probable data for an
intellectual history of Columbus. What interests us about this
repertory is the tentative system Las Casas builds about an errant
New World. If Las Casas pursues a rational (natural) explanation
of the genesis of the discovery, what counts as evidence is geared
toward investing the New World with the same ideal primitivism
he derives and emphasizes in his transcription of Columbus's
Diario. Thus the anticipations of the discovery of the Indies that
Las Casas prefers are related to myths about a golden age or
paradise. For example, Las Casas compares the Amerindians to a
prelapsarian state that lasted six hours for Adam: "Parecía no
haberse perdido o haberse restituido el estado de inocencia (en
que un poquito de tiempo, que se dice no haber pasado de seis
horas, vivió nuestro padre Adán)" [It seemed that the state of
innocence had never been lost or that it had been recuperated (in
which for a very short time, which some say did not exceed six
hours, our father Adam lived)] (1:202).

Another instance, taken from classical literature, appears in a
marginal note (1:205) where Las Casas compares the Indies to
the marvelous islands in Diodorous where islanders had their
tongues split, and thus could dispute with two men simultaneously, and sang like birds. Beyond this fabulous motif, Diodorous affirms that they did not die because of illness or old
age, but committed suicide; moreover, women were held in
common and they lacked private property. These comparisons to
biblical and legendary topoi underscore spatial and temporal
differences that define the Indies as ontologically different from
Europe. By means of these analogies, Las Casas materializes, in

the New World, the locus of myths that refer to a prelapsarian state of innocence. Henri Baudet has accurately defined this transition of ideal primitivism from imaginary peoples to reality: "As we have seen, this idea had also existed in the Mediterranean era, but then it concerned dream peoples and figures. And although it is true that it also represented a reality for Europe, it was a mythical reality."[66] The substance of myth, as with Columbus, becomes, if not empirically verifiable, a rhetorical and political figure.

But the differentiating aspect of the New World as well as its topical values are not systematically drawn until the *Apologética*, where Las Casas isolates physical, cultural, and climatic specificities for constructing his ethnology. The *Apologética* is divided into three books and an epilogue. Book 1 treats of the climate of Hispaniola and gives a geographic foundation for the demonstration of the Amerindians' physical fitness in book 2, which in turn serves to argue for the cultures discussed in book 3. The epilogue dismantles the concept of barbarism.

I consider books 1 and 2 the most original in Las Casas's treatment of the New World. While book 3 contains a compilation of various ethnographies from different authors and areas of America, the interpretation and organization of the materials are determined by a chain of causality initiated in the first books: climate produces bodies, which effect culture. The descriptions of geography, physiology, and culture are affected by the initial demonstration of climatic excellencies: for instance, Las Casas depicts creeks as smiling (*riachuelos risueños*) and complements the beauty of meadows with cheerfulness. The painter's vision predominates in the following description reminiscent of Columbus's picturesque landscapes, where Las Casas again equates nature with the care and orderliness of a garden, and climate with a perpetual spring:

> Está toda pintada de yerba, la más hermosa que puede decirse, y odorífera, muy diferente de la de España. Píntala de legua a legua . . . arroyos graciosísimos que la atraviesan, cada uno de los cuales lleva por las rengleras de sus ambas a dos riberas su lista o ceja o raya de árboles siempre verdes, tan bien puestos y ordenados como si fueran puestos a mano. . . . Y como siempre esté esta Vega y toda la isla como están los campos y árboles en España por el mes de abril y mayo . . . , ¿quién no concederá ser el alegría gozo y consuelo y regocijo del que lo viere, inestimable y no comparable?

[It is all painted with grass, the most beautiful that can be spoken, and fragant, very different from the one in Spain. It is painted by charming creeks that traverse it from league to league . . . [and] each one carries on both borders of its banks a strip or eyebrow or line of trees that are always green, and so well placed and ordered as if they had been placed by hand. . . . And as this fertile lowland and the whole island always are as the fields and trees in Spain in the months of April and May . . . , who would not concede that the happiness, joy, and consolation and jubilation of one who may see it would be inestimable and beyond compare?][67]

From this genre of picturesque descriptions of the island of Hispaniola, Las Casas moves on to a series of chapters that draw causal explanations for the natural excellencies. He extends a generalization of these qualities to the whole New World and infers a universal statement about its superiority: "Y así diremos con verdad que todas esta Indias son las más templadas, las más sanas, las más fértiles, las más felices, alegres y graciosas y más conforme su habitación a nuestra naturaleza humana, de las del mundo" [And therefore we can truly say that these Indies are the most tempered, the most healthy, the most happy, cheerful, and gracious, and their habitat the most agreeable to human nature in the whole world] (1:108).

Thus Las Casas establishes an abstract of the New World in terms of temperateness and cheerfulness from which he can infer a causal relationship between climate and disposition. Physiology becomes a mirror of the soul:

Así que, pues como todos los moradores destas Indias, por la mayor parte, y especial en los niños y niñas y adolescentes, sean de buenos aspectos y acatamientos, de hermosas caras y proporcionados miembros y cuerpos, y esto desde su nacimiento, como el filósofo dijo, se muestra, siguese haberles Dios y la naturaleza dado y dotado y concedido nobles ánimas naturalmente, y así ser bien razonables y de buenos entendimientos.
[Consequently, since all the inhabitants of these Indies, for the most part, and especially the boys and girls, have a good semblance and concordance of beautiful faces and proportioned limbs and bodies, and this since birth, as the philosopher said, it demonstrates, it follows that God and nature gave and endowed and granted them by nature with noble souls, and therefore [made them] to be very reasonable and of good understanding.] (1:179)

The transition from physiology to *nobles ánimas* (noble souls) is woven out of a theory that the soul's potentialities are determined by body structures. This enthymeme (an imperfect syllogism lacking the middle term) thus allows Las Casas to integrate the metaphor "noble" into his characterization of an ideal primitivism: the Amerindians have not merely rational souls but "natural nobility" as well. This predication of "nobility" is among the earliest expressions of a noble savage theme that Hayden White has conceived "as a moment in the general history of fetishism."[68] By means of the noble savage figure, Las Casas augments the "vileness" of Spanish domination and the superfluity of Western civilization. The errancy of the motif from a temporal to a spatial embodiment returns to Europe in the oblique critical function of utopia characterized by Baudet: "It was criticism of our society and of our culture in general."[69] (We can gloss over Baudet's all-too-European "our.")

On the other hand, colonialist utopias carry an equally destructive impulse as they project a social order on an indigenous population.[70] In this regard, the noble savage figure implies the utopian experiments that Las Casas implemented in Cumana, in present-day Venezuela (1520–21), and Vera Paz, Guatemala (1537–50). We shall not dwell here on the feasibility of these social experiments and the peaceful evangelization of Las Casas.[71] Ultimately, as Phelan, following another line of analysis, has underlined, Las Casas ends up serving the interests of the crown concerned at this point with the autonomous, political aspirations of the settlers: "La Corona escuchó con complacencia las vigorosas protestas de Las Casas, para inquietud de los colonizadores" [The crown listened with complacency to Las Casas's vigorous protestations, to the uneasiness of the colonizers].[72] Las Casas serves the centralizing interests of the crown, and consequently the established hierarchy. We must recall, however, that the *Apologética*, which postdates the experiments of Cumana and Vera Paz, defines a theoretical and political transition to a later Las Casas that condemns outright the Spanish colonization of the New World and calls for a full restitution of Indian sovereignty.[73]

As I have argued elsewhere, although the primitivism of the Amerindians certainly suggests potential ideal Christian subjects, the figures of the *noble savage* and a paradisiacal *natural garden* in the *Apologética* are not defined in terms of a new Spanish order.[74] On this theoretical and political change depends whether the *noble savage* figure functions as fetishistic reification or as a textual form of utopian practice. In brief, my argument goes as follows. If "noble" encompasses Christian and civilized values, which is certainly the meaning Las Casas gives to the term when he attributes it to the Amerindians, the nobility of the savage (future new converts, non-noble) cannot be sustained in a society defining aristocracy with *viejos cristianos* (Old Christians, nonsavage) and effecting a meticulous *limpieza de sangre* (blood purity). If, as has often been said, Las Casas was a converso, a Jew who converted to Christianity, then the invention of the noble Amerindian makes of the converso a "savage" without nobility.[75]

As an "empirical primitive" that would argue for the feasibility of a social experiment, the *noble savage* of Las Casas is fetishistic. The *noble savage* figure, however, can also be read as a form of utopian discourse. The *noble savage* and the paradisiacal *natural garden* in the *Apologética* have similar critical function to the perfect islands, lunar states, or austral continents of utopian texts. As Louis Marin has argued, those fictions reveal "the very possibility of uttering such a discourse, of the status and contents of its enunciating position and the formal and material rules allowing it to produce some particular expression."[76] Accordingly, the *noble savage* and the *natural garden* figures would function as neutral terms that manifest the semantic field from which the opposition between "nature" and "culture," "civilization" and "savagery" emerged in the first place — that is, the ideological underpinnings of a binary opposition. The *noble savage*, then, would not be an opposite of barbarism, but rather would mark the passage from a concept of civilization to barbarism by including in the double negation "noncivilization" and "nonbarbarism." In fact, these figures are rhetorical and discursive fictions that dismantle the possibility itself of predicating the need of imposing a new order on the Americas. Moreover, the analysis of these figures should ultimately render the semantic field from which the "West" defines the "rest" and posits itself as a universal cultural model.

Let us now move to examine how the *noble savage* and the *natural garden* are invented in the *Apologetica* as specifically New World figures. Whether in the fetishistic or the critical mode, the logic producing the effect of an exotic New World is impeccable. The fascination over the centuries with the *noble savage* figure posited by Las Casas in a New World landscape proves the success of his use of enthymemes.

Las Casas opens his arguments by proposing similarities between Old and New World phenomena and with data from ancient histories, and proceeds to punctuate differences. In this respect the process we outlined above in Oviedo, from ready-made metaphor to the description of ineffable particularities, is parallel to the enthymemes of Las Casas. Las Casas is not an experimental "glutton" à la Oviedo; his strokes depicting American nature are impressionistic and subservient examples to a demonstration of the natural qualities of Hispaniola. Without entangling himself in the depiction of particularities, Las Casas builds and enriches his abstract propositions with sensual imagery. Although in breadth the *Apologética* is an encyclopedic text, in detail it is a philosophical anthropology.[77] His collection of ethnographies from all over the New World would ultimately document his physiological and cosmological arguments on the Amerindians' natural disposition to virtue.

Chapter 22 of book 1 serves as a transition to book 2 and exemplifies well Las Casas's style of argumentation. After concluding chapter 21 by stating that the Indies are the best lands in the world, Las Casas opens the new chapter with the following proposition: "Prueba y confirma todo lo que habemos dicho de la fertilidad de todas estas Indias, ser parte y la postrera de las verdaderas Indias, de cuya felicidad tantas maravillas escribieron los historiadores antiguos, la India digo *ultra* o *extra-Gangem*, la cual según sentencia de Solino en su *Polystor*, capítulo 65, por muchos años fue estimada ser la tercera parte de todas las tierras" [All we have said about the fertility and felicity of all these Indies proves and confirms that they form part and are the last of the true Indies, about the felicity of which many ancient historians wrote marvels, the India I say *ultra* or *extra-Gangem*, which according to a sentence by Solinus in his *Polystor*, chapter 65, was for many years considered to be the third part of all the lands] (1:109).

At once, Las Casas formulates a statement of truth and exploits the reader's delight by evoking the legendary "India *ultra Gangem*" described in ancient histories. But if the metaphoric identification of the Indies intends to stimulate a European audience avid for exotic associations, the chapter progressively moves toward accentuating the lack of correspondence between even more "delicious" imagery from the Indies and accounts recorded in ancient histories.[78] The initial "fact" soon dissolves into an object for speculation:

> Pues corriendo dos mill leguas y que sea mill y quinientas, desde donde comienza la India que dicen *extra-Gangem*, harto vecinas pueden parecer las postreras partes que se han descubierto de nuestras Indias, sin haber parecido el cabo, como podrá ver cualquiera que especulare el globo en que se figura o pinta toda la tierra. Y ésta puede ser una de las razones que se pueden traer por argumento de que aquestas Indias nuestras son cabo de la que antiguamente se llamó India.
>
> For traveling two thousand miles and let it be fifteen hundred, from where begins the India that is called *extra-Gangem*, very close might seem to be the hindermost parts of what has been discovered of our Indies, without the end in sight, as whosoever speculates on the globe where the whole earth is figured or painted. And this can be one of the reasons for arguing that our Indies are the end of what the ancients called India. (1:109)

Las Casas has moved from the initial authoritative position *prueba y confirma* (proves and confirms) to a wandering gaze over an incomplete globe. A dubious mood sets in with *esta puede ser una de las razones* (this can be one of the reasons). Other possible arguments for such a thesis follow this passage, among which the descriptions of climate, physiognomy, and culture given by Pliny, Diodorus, Herodotus, and Solinus are included as apparently supportive data. But Las Casas breaks our expectations of a demonstration with one stroke, which cancels the seemingly deductive process with an affirmation of difference: "De aquí parece que nuestras Indias alcanzan mejor aspecto de cielo, y mejor disposición de tierra y clemencia de aire y otras cosas particulares, por consiguiente son las tierras más templadas, pues las gentes dellas tienen mejor color y más llegada a la mediocridad de los extremos dos, negro y blanco, que ninguna de India, que ha sido siempre tan nombrada y celebrada" [Consequently, our Indies have better appearance of sky, and better disposition of earth and clemency of airs and other particularities, and consequently they are the most temperate lands, since their peoples have the best color and are nearer to the median between the two extremes, black and white, than any other people from the India that has always being so named and celebrated] (1:111). A simple argumentative retort (all of the above proves the association wrong) established the terrain for a contiguous reality to the Old World.

By thus negating and canceling a metaphoric mode of proceeding, Las Casas concludes the book dedicated to the geography of Hispaniola and announces the topics treated in the succeeding books under the following equation: "Y así parece que de la color destas gentes podemos la templanza deste orbe, y de la templanza misma su color y también sus costumbres y sus entendimientos, como luego veremos, arguir" [Therefore we can argue from the color of these peoples the temperance of this orb, and from the temperance itself their color, as well as their customs and understanding, as we will see later on] (1:112). Geography, in the *Apologética*, might have been at fault, but Las Casas definitely draws the specificity of *deste orbe* (this orb), and pronounces the superior physical and cultural qualities of *nuestras Indias* (our Indies).

Indeed, Las Casas is less concerned with asserting the equality of races than with constructing an image of the world divided by climatic belts and racial topologies. All persons may bring into act all their potentialities, and as humans, all possess senses, imagination, and intellect, but, for Las Casas, certain individuals and peoples have senses and imaginations better fit for developing a fine intellect. Following Aquinas, and in general an Aristotelian tradition, Las Casas states that if the soul is the same in all humans, it is not developed the same, nor does it partake of an equal potentiality, implying accidental variations rather than difference in species. Variations differ according to the bodies the soul communicates with. Insofar as the intellect depends on the senses, the "shape" of the body determines the form of the soul. Thus the first book in the *Apologética*, praising the climate of Hispaniola, prepares the ground for exalting the bodies of the Amerindians. One might say that a royal road to racism opens with this doctrine; certainly, the attributes linked to black skin by Las Casas are a case in question.[79] But blond or red hair, blue eyes, thin hair, or ugliness, among other traits, imply excess and the distortion of images informing and imprinting an originary state of the mind as a tabula rasa: the mean, what is temperate, defines the best body—that is, the Amerindians.[80]

The primacy of climate and physiognomy in the determination of habits makes history insignificant (a position hard to reconcile with the Thomist tradition from which he writes) in the configuration of cultural practices. On the one hand, ethnography itself is not only redundant, since climate already predicts what may be said of peoples, but also becomes irrelevant to conversion. As was already implied in the title of his tract on evangelical methods—*De unico vocationis modo* (c. 1536), which informed his experiment in Vera Paz—it never was a question of knowing the "Other" in order to extirpate beliefs, but of inculcating Christian habits and teaching the good lovingly.[81] Thus Las Casas's social utopia implied that "evil" would automatically disappear while the best of the old habits would remain. On the other hand, ethnographies and histories of the Amerindians are collected in the *Apologética* for a comparative anthropology and not for purposes of indoctrination. Las Casas uses them to demonstrate the uniqueness of New World cultures and argue against those who claimed that the Amerindians were incapable of governing themselves.

Book 3 espouses two universal notions about gentile nations: all men know God by natural reason but, because of a lack of revealed truth, the devil likewise induces all of them to distort the initial intuition with idolatry. To demonstrate the common situation of all pagan nations, Las Casas draws a repertoire of idolatrous social practices from the Old World and compares them to the New, to the benefit of the latter. A glance over the individual chapters in book 3 reveals a movement from these parallelisms to a praise of the Indies. The concluding remarks to book 3 summarize the point in question: "Nosotros mismos en nuestros antecesores fuimos muy peores, así en la irracionalidad y confusa policía, como en vicios y costumbres brutales por toda la redondez desta nuestra España, según queda en muchas partes arriba demonstrado" [We ourselves were in our forefathers much worse, both in the irrationality and confused polity as well as in the vices and brutal customs throughout the face of our Spain, as it stands demonstrated in many places above] (2:633). Obviously the benefits of Christianity would hardly prove, according to Las Casas, the superiority of the Spaniards as such, nor would a divine apportionment justify the iniquities of conquest. This negative judgment of Spanish ancestors would ultimately apply to the behavior of Spaniards in the New World.

Although the climatic belt encompassing the Mediterranean partakes of a mean close to that of the Indies, the cultures (Egyptian, Greek, or Roman) are inferior. Indeed, the physical minutae deployed in book 2 are all geared to glorify the bodies of the Amerindians, who according to Las Casas possess an angelic semblance: "Las gentes de las islas de los Lucayos, que el Almirante descubrió las primeras . . . eran de aspectos angélicos; las de la isla de Cuba y más los de la isla de Jamaica, lo mismo" [The people from the islands of the Lucayos, the first discovered by the admiral . . . had angelic faces; the ones from the island of Cuba and furthermore the ones from the island of Jamaica as well] (1:178). Las Casas includes New Spain, Peru, Nicaragua, and others under the same category, along with the specific accidental variations. I feel the above suffices to grasp the form of argumentation by which Las Casas differentiates the Amerindians from all other peoples in terms of the determination of climate over body and culture. Las Casas brings an errant concept (noble savagery) of the New World into the foreground in order to systematize it under the symbol of an ideal primitivism conditioned by a paradisiacal climate. Hence the New World is ultimately invested with the imagery pertaining to a best of all possible worlds.

In the *Apologética*, the figures of the *noble savage* and a paradisiacal *natural garden* are utopian fictions that reveal the semantic field upon which barbarism is predicated on the Amerindians and which thus structures the New World as a colonial discourse. In this regard, Las Casas deconstructs the grounds upon which the text-work of colonialist historiography superimposes binary oppositions to what otherwise would be ethnographic information. The barbarian, then, would be a product of writing about a culture that is initially posited as an "Other" (as a historiographic precondition) but not necessarily in terms of "civilization" versus "savagery." Quite the contrary, all suggests that "savagery" is invented as a consequence of an excess (a body of pleasure, as de Certeau puts it) that the will to truth cannot accommodate within its parameters. The concept of savagery, of course, can once constituted inform the selection, description, and evaluation of cultural practices. And yet Oviedo's thick-skulled "savages" or Sahagún's "conniving neophytes" do not preclude the will to knowledge. The exotic and the millenarian as dominant motifs do not foreclose in any way an objectification of the New World. Objectivity does not necessarily imply impartiality or a set of universally valid procedures (which are in fact a myth), but an epistemological condition in which a self-critical subject produces an object of knowledge according to consistent criteria of truth.[82]

Las Casas does not refute the "facts" about cannibalism and human sacrifice that one could find in Oviedo, the Franciscan ethnographers, and other encyclopedic texts on the New World; rather, he produces a fiction that not only provides an alternative interpretation but also dismantles the criteria upon which one could articulate a colonialist discourse.[83] As has been often pointed out, Oviedo as a naturalist or Sahagún as an ethnographer are in many ways better historians than Las Casas. The latter, however, invents a form of utopian discourse. But Las Casas remains vulnerable to a general characteristic of all utopias; to put it in Louis Marin's words, "Utopia is an ideological critique of ideology."[84] Our contemporary distrust of the *noble savage* figure is, in itself, symptomatic of its long history and the privileged role it has played as an ideologeme in the "Europe and its others" cultural complex.

I have purposely refrained, in this part of the book, from making comparisons based on influences or reactions to previous positions. Each writer and corresponding theme has been seen as a discrete entity. Together they represent dominant perspectives of the New World, where meaning, symbolism, and imagery are errant, that is, wandering without a fixed, univocal meaning. Beyond their undeniable literary value, early encyclopedic compendia of the New World reflect systematic forms of writing as well as an unstable exchange of information and a fertile terrain for fantasy. Within the initial metaphors, the early tendency to say *this is that*, lurked the strange and the marvelous that crystallized in the encyclopedias. Thus we are on our way to understanding how during the sixteenth century the arsenal (the thesaurus of memory) of European knowledge was refurbished with American motifs that have contributed to the formation of a Eurocentric worldview.

CHAPTER 5

Allegories of Atlas

PALIMPSEST, DECONSTRUCTION, AND THE
HISTORICAL EYE OF THE WORLD

Although Abraham Ortelius in his *Theatrum orbis terrarum* (1570) was the first to organize a standardized compendium of maps in a book format with a narrative supplement, it was Gerhard Mercator who first coined the term *atlas* after the mythical king of Mauretania "who was supposed to have made the first celestial sphere."[1] As Mercator points out in "Preface vpon Atlas," he intended his *Atlas* to cover five parts: "Creation," "Coelestial things," "Astronomicks," "things Elementarie," and "Geographicks."[2] Mercator died before completing his task; his heirs first published an incomplete version in 1595 with the title *Atlas sive cosmographicae meditationes de fabrica mundi et fabricati figura*. The heirs and later owners of the plates, as well as Henry Hexham, translator of the 1636 English edition, erased information, made corrections, and added visual details to maps and frontispieces while expanding the written sections. Insofar as the different contributors are not always identifiable, I am, for convenience's sake, attributing all quotations to Mercator with the exception of those where the translator, Hexham, expresses an opinion about his task.[3] Literally speaking, the *Atlas* is a palimpsest. But a figurative use of the term *palimpsest*, as defined by Gérard Genette, opens the *Atlas* to an allegorical reading: "This object duplicity, in the order of textual relations, can be figuratively represented [*see figure*] with the old image of the *palimpsest*, where one sees, on the same parchment, a text being superimposed on another, which in fact is not concealed but allowed to be seen by transparency [*par transparence*]."[4] I am following Quintilian's definition of allegories where "meaning is contrary to that suggested by the words" (8.6.54).[5] These definitions of palimpsest as duplicity and allegory in terms of irony inform the critical moves and terminology organizing this chapter.

As far as I know, there is no history of the atlas as a genre. Insofar as such a history might turn out to be important for clarifying the question of Eurocentrism, I believe that an analysis of Mercator's *Atlas* is a necessary preparatory task. I also believe that the *Atlas* manifests the main constituents that have defined Europe as a privileged source of meaning for the rest of the world. Eurocentrism, as I will try to point out with respect to the *Atlas*, is more than an ideological construct that vanishes with the brush of the pen or merely disappears when Europe loses its position of dominance. The trace of European expansionism continues to exist in the bodies and minds of the rest of the world, as well as in the fantasies of the former colonizers. The transposition of the image of the palimpsest becomes an illuminative metaphor for understanding geography as a series of erasures and overwritings that have transformed the world. The imperfect erasures are, in turn, a source of hope for the reconstitution or reinvention of the world from native and non-Eurocentric points of view.

For the purpose of this essay the palimpsest nature of the *Atlas* manifests the unlimited combination of motifs that characterizes the fourth moment in the invention of America. In composing the *Atlas*, Mercator drew from Spanish texts and encyclopedias that were circulating all over Europe in translation in such collections as Ramusio's and Hakluyt's. In the areas that correspond to Spanish America in the *Atlas*, it is obvious that Mercator depended on previous Spanish maps. It is not by chance that the profusion of details surfaces in the interior of European maps after 1569, when Spain carried out an extensive survey of its domains in the *Relaciones geográficas*.[6] The *Relaciones* were designed to obtain information by means of a series of formal questionnaires asking for not only geographic data but also historic and ethnographic information. In the words of Clinton R. Edwards, the *Relaciones* constituted an extraordinary effort to map by questionnaire, despite the shortcomings, in a "superbly bureaucratic style."[7] The number of items varied, according to the cosmographers in charge, from an initial thirty-seven questions to two hundred in its most ambitious format.

These questionnaires—dating from 1569, 1571, 1573, 1604, and 1648, just to mention the ones pertinent to the sixteenth and seventeenth centuries—traveled to the most remote regions and involved the concerted effort of the whole state machinery, from the viceroys down to minor crown officials and indigenous leaders. Necessarily, the questions were expressed in simple language with accessible instructions designed to produce relevant data about particular locations for a mapping of the whole back in Spain. *Pinturas* (town plans and maps of regions) were solicited with color details and features of the landscape. Since the informants were not told about the cartographic intent of the questionnaire, they often neglected important details; the sources voicing these concerns would ultimately betray a Eurocentric understanding of geographic space. But their accuracy need not concern us here; with respect to Mercator it is important, rather, to highlight a question of "style" and the strata of palimpsests underlying cartography. What might be erroneous from a geographic perspective constitutes a collection of invaluable sources from an ethnohistorical point of view. For our concerns, we need to define the modes of organizing and appropriating the data that differentiate the procedures in the *Relaciones* from those of Mercator.

The *Relaciones* can be seen as the epitome of Philip II's bureaucratic machinery and effort to keep control over the empire. It is not inconsequential that this cognitive preoccupation corresponded to a policy shift from conquest to pacification. The conquest was taken as an accomplished fact (which translates into a limitation of social mobility among the settlers); on the other hand, unsubdued indigenous communities were taken as pockets of rebellion to be subjected by military campaigns orchestrated by the crown (which often bordered on extermination). Along with these internal preoccupations implying both a dominion over Spaniards and an indigenous resistance, there was a growing concern for piracy. Within the established geographic boundaries, the questionnaires charted areas of inquiry for a semantic definition of the territories. These inquiries, like the earlier ethnographic inquests under Sebastián Ramírez de Fuenleal in the 1530s, produced a mass of documents that were drafted in terms of an indigenous understanding of the territories. By means of an ample distribution of a homogenous questionnaire, the *Relaciones* sought to collect raw materials for an objective picture; the official cosmographers would thus avoid the mediations and interested versions of the earlier encyclopedia ensembles. Nevertheless, the possibility of framing the questions depends on the stock of information contained in the encyclopedias, and thus the conditions of possibility of the *Relaciones* would exemplify the fourth moment of the invention of America.

Thus the *Relaciones* embody the will to know indigenous geographic, political, and genealogical texts. These indigenous representations were ultimately assimilated and translated into Western conventions in the process of producing the official chronicles and maps. There is never, however, the suggestion of a view of the indigenous communities as "blank pages." On the contrary, the inquiries presuppose indigenous texts, but they also generalize the practice of writing as a form of inscribing an order of the world on a blank page. These inevitably hybrid textualizations are, in turn, appropriated by the officials of the Consejo de Indias.[8]

Despite efforts to safeguard the secrecy of the information, the data filtered out. As knowledge derived from Spanish texts appears in Mercator, it is not so important to know his sources or even to evaluate the updatedness of the *Atlas*, but to observe how data were appropriated within a new geographic system, which is what the name Mercator boils down to in this study.

Given the rhetorical self-consciousness of Mercator, a deconstructive reading of the *Atlas* would seem to offer not only a suitable theoretical framework for an analysis of the rhetorical strategies of the text but perhaps also a means of delineating a series of blind spots from which counterdiscourses to Eurocentrism may take form.

Some practitioners of deconstruction reify the same Eurocentric canons and categories they set out to dismantle. Corrective criticism of reified approaches would be limited to questionable themes, motifs, concepts, notions, or privileged cultural ensembles. But one must not define deconstruction if one wishes to avoid reducing a salutary and rigorous critical practice into an authoritarian discipline. Nothing, however, appears farther from the practice of deconstruction than a value-free form of criticism that would exclude the need of an ethico-political position. It is evident today in the United States and Europe that many critics across the political spectrum operate under the auspices of deconstructive criticism. Political naïveté does not mean the absence of a position. Gayatri Spivak and the late Paul de Man represent two extreme cases. While Spivak's reading of Derrida's response to John Searle[9] sets a precedent for questioning authoritarian reductions, de Man is the foremost exponent of a new, deconstructivist school of criticism in his *Allegories of Reading*. The phantom of the suffix *-ism* is latent to de Man's deconstructive project, despite the brilliant intricacies so characteristic of his thought. My analysis of the *Atlas* sets off from de Man's general principles but, in the framework of Derrida/Spivak, beyond repetition I will aim to iterate the model and possibly open new areas of research disregarded by de Man.

De Man's notion of poetic writing as the "most advanced and refined mode of deconstruction" and his call for a deconstruction of literature as "the task of literary criticism in the coming years" pretty well characterize his brand of "deconstructivism." De Man privileges poetic writing, or in more general terms the *literary*, in the following terms: "A literary text simultaneously asserts and denies the authority of its own rhetorical mode." De Man's deconstructivism thus takes the semblance of an open book, a thesaurus of deconstructive commonplaces drawn from the self-reflexive passages of the great masters. But such a compilation depends on the epistemological and political naïveté of an objective reading: "The deconstruction is not something we have added to the text in the first place . . . but reading the text as we did we were only trying to come closer to being as rigorous as the author had to be in order to write the sentence in the first place."[10]

In this respect the *Atlas*, as I will attempt to show in this chapter, assumes an exemplary function as palimpsest (an iteration and deconstruction of primitive texts); moreover, its objectification of the world has validity only insofar as it is intended as and limited to subjective appropriations by a plurality of addressees. Indeed, the *Atlas* builds the semblance of an always inaccessible totality of the world, which can be visually grasped only by particular configurations of perceived fragments. At once it represents the whole and undermines the possibility of a world map. Thus the *Atlas* implies the assertion and denial of claims that define the literary according to de Man, but blindness is integral to the project and excludes anxiety over aporias or the undecidable: the world, the *Atlas*, is not designed to be interpreted for a univocal meaning, but to be subjected to active translations by the readers. The possibility of multiple rearrangements of particulars presupposes a conception of the world as a semiotic invention rather than a representation of reality that would purportedly reflect natural spatial relations.[11]

If my analysis of the *Atlas* is correct, the literary as defined by de Man loses the regional specificity of literature and criticism, and expands over a variety of cultural artifacts that may serve as instruments of colonialism. Not only does my analysis bring ethico-political implications into the realm of the literary, but it also implies that the limits a critic imposes on the deconstruction of a text are political as well. From the *Atlas*, the ahistorical critic learns that the "eye" of the poet is historical and that the poet's field of perception entails an unconscious dimension that eludes self-reference. Irony and deconstruction carry a historical precondition: they must operate within a specific cultural state where elements from a given cluster of signs are recognizable and comprehensible in discursive configurations. One cannot deconstruct or be ironic about what is not yet, nor can one assume those stances during the work process. Similarly, the areas of non-signification in a given discourse can be demarcated only in terms of a deviation from or transgression of the communicable. At the farther side of the communicable lies inaugural writing and the impossibility of knowing or intending what is in the offing.

Beyond a desire to graft onto the literary a wider variety of cultural artifacts, the above remarks introduce a historical precondition to deconstruction and irony: their condition of possibility depends on an encyclopedic stock of information on a given subject. The exclusion of genetic considerations by de Man further lends the semblance of a monumental anthologizing to his project.[12] I will return to the question of history at the end of this chapter. For now, I will move on to the analysis of the *Atlas* and prepare the ground for a discussion of the relationship between history and deconstruction.

A cursory glance at Mercator's world map (fig. 13) uncovers a plurality of semiotic systems and semantic levels interacting with each other. The map functions as a mirror of the world, not because the representation of the earth has the status of a natural sign, but because it aims to invoke a simulacrum of an always inaccessible totality by means of an arrangement of symbols.[13] Thus Mercator, after enumerating the different sections of the *Atlas*, tells us in "Preface vpon Atlas" that his work "(as in a mirror) will set before your eyes, the whole world, that in the making use of some rudiments, ye may finde out the causes of things, and so by attayning unto wisedome and prudence, by this meanes leade the Reader to higher speculation." As such the world map itself organizes different semiotic systems for creating a play of mirrors that would ultimately lead the reader to speculate on the creation of the world and the godhead; only topics from the part of the *Atlas* on "Creation" are not allegorically coded on the margins of the world map.

The elucidation of an ideological content in the allegories accompanying the *Atlas* is a facile task to perform. However, the ideological dimension that allegories introduce into the cartographical description of the earth itself remains hidden.[14] We must understand the map, and the *Atlas* in general, as simultaneously constituting a stock of information for a collective memory and instituting a signaling tool for scrambling previous territorializations. Memory and systematic forgetfulness, fantastic allegories and geometric reason coexist in the *Atlas* without an apparent disparity. I will attempt to show how an effect of objectivity neutralizes the contradictoriness of these operations, and how such an effect depends on a generalized form of blindness.

Since the totality of the world can never be apprehended as such in a cartographical objectification, maps have significance only within a subjective reconstitution of the fragments. The *Atlas* stands out as an ironic allegorization of this blind spot inherent in a cartographical enterprise. As a palimpsest, the *Atlas* conveys the irony of a bricolage where the interpreter is caught up in an open-ended process of signification and where the loose fragments derived from earlier texts allow for a plurality of combinations.[15] Memory and systematic forgetfulness suspend the elucidation of a stable structure and define the need for an active translation.

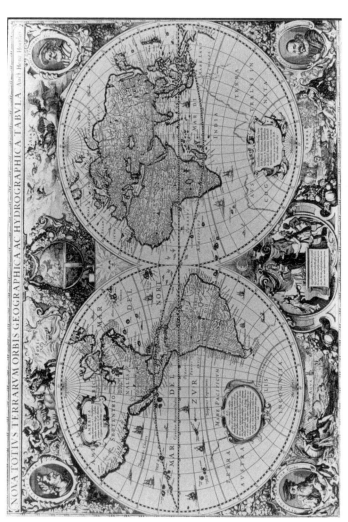

Figure 13. The ideological dimension that allegories introduce into the cartographical description of the earth itself remains hidden. *World Map. In Gerhard Mercator, Atlas; or, A Geographicke Description of the World (London, 1636). Courtesy Nico Israel/Theatrum Orbis Terrarum.*

An inside and an outside constitute two planes of content and expression for reading the map. The outside consists of an allegorical decoration that offers a narrative illumination to the portrayal of the earth. A title, portraits, proper names, allegories of the elements, a celestial sphere, instruments of measurement, a sun, a moon, and an allegory of the four continents frame the world with historic, cosmographic, and anthropological categories. These registers introduce a series of strata into an apparently homogenous and flat representation of the globe. The frame functions both as a decoration and as a content to be read in the map. Likewise, the separation of the world into two circles (the Old and the New World) tabulated by meridians, parallels, and the line of the zodiac not only structure the totality of the world for locating names and points in space but are also particular expressions of the celestial sphere represented in the frame itself. As a result, the map mirrors the course of history and the macrocosmos. Under closer inspection, we find the inside and the outside organized in terms of a binary opposition between the eternal and the contingent, between hard and soft parts.[16] Without exhausting the binary oppositions organizing the map, the following samples exemplify the hierarchical arrangements:

Hard	Soft
moderns	ancients
Europe	the rest of the world
Old World	New World
masculine	feminine
coordinates	contours
macrocosmos	microcosmos

These binary oppositions must be understood as independent realms interacting with one another and inseparable for portraying the totality of the cosmos and the whole circle of the Earth. In the following discussion we will often see soft and hard characterizations of the written and the visual, of geography and history, shift positions.

In the use of *nova* (new) in the title of the map we find a clue to the inseparability of the soft and the hard. Nova points to the commitment cartographers have toward modifications; this open-ended process of mapping that constantly requires the insertion of novelties introduces a soft dimension within the solid coordinates reflecting the unchangeable structure of the stars. A Mercator projection establishes a systematized totality that guarantees, along with a new mode of navigation through homogenous space, the accurate location of particulars within an ongoing refinement of contours as well as the transposition of data into other projections.[17] A survey of Juan de la Cosa's 1500 "World Chart" (fig. 14) reveals the radical shift of perspective a Mercator projection introduces into the European experience of the world.[18] Not only are the top and bottom in different directions (for instance, both Europe and Africa constitute a top depending on the direction one looks at the map), but the movement from east to west in de la Cosa's chart points to an unknown amorphous mass without boundaries, destined in its elucidation to topple previous geographic notions and configurations of the earth. In contrast, for Mercator, *Terra australis incognita* is an invention in need of precise contours within a stable structure of the world. It is merely a question of time (exploring and naming) before the historic and geographic nature of this region surfaces within the system organizing the totality. Although de la Cosa's map could be seen as a deconstruction of Ptolemy's *oikoumene*, de la Cosa could not be ironic about his charting of the New World. The faces of invention that we have traced in this essay mark the passage from de la Cosa's world chart to Mercator's world map. One cannot be ironic about, nor can one deconstruct, what does not exist. An ironic and deconstructive description of the totality of the world presupposes a semiotic and semantic stability, that is to say, a cultural state where elements from a cluster of signs can be recognized and comprehended in discursive configurations.

Let us now observe in the following analogy between cartography and the art of painting how the historical is indissoluble from the geographical in Mercator's *Atlas*:

> For as the Painter will not have satisfied his profession, that had represented a man according to the proportion of his limbs, but neglecting the colours and Physiognomick signes left unto us his nature and passions hidden, in like manner he will shape us a Geographick body, dead and senseless, that setting down the description of places shall forget the relation and proportion which they hold together. Therefore, I have principally endeavored to

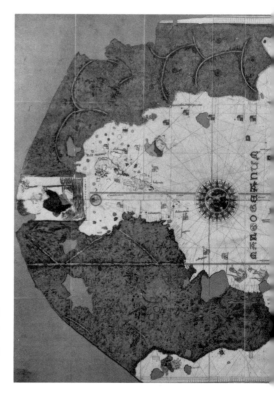

Figure 14. De la Cosa could not be ironic about his charting of the New World. *Portolan World Chart (1500), Juan de la Cosa. Courtesy Newberry Library.*

describe before every Mapp the order & nature of the most remarkeable places in every Province, the better to profit, the studious, and carefull of Politick matters and State affaires. (2:269)

For Mercator, the written defines differences in what otherwise would be a homogenous space. As a result, knowledge and power merge "to profit the studious, and carefull of Politick matters and State affaires." The written solidifies locations while supplying meaning to the visual. Writing as such is both a soft and a hard component of the *Atlas*. Inscriptions precede and determine the visibility of the contour, but they also flesh out the abstract frame. The possibility and the significance of the map thus depend on history. The inscription of the map gives place to its silhouette, but its silhouette is historical and meaningful only when it evokes a European history. In this light Mercator explains in "Preface to the Reader" the scope of the *Atlas*: "This

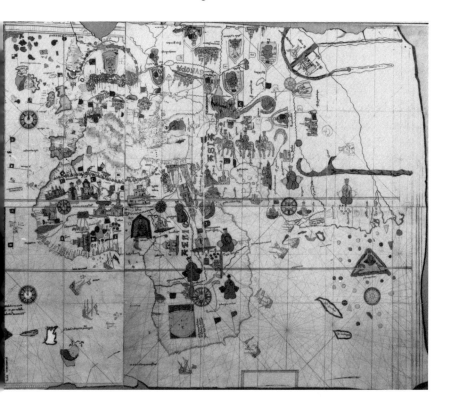

work then is composed of *Geographie*, (which is a description of the knowne Earth and parts thereof) and *Historie*, which is (*Oculus mundi*) the eye of the World." The personification of geographic space in terms of a Eurocentric perspective is inseparable from the above definition of history as a visual function: "the eye of the World." This catachresis parodies Ortelius's visual complementarity of geography: "The knowledge of *Geography* is . . . called *The eye of History*."[19] Indeed, Mercator historicizes the "eye" of the geographer; the metaphoric correlation of the two disciplines in Ortelius is replaced by an understanding of geography as description constituted by writing and history.

The visual and the written ironically jumble up time and space within this paradoxical understanding of history, and the "eye of the world" takes a plurality of meanings depending on three points of reference:

1. Travel narratives prefigure the data of the *Atlas*.
2. History introduces a soft component into the maps for a qualitative determination of space.
3. Mercator defines cosmography as the light of history.

Whatever alternative, the metaphorical nature of the maps explodes into a spatiotemporal reversibility: time becomes spatial and space becomes temporal. Cosmography is the light of history, while history illuminates the spatial representation of the Earth. But a true cosmography depends in turn on a true (Judeo-Christian) narration of the creation of the world that ultimately refers to a germinal preexistence of times to come in the godhead. A constant sliding of time and space replaces one explanatory level with another, while the spatiotemporal distinction of these realms depends on the perspective taken. But there is nothing ironic in these categorical shifts, nor in a comprehension of the process of nature in terms of an alternation between *natura naturans* and *natura naturata*, if they are not linked to a privileged Eurocentric organization of geographic space. The irony expressed in the catachresis quoted above depends on the implicit reduction of the description of space and the existence of the world to a European history. The *Atlas*, however, constitutes a mnemonic device while simultaneously instituting a systematic forgetfulness of antecedent spatial configurations.

RHETORIC AND THE UNIVERSALITY OF EUROPE

Along with an ideological stance, the *Geographie* and *Historie* of the *Atlas* convey a planetary strategy wherein knowledge and representation indissolubly institute and erase territories. If specific political configurations establish boundaries and national identities for a European geographic space,[20] then the rest of the world acquires spatial meaning only after the different regions have been inscribed by Europeans. History, "the eye of the world," on an ideological level defines the national character of territories depicted. History thus naturalizes paticular national formations and institutionalizes forgetfulness of earlier territorializations in the perception of the world. Next to this ideological, or mythological, reification of space, the *Atlas* opens the territories to a qualitative appraisal of demographic, commercial, ethnographic, religious, political, and military details for strategic arrangements. Ideology naturalizes history insofar as it places national configurations and the destiny of European domination *sub specie aeternitatis*. Accordingly, the signaling power of the *Atlas* reopens territories to domination and appropriation within a historical dimension.

Underlying these ideological and instrumental facets of the historical within the *Atlas* is the ironic reversibility of time and space that I have mentioned above. Inasmuch as the historical at once solidifies the world into a particular perspective and opens space to temporality with new global strategies, the *Atlas* institutes a teleology and temporalizes geographic configurations. I must now isolate a rhetoric of the *Atlas* in order to explicate how these contradictory movements reconcile themselves within an effect of objectivity. To the ideological and instrumental levels of spatial determination, the rhetorical introduces the addressee. To a universal fabricator corresponds a universal addressee; theoretically speaking, then, the mapmaker encompasses the totality and leaves no trace of a particular point of view in the process of objectification, if he is to appeal to a universal audience.

The geographer's "spatial omnipresence" requires the book format of the *Atlas*, where the totality represented in the world map must be broken up into particular chorographies. Not only is the shape of the totality built from a sum of partial perceptions, but the omnipresent consciousness of the geographer refers to an ideal universal subject encompassing a totality and present throughout the fragments. The illusion of a geographic subjectivity that is at once transcendental (grasps the whole) and immanent (links the fragments) depends on a consistent method and mode of representation. The effect of omnipresence lends support to this illusion of a value-free objectivity. But in fact it is not a reflection of generic *man* that we find in the *Atlas*, but of European *man*. It is specifically the Christian European *man* who can offer the mirror of the world and hold a privileged position throughout the universal semblance of the *Atlas*: "Here [in Europe] wee have the right of Lawes, the dignity of the Christian Religion, the forces of the Armes. . . . Moreover, Europe manageth all Arts and Sciences with such dexterity, that for the invention of manie things shee may be truely called a Mother. . . . She hath . . . all manner of learning, whereas

other Countries are all of them, overspread with Barbarisme"
(1:42). Let us leave aside for the moment the *Mother Europe*
attribute. This passage makes manifest how global histories and
geographies, despite their "introduction" of other regions into
the world scenario, always retain a Eurocentric perspective that
defines the position and value of the rest of world. In this respect,
the project of the *Atlas* seals an epoch that began with Columbus:
the pulsating utopian and millenarian disruptions of European
history that the discovery of the New World provoked in Spanish
historiography are long gone from the totalizing global vision of
Mercator.

The historical records of the Spanish conquest of the New
World become a substratum of information for ideological and
instrumental rearrangements of the planet. In the process, the
"experience" of the New World, or even the possibility of an
analogous disruptive phenomenon of a New World, vanishes. A
series of geographic, anthropological, and natural categories
precedes and determines the assimilation of "novelties." Regions corresponding to *terra incognita* may lack precise contours, but not a previous allegorization, as we can observe in the
frontispiece (fig. 15) where the Magalanica (after Ferdinand
Magellan, the inhabitants of *Terra australis incognita*) stand
next to other peoples. The *Atlas* thus constitutes a world where
all possible "surprises" have been precodified.[21] Along with a
projection of the monsters and marvels populating terrae incog-
nitae in the Middle Ages, categories and images generated out of
the encounter with the New World constitute a stock of motifs
and conceptual filters prefiguring any possible discovery. Ironically, a "surprise" discovery at this time would correspond to
something like finding Francis Bacon's scientific utopia some-
where in the South Pacific. As in Bacon, the future of geography,
according to Mercator, is summed up in the coordination of
knowledge and power. The task is a collective project involving
different disciplines.

To a Eurocentric measurement of all territories by a universal
consciousness corresponds an equally universal addressee composed of monarchs, nobles, merchants, soldiers, divines, naviga-
tors, physicians. "In fine, this booke is usefull for all men, of
what profession, quality, or condition so ever they bee" ("Preface to the Reader"). By the same token, the reader can learn

Figure 15. The emblem of the geographer as Atlas represents the task of cartography as moving from one stable global totality to another where details are corrected. *Frontispiece. In Gerhard Mercator*, Atlas; or, A Geographicke Description of the World *(London, 1636). Courtesy Nico Israel/Theatrum Orbis Terrarum.*

more from the *Atlas* than from traveling and, furthermore, the *Atlas* becomes a surrogate mode of traveling. According to needs and interests, the addressee can not only reshuffle the maps, but "by speculation in his closset, may travell through every Province of the world" ("Preface to the Reader").

"Closset" traveling had become a commonplace in medieval literature since Sir John Mandeville's *Travels* (1370). Mandeville set a paradigm for a series of works using itineraries for expounding geographic and cosmographic ideas.[22] Mandeville intended his *Travels* to fulfill a desire for traveling and to fill a vacuum of information about the Holy Land and the East due to a defeat of the Crusades by the Ottoman Empire.[23] It is important to notice that Mandeville's *Travels* simulates a firsthand experience in an imaginary voyage to the East by a particular subject. It is the writer himself who travels in the "closset." The reader follows a particular itinerary, often repeated by later imitators, which is, in itself, a variation of the actual journeys of Franciscan missionaries such as Giovanni da Pian del Carpini, Willem van Ruysbroek, and Odoric of Pordenone. The travel depends on a fidelity to a prototypical itinerary, ultimately referring to the structure of romance and a Christian eschatology.[24] Hence the world given by Mandeville is not intended for a subjective rearrangement by the addressee, but rather depends on the recognition and comprehension of well-known motifs and themes within the variant version Mandeville offers. Thus Mandeville's itinerary carries an eschatological organization of space with Jerusalem in the midst of the world and the terrestrial paradise at the end of the Far East.

The personal note with which Mandeville infuses both information derived from previous accounts and the eschatological orientation of the medieval world map creates an illusion of actual travel that remained unquestioned for the larger part of the fifteenth and sixteenth centuries. Next to Marco Polo, Mandeville was the major source of information about the East for Columbus. Mandeville's vividness, immediacy, and romantic emplotment of a journey to the end of the world radically differ from the distancing effect the objective illusion generates in Mercator. In this respect, Mercator's view of the *Atlas* as a vehicle of travel from the "closset" seems to parody the earlier prototype. Mercator replaces a personal experience of the world with a description that lacks any trace of subjectivity. A world encompassed by an ideal universal subject implies an equally universal addressee who can project variegated interests and organize particular configurations without jeopardizing the objectivity of the *Atlas*.

There is also a reverse mode of transforming antecedent texts. For credibility Mandeville depends on rationalizations and additional "experiential" ingredients that amplify and give further substance to passages from the texts of his predecessors.[25] Mercator, on the other hand, proceeds by abbreviation: he expurgates personal experience from the sources of information, and he omits the problems involved in the production of information. Paralleling a method of navigation from one spatial point to another that a Mercator projection makes possible, the data stocked in the *Atlas* become isolated points of reference to be interconnected by means of particular interests. This openended side of the *Atlas* does not interfere with the illusion of objectivity; rather, the systematic simulacrum of a totality intends a subjective appropriation.

A methodological arrangement of topics includes a need for abbreviation in the written section of the *Atlas*. Mercator's taxonomical headings structure and sift available information for a reductive vision of the territories. Hexham, the English translator of the *Atlas*, praises Mercator's method for its succinct clarity and pragmatic dimension:

Now to observe my Authors Methods in these, and all other Geographick descriptions, first is given you the name, then the Site, the Largeness, the Bounds, the Fertilitie, the chief Citties, Townes, Castles, Forts, Villages, Rivers, Mountaines, Woods, Forests, Cattel and strange beasts of every several Kingdome, Countrie and Region of the World, the diverse rarities and wonders in nature, more in one Countrie, then in an other, the Religion, Customes, Manners, Conditions and Qualities of the sundry nations of the Earth. Here then the great Monarches, Kings and Princes of this Universe, may representively in their Cabinets take a view of the extension, and limits of their owne Kingdomes, and Dominions: yea, and to see the Genealogie of diverse Princes, and the Politicke Government of their Estates. And if they be in hostility with their neighbour Princes may peepe upon those places, towns and Forts, which lye most advantagious & commodious to satisfie their ambition, and what memorable and warlike actions, during the Monarchies of the world have hapned. Here the Noble-man and Gentle-man by speculation in his closset, may travell through every Province of the World. ("Preface to the Reader")

Regardless of the paratactic alternation from cultural to natural phenomena, or the particular data filling in these abstract niches, we can, from a formal perspective, trace the intent to supply a "visual" supplement for an evaluation of the cartographical details. We also gain a better understanding of the "eyelike" definition of the historical: the written provides in the above list a means to "representively . . . take a view," to "peepe" into the territories and histories of others, and to travel "by speculation," that is, by looking at. The historical specificity of the different regions (for the most part erased under names and the homogeneous structure that parallels and meridians effect) lends substance to abstract symbols denoting towns, cities, forts, and so on, or to orographic and hydrographic particulars represented in the maps. Thus the *Atlas* aims to form a mnemonic device with a highly concentrated accumulation of information in a minimum of space. The taxonomical table organizes and synthesizes an infinitude of details that otherwise would spill out over the written description. In the process of abbreviation, data about the present and the past constitute a sort of genetic code for the different regions. The *Atlas* simultaneously purveys an open-ended view of the world and fashions an addressee dislocated from an everyday experience of the world. The addressee can, nevertheless, master the universe from the "closset," or the "cabinet." In fact, the universal addressee is expected to draw a plurality of equally valid hypotactic rearrangements—including fancy, of course. As such, the so-called age of reconnaissance concludes with a reification of the planet and European consciousness.

On the other hand, the need for abbreviation is a requirement for all cartographical transpositions of textual passages into spatial configurations where legends offer a minimum of information taken from the written sources. Mercator himself exemplifies this practice in his attempt to trace historical strata in the maps. We find transpositions of narrative descriptions into a cartographical representation as early as the so-called Catalan Atlas (1375), where the information derived from the narratives of Carpini, Willem van Ruysbroek, Marco Polo, and Mandeville gave place to the first known medieval attempt to describe the contours of the world.[26] Ptolemy himself proceeded in a similar vein. But while the expansion of knowledge came to contradict

Ptolemy's *oikoumene* almost simultaneously with his rediscovery, Ptolemy provided a method for representing the world according to linear perspective.[27] In Mercator's *Atlas*, knowledge of the world, new and old, conjoins Ptolemy's geometric filter for a verisimilar flat representation of the terrestrial globe that homogenizes space.

In Mercator's maps, previous names accompany contemporary usages. The different regions of the world reflect a temporal disparity according to the periods when the sources of information were produced. Generally speaking, Mercator also displays a tendency to make space historical by incorporating legends into the empty areas in the maps. This practice ensures a centrifugal movement from the name-laden Europe to the periphery, where legends and drawings characterize vast territories without history. In the periphery itself, the concentration of names serves as an index of colonialization. For instance, the map of Central Asia, *Tartaria* (fig. 16), remains the world experienced by Carpini, Willem, and Marco Polo, while the map of New Spain (fig. 17) is analogous to Europe insofar as there is a movement from the colonized areas to the regions populated by "savages." In *Tartaria*, Gog and Magog are located; legends refer to bizarre passages in the travel narratives; and miniature tableaux of life in the steppes substitute for a lack of knowledge, that is, an absence of colonialist penetrations. Brazil, the interior of Africa, and Iceland, likewise contain in the *Atlas* the medieval projections of monsters, marvels, and anomalies associated with the far corners of the Earth.

This population of certain areas with monsters does not simply correspond to a lack of knowledge. The presence of the monstrous also points to sedimented symbolic associations of topographical regions with the fantastic and the demonic. For instance, since antiquity deserts have coincided with the infernal regions of the Earth. In some passages, the *Atlas* displaces infernal symbols with a rational explanation; for instance, Mercator explains the abundance of monsters in Africa in biological terms that suggest feasts where the different species mingle: "There are also diverse sorts of Monsters, the variety & multitude of them is ascribed to the want of waters, all kinde of Beasts being there by force to meete at the next Rivers, Broches or Fountaynes for to stanch their thirst. From whence this vulgar

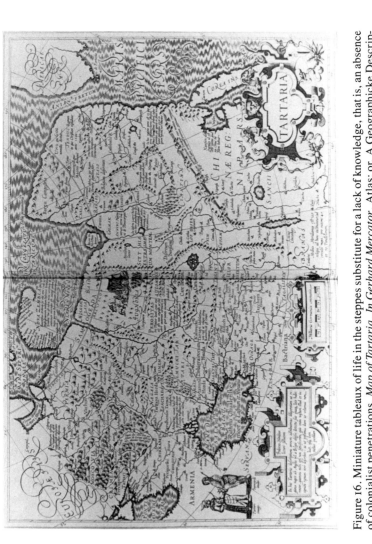

Figure 16. Miniature tableaux of life in the steppes substitute for a lack of knowledge, that is, an absence of colonialist penetrations. *Map of Tartaria.* In Gerhard Mercator, *Atlas; or, A Geographicke Description of the World* (*London, 1636*). *Courtesy Nico Israel/Theatrum Orbis Terrarum.*

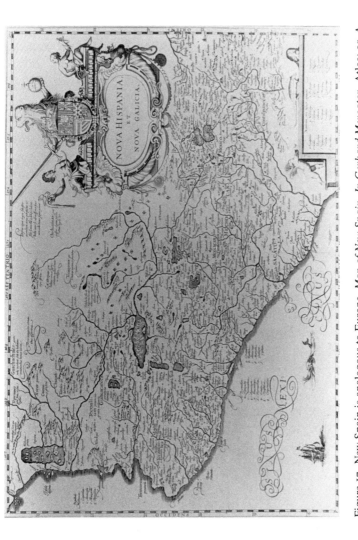

Figure 17. New Spain is analogous to Europe. *Map of New Spain.* In Gerhard Mercator, *Atlas; or, A Geographicke Description of the World* (*London, 1636*). *Courtesy Nico Israel/Theatrum Orbis Terrarum.*

proverbe came, *That Africa allwaies breedeth some new thing"* (2:425; Mercator's emphasis). Deserts remain as a favorite locus of the monstrous, but the infernal determinant gives place to hybrids that naturally result from a scarcity of water. As Georges Canguilhem has put it: "Life is poor in monsters. The fantastic is a whole world."[28] A homogeneity brought forth by the schematization of space in a Mercator projection, far from excluding the monstrous, merely fashions a different scenario for its proliferation in alien territories.

The normality and supremacy of Europe, however, are not perceptible in the bare frame of the world. We have already seen how the written—names and legends—index the higher position of Europe insofar as a hierarchy of space moves from an agglomeration of names to vaguely defined contours, and the newly discovered territories acquire semanticity in terms of their inclusion within a European perspective. Legends in the world map remind us of this: "AMERICA: Anno Domine 1492 a Christoforo Columbo nomine Regis Castillae primum detecta, et ab Americo Vesputio nomen sortita 1499" [AMERICA: first discovered by Christopher Columbus in the name of the kings of Castille in A.D. 1492, and the name was chosen from Amerigo Vespucci in 1499]. One wonders if this legend fulfills an aesthetic principle, reveals a baroque phobia for empty space, or seeks to establish an understanding of the New World in terms of the regions discovered by both Columbus and Vespucci. One thing is for certain—no region must be left uncharted. Accordingly, the unknown (*Terra australis incognita*, most of *America septentrionalis*) must be prefigured, invented for a hesitant totalization of the shape of the Earth.

The book format does not limit itself to a display of chorogaphies, but points to the limits of a flat representation of the terrestrial globe. An adequate representation of North America requires a map of the Arctic region, which in the map of America is juxtaposed with a legend referring to an even more detailed map (fig. 18), "Borealiores Americae tractus cum hac tabula comprehendi nequirent nisi forte istas regiones minoris forme ambitu concludere et describere voluissemus nos iis tabellam seorsim destinavimus supra delineatam cui et Polus Arcticus includitur" [The more northern parts of America were not able to be described with this chart unless, perhaps, we wished to enclose and describe those smaller regions with a round form. For these smaller regions we

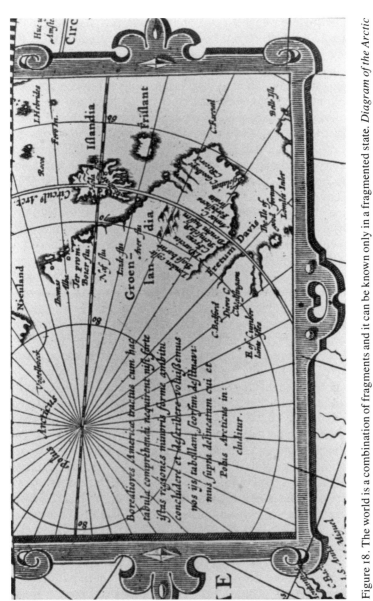

Figure 18. The world is a combination of fragments and it can be known only in a fragmented state. *Diagram of the Arctic Pole.* In *Gerhard Mercator,* Atlas; or, A Geographicke Description of the World *(London, 1636). Courtesy Nico Israel/Theatrum Orbis Terrarum.*

designed a chart drawn above on which even the Arctic Pole is included]. Here we meet again an ideal subjectivity encompassing a totality that cannot be adequately represented on a flat surface, nor could it be the object of an intuition. The world is a combination of fragments in the *Atlas* and it can be known only in a fragmented state. Therefore, the ideal subjectivity omnipresent throughout the fragments concurs with an ideal universal addressee destined to arrange the fragments of the world according to particular interests. However, these subjective idealities enhance rather than negate the objective simulacrum: the ideal fabricator guarantees the verisimilitude of the fragments and thus projects an objectivity that remains unimpaired despite, and on account of, the possible particularizations by an ideal addressee. Their common denominator is European subjectivity.

Europe appears destined to receive the gifts from the other continents in the allegory at the bottom of the world map (fig. 19). All the continents are represented by women in a hierarchical arrangement in terms of the emblems and amounts of garb worn. The representation of Europe takes supremacy, not only because of her position on the throne, but also in the allegorical investments that subdue her to the male principle. For Mercator differentiates the male and female principles as follows: "Willing then, that the inferior world, to wit, the earth, the water, & the ayre was the mother of all things, which ought to be engendered, and that the Superiour, was the Father endowed with masculine vertue, that is, willing to ordayne a feminary reason in the Elements" (1:13). Dressed and learned in the sciences, Europe rules and supersedes Asia, the origin of science, art, and religion. In contrast, Africa and America in their nudity testify to the dominance of the feminine and typify barbarous states that are, nonetheless, full of treasures for Europe. This inversion of a century of imperialistic exploits that shaped the globe emblazons an ironic finale to the invention of America. The work process of a colonialist machinery disappears under the facade of the world offering its riches to Europe. Our new European subject may likewise now "peepe" into the world from his "closset" and "contemplate" the flow of riches without entangling himself in their production. The world becomes an "out there" to be appropriated and conquered by means of particular arrangements of military, commercial, and theological strategies.

Figure 19. The work process of a colonialist machinery disappears under the facade of the world offering its riches to Europe. *Allegory of the Four Continents. In Gerhard Mercator*, Atlas; or, A Geographicke Description of the World *(London, 1636). Courtesy Nico Israel/Theatrum Orbis Terrarum.*

It is interesting to note in the frame of the world map (fig. 13) that while Ptolemy, Mercator, and Hondius carry a national identification next to their names, Caesar, a symbol of imperialism, stands open to national determination. While Ptolemy is dressed in a Renaissance fashion, Caesar's laurel crown takes a transhistorical and transnational dimension. Caesar functions as an empty slot where different leaders may inscribe themselves. The merging of geography and history, of knowledge and power, have Caesar as a prototypical incarnation of world domination: "These two [Geographie and Historie] are of such singular use, that *Julius Caesar* began with Geographick descriptions his commentaries of his warres against the *Gaules*" ("Preface to the Reader"). Like the symbol of Caesar, the world revealed by Mercator's *Atlas* is a transhistorical and transnational theater where imperialist configurations take form by means of particular national appropriations. Beyond rationalization, the *Atlas* establishes a world subject to national translations. Hexham formulates the malleability of the *Atlas* in the following terms:

> At their request I have undertaken, and by the helpe of God, according to my weake abilitie, translated their *Atlas Major* into English, for the good of my Countrie-men, and by their direction (who have most interest therein) have enlarged, & augmented it, out of many worthy Authours of my owne Nation, where it was most needful and requisite, and amended some errours in it, which were escaped in the former editions, & they for their parts have adorned it with new and exact Maps. ("Preface to the Reader")

The "Englishing" of the world rests on the translatability of Caesar and the imperialist regard. The role of the translator corresponds to the formulation of a planetary strategy from a national point of view. Under the objective simulacrum of the *Atlas* flows an ironic commentary to the papal bulls that partitioned the unknown world between Portugal and Spain. The Iberian discoveries, conquests, and tentative location of places for a determination of sovereignty slowly shaped and mapped the totality of the globe. Such a totality became a theater for contention as European nations came to disregard the pontifical division of the Earth.

Mercator's disregard for an Iberian determination of the world is representative of this new state of affairs. I have pointed out how, in the *Atlas*, an effect of objectivity introduces an open-ended definition of geographic space for appropriation by variegated interests. In this respect, the *Atlas* could be studied as a most suitable companion for the free trade policies elaborated by Holland in the course of the seventeenth century. While the *Atlas* is symptomatic of an age when objects of utility were still imbued with a symbolic and magical dimension, it is also an accomplished product of nascent capitalism insofar as the production of atlases was aimed at a universal consumer within a competitive market.

Not only are the allegories in the *Atlas* an integral part of cartography, but the *Atlas* as a whole stands as an ironic allegory of the geographer's project to encompass the totality of the world. Atlas, king of Mauretania, the legendary first constructor of a globe, becomes a symbol for a particular genre of the Renaissance "book of the world."[29] In the process, the ancient male geographer is transformed into a feminine flat representation of the world where Europe ultimately figures as the mother of "all manners of learning." As I have pointed out, in the allegory of the four continents the presence of the male principle in the female personification of the continents formulates a hierarchy in terms of their subordination to masculinity. Asia, Africa, and America in their degrees of nudity lack properness; that is, their selfhood depends solely on European imprints and a consequent mimicry of European space.

From the invention of America emerges a new Europe. The millenarian dream whereby the Franciscans transfered the geographic realization of history to the New World now, with Mercator, returns the locus of universal history to Europe; the angelic nature of the natives is replaced with a universal subjectivity that is indispensable to the knowing of truth and thus constitutes the apex of history. Europe, which in analogous allegories is invested with a sphere and a cross emblematic of Catholicism, assumes a secular version where science and knowledge define her supremacy and universality. The remaining parts of the world are posited outside of truth, since Europe holds the secret of their being. Moreover, the allegory of the four continents suggests a historical axiology of the exotic moving from savagery to barbarism. Likewise, exotic products are gratis raw materials whose secrets Europe possesses as useful for the manufacture of normal goods. As raw materials conjoin a native willingness to provide Europe (exploitation suppressed), the theme of the noble savage redefines European sovereignty as extending beyond the Holy Roman Empire. The same themes that enabled Columbus to produce the notion of a *new world* now operate within a secular totality that dismantles the authority of the pope to divide the world between Spain and Portugal.

In the analyses of Ovicdo's and Sahagún's historiographies, we have already seen how they constituted taxonomies that left their books open to additions from other writers. What is particular to Mercator's *Atlas*, however, is that it reintegrates America into a global perspective that not only privileges Europe but also institutes European subjectivity as universal. One can no longer trace the Amerindian voices recorded in Franciscan ethnographies or even in the hybrid texts of the *Relaciones*. And certainly Mercator does not deconstruct the "Europe and its others" cultural complex in the ways of Las Casas's noble savage. In these regards, the *Atlas* is not a historiographical advancement over Spanish encyclopedias. However, Mercator invents a different form of writing the world that fully seeks to engage the reader in the production of meaning. The *Atlas* as an example of the book of the world constitutes not so much an encyclopedic compendium as a system for an open-ended encyclopedia of a "new sayable world." In the light of Michel Beaujour's observations on the *genus universum* represented by the Renaissance book, we can characterize the *Atlas* as follows: "The deliberate and functional primitiveness of the new books might be called *neoteny*: they would be brought to completion *after* their publication."[30] The *Atlas*'s representation of the totality of the world remains latent insofar as it is significant only through a particular reading.

The allegories of Atlas eventually disappeared in the process of completion. The complacency of European universality solidifies as the art of cartography retains an indelible truth value up to our day, and ignores the ideology that defined the significance of mapped spaces in the first place. Isolated deposits relevant to a discourse of conquest will remain dormant (within the distant position of the *Atlas*) until the so-called second wave of imperialism, when Africa, India, and China, among other regions, will be reinvented for conquest.

If Europeans retain the universal key, nothing keeps the *Atlas* from being translated into a non-European idiom as its ultimate irony within a historical horizon. This is not the place to elaborate on the "writing back" of the colonized,[31] but my analysis depends on the possibility that the universal addressee of the *Atlas* includes readings not confined to a Eurocentric point of view. The meanings of humanity, the world, and history become undecidable beyond a European battleground. Universal history is undecidable, not on account of a theoretical deconstruction of teleology and eschatology, but because of an ever-present deconstruction of Eurocentric world views by the rest of the world. As it were, the empire has always been writing back.

The allegorization of the four continents suppresses the colonialist machinery and fabricates an omnipotent European subject who can dominate the world from the cabinet, but it also produces a blind spot that dissolves history as a privileged modality of European culture.[32]

The ironic assertion and denial of claims in the *Atlas* carry an area of blindness that could not be anticipated in the opening of the world within the context of nascent capitalism. The *Atlas* also fails to acknowledge that the self-definition of the European depends solely on the production of differences from a silent other. Despite the lucid historicizing of geography, Mercator and company reify an open vision of the world and a universal subjectivity that ignore the historicity of their ethnocentric premises. I believe that this bearing of an unconscious element in writing is ultimately more important for a deconstructive project than the elusive full presence of self-reference.

The deconstructive moves I have isolated in the rhetoric of the *Atlas* make de Man's reduction of the literary to literature and criticism untenable. De Man's postmodern definition of the literary can be expanded from a postcolonial perspective to cover a wider variety of cultural artifacts, which, as in the case of the *Atlas*, have been instrumental in the formation and perpetuation of Eurocentric totalizations.[33] Literature and criticism exemplify varieties of such totalizations whose significance depends on the European canons and categories that lend them substance. It has not been my concern here to show how detrimental these particular cultural ensembles could prove to be with respect to the European invention of its others, but to dissolve the privileged position given to them by de Man in order to trace the literary at work in the heart of Eurocentrism.

Political and historical asepsis in criticism, far from repeating the deconstructive moves in a text, appears condemned to iterate them within "eternal" notions of the subject, language, and culture. All this suggests that philological and historiographical questions should not be extraneous to deconstruction if the critic wants to avoid a delusive repetition of the same, no longer in terms of a glorification of literature, but in a broader range of cultural artifacts that under analysis might turn out to be not so glorious after all.

Epilogue

In a somewhat pardoxical statement, Father Joseph de Acosta expresses an aging of New World phenomena in the "Proemio al lector" in his *Historia natural y moral de las Indias* (1590): "Así que aunque el Mundo Nuevo ya no es nuevo, sino viejo, según hay mucho dicho y escrito de él, todavía me parece que en alguna manera se podrá tener esta Historia por nueva" [Even though the New World is not new anymore, but old, since there is much written about it, it still seems to me that this history can be taken for new].[1] As Acosta points out, novelty wears out with writing and speech, but by the same token the available thesaurus may still be subjected to a new discursive configuration in a new history: Acosta's *Historia* draws a self-conscious variant interpretation, ipso facto, a New World represented. I am interested here not in the particular interpretation of the *Historia* but in suggesting two terrains addressed by the oxymoronic expression "the New World is not new anymore, but old," which summarizes well the discursive conditions of the moments in the invention of America we have charted in this essay.

Acosta's accommodation of Amerindian peoples to a common ancestry of all humanity in Noah, by postulating a migration through the Bering Strait, best exemplifies the affinity we may find between his view of America as a continental landmass and our own geographic and anthropologic understanding of the Western hemisphere. But Acosta also faces the task of explaining how the descendants of Noah became the idolatrous barbarians of the New World. For this he provides a theory of their degeneration to a state of savagery and a posterior reinvention of culture under the tutelage of Satan. Acosta designs different programs of conversion according to an evolutionary classification of Indian societies that roughly corresponds to nineteenth-century anthropology's savagery, barbarism, and civilization.

Within a historical schema, Europe, obviously, is the most achieved form of civilization. Ancient civilizations of Mexico and Peru are inferior to antiquity because they not only lacked Christianity but "les faltó también la filosofía y doctrina natural" [also lacked natural philosophy and doctrine] (216). On the lower rungs of the ladder, Acosta locates Amerindian chiefdoms and defines nomadic "savages" as those people "que es necesario enseñallos primero a ser hombres, y después a ser cristianos" [who must be taught how to be men first, and then Christians] (320).

Acosta's model of evangelization entails a developmental understanding of society and an evolution through a series of stages. As degenerates from higher cultural forms, Amerindians would be especially susceptible to the influence of the devil. Ultimately, Amerindians were perceived as problematic neophytes that could not be trusted. In the course of the sixteenth and seventeenth centuries blood purity (*limpieza de sangre*) became a metaphysical principle for excluding Indians, Jews, Moors, and other infidels from many forms of social life, if not barred altogether from Spanish soil or colonies—their "evil" came to be conceptualized as hereditary.[2]

Acosta's evolutionary model of development is fully consequential with a Eurocentric concept of history and subjectivity that, if not repeated literally (mainly because its religious language does not fare well with modern science), in substance still informs nineteenth- and twentieth-century anthropologies and theories of development. Indeed, the "let's save brown women and little folk from abusive brown men" syndrome can still be heard among theorists of development who have only recently come to postulate patriarchy as a specifically noncapitalist social formation; now it is not missionaries who come to the rescue but multinational corporations.[3] This last example should convey how prevalent is Acosta's developmental model and how pressing is the task of reinventing America.

This study has traced a series of textual layers that coexist as they build upon each other in the likeness of a palimpsest. It has analyzed four different moments where the production of a New World assumes different forms and presupposes different semiotic preconditions. These moments demarcate different places of enunciation with respect to the stock of information and what was available to observation. Thus the differences and similarities between texts cannot simply be attributed to different attitudes, experiences, or outlooks. As I have examined the production of categories, themes, motifs, and conceptual devices in descriptions of the New World, I have critiqued the grounds that inform narratives of a progressively more accurate or authentic American text. There is certainly an accumulation of information and a formation of a conceptual apparatus that makes certain forms of knowledge and power possible — and by the same token, more like the present. Whereas traditional narratives of the historiography of America valorize and emphasize how individual figures have contributed (more or less) to our contemporary worldview, I have isolated contemporary forms of discourse in places that are not readily identifiable as "modern," "scientific," or "postmodern."

Thus, in my readings, Columbus's descriptions of nature and culture partake of "our" sensibility; Cortés elaborates an anthropological discourse where mapping and dialogue complement each other; the encyclopedic compendia elaborate taxonomies that enable future writers to actualize entries with new information; Las Casas's figures of the *noble savage* and the paradisiacal *natural garden* elaborate a critique of the ideology that underlies the opposition "savagery" versus "civilization"; Mercator's self-deconstructive moves ultimately reveal a blind spot in the midst of Eurocentrism that would enable a decolonization of subjectivity in the mode of a non-Eurocentric invention of the world; and finally, Stradanus's allegory provides a play of mirrors that betrays how the project of an archeology or, for that matter, of deconstruction, as Derrida has put it, "always falls prey to its own work."[4] As such, this essay on the invention of America provides an alternative history, a fiction that undermines the universality of European history and subjectivity — not with factual contradiction, but rather by elaborating a narrative that maps out blind spots and opens areas for counterdiscourse while decolonizing our present picture of the world.

Eurocentrism, Western metaphysics, and racism constitute overhanging determinants of contemporary thought. Their ramifications are so overwhelming that the project of defining Eurocentrism would constitute an elusive knowledge, if not a mere repetition. We may compare this study's approach to

Michel de Certeau's distinction between, on the one hand, seeing and representing Manhattan from the 110th floor of the World Trade Center and, on the other, the art of walking through the city and inventing new spaces, forms of transgressing an urbanistic order imposed upon the walk.[5] From the ground we are blind to the totality, but we may trace places for counter-discourse — as it were, invent within an invention. Inventions are at once real (racism is a clear instance) and the locus of phantasms (the perverse forms of the other). Invention also corresponds to the art of finding topics, as well as of producing new ones. In this sense inventions comprise inherited logics, statements, and terms, such as the cultural complex "Europe and its others," the logic of "historical dialectics," the terms "savage," "native," "Amerindian," "the West," and so on, which this essay has attempted to displace while heuristically using them.

This study has argued that the invention of an unknown part of the world implied its inscription within a preexistent representation of the globe. Not only did the emergence of America affect the cartographical image of the world, but it also brought forth a redefinition of previously known regions. In the process, European subjectivity surfaced as a privileged perspective and definer of the totality. The power behind this objectification of the planet and its peoples has continued to refine itself without reprieve up to our days. The errancy of New World motifs, themes, and Eurocentric conceptual devices congealed as integral elements of the objective picture of the world in sixteenth-century cartography. In the long run, the representations of "imaginary" constituents vanished from "realistic" accounts and maps, but as this study has shown, the passage that *naturalized* the West's history and picture of the world has never been complete and can always be redrawn. From this standpoint, the dismantling of how America was invented in the sixteenth century, and continues to be invented, is through and through a historical practice that seeks to open horizons for countering Eurocentrism.

By emphasizing the production of America, this investigation has charted a series of blind spots within an unavoidable Eurocentric point of departure. Needless to say, such areas of blindness imply possible marginal positionings and oppositional practices: that is, recenterings. I have chosen, however, to elaborate my analysis from within the dominant system of representation in order to affect the conditions from which a Eurocentric universality produces and reproduces its criteria of truth. On the basis of a teasing caption to Stradanus's allegory, this study opened its discussion with attention to paradox. This allowed it to begin dismantling the Eurocentric edifice without presupposing a positive ahistorical exteriority.

Perhaps the curious notion of an awakening of America can sum up the intention of this essay: America as a regime of signs and self-evident facts about its discovery must be "reawakened" with an interrogation about the geographic, cartographic, and historic constituents underlying our present picture of the world—not to demystify, but to invent the *Americas* anew.

Notes

THE CRITIQUE OF COLONIAL DISCOURSE:
AN INTRODUCTION

1. See Peter Hulme, "Subversive Archipelagos: Colonial Discourse and the Break-up of Continental Theory," *Dispositio* 14:36–38 (1989): 1–23; Svetlana Alpers, *The Art of Describing: Dutch Art in the Seventeenth Century* (Chicago, 1983); and Elizabeth Sewell, "Bacon, Vico, Coleridge, and the Poetic Method," in *Giambattista Vico: An International Symposium*, ed. Giorgio Tagliacozzo and Hayden White (Baltimore, 1969).

2. For O'Gorman's discussion of the terms *invention* and *discovery*, see *La invención de América: Investigación acerca de la estructura histórica del Nuevo Mundo y del sentido de su porvenir*, 2d ed. (Mexico City, 1977), 57–76 and passim. O'Gorman's classic study still holds that there is an authentic version of America. O'Gorman brilliantly states the problem of reconstructing the "discovery of America" by questioning in the first place whether the notion that America had been discovered is an adequate explication of the event. Leaving aside the question of whether his critiques of earlier interpretations are accurate or not, this transformation of the problem has cleared the ground for examining the reconstructions and reinterpretations of the "discovery" no longer in the light of a correct version but according to the systems of representation prevalent during specific historical moments. It has also provided the basis for considering the emergence of the New World as an invention—a historical product of the sixteenth-century imagination, which obviously also includes specific, very real forms of colonization and exploitation. Notwithstanding my affinities with O'Gorman's thesis, his is still one more invention of America that seeks to outdo other versions. There is no room in O'Gorman for alternative histories to the universality of Western culture nor, consequently, for a culturally pluralistic America.

O'Gorman associates invention with a historical destiny and ontological structure that defines the United States as the authentic America: "En la América anglosajona se cumplió la promesa que, desde el siglo XV, se alentaba el mesianismo universalista propio a la Cultura Occidental" [In Anglo-Saxon America was fulfilled the promise that, since the fifteenth century, inspired the universal messianic vocation proper to Western culture] (158; my translation). Let it stand as a description of a history, but not of a destiny. In this essay I do seek, not to substitute another more authentic evolution, but to counteract the possibility of defining a historical apex, and thus reducing the rest of the world to imperfect or inauthentic manifestations of a universal development. Indeed, in inventing America, we must avoid the transformation of criticism into persecution that haunts O'Gorman's praise of freedom *à la Americana* as the end of world history: "Que el alcance de esa meta implique un recorrido de violencia e injusticia, que durante él se corra, incluso el riesgo de un holocausto atómico, no debe impedir la clara convicción acerca de la autenticidad de aquella suprema posibilidad histórica" [That the achievement of this goal implies a path of violence and injustice, that meanwhile one runs even the risk of an atomic holocaust, should not impede the clear conviction about the authenticity of that supreme historical possibility] (159; my translation). For a discussion of the limits of the notion of invention, see José Piedra, "The Game of Arrival," *Diacritics* 19:3–4 (Spring 1989): 34–61, esp. 38–39; and Fernando Coronil, "Discovering America Again: the Politics of Selfhood in the Age of Post-Colonial Empires," *Dispositio* 14:36–38 (1989): 315–31; esp. 325–30. Cf. the use of the term "inventing America" in the cartographical sense of a plotting, drawing, mapping, and so on that results from the "discovery" in William Boelhower, "Inventing America: A Model of Cartographic Semiosis," *Word & Image* 4:2, special issue on *Maps and Mapping*, ed. Stephen Bann and John Dixon Hunt (April–June 1988): 475–509.

3. See Roberto González Echevarría, *Isla a su vuelo fugitiva* (Madrid, 1983), 13–15, and Edmundo O'Gorman, "Prologo a la primera edición," in Joseph de Acosta, *Historia natural y moral de las Indias* (1590), 2d ed. (Mexico City, 1962), xcix–ci.

4. See González Echevarria, *Isla*, 15. Cf. Enrique Anderson Imbert, *Historia de la literatura hispanoamericana*, vol. 1 (Mexico City and Buenos Aires, 1962), esp. 19–21; Alfonso Reyes, *Letras de la Nueva España*, in *Obras completas*, vol. 12 (Mexico City, 1960), 311–21; the collection of essays in *Prosa virreinal hispanoamericana*, ed. Raquel Chang-Rodríguez (Barcelona, 1978); Stephanie Merrim, "Historia y escritura en las crónicas de Indias; ensayo de método," *Explicación de textos literarios* 9:2 (1981): 193–200; Enrique Pupo-Walker, *Historia, creación y profecía en los textos del Inca Garcilaso de la Vega* (Madrid, 1982); and idem, *La vocación literaria del pensamiento histórico en América: Desarrollo de la prosa de ficción, siglos XVI, XVII, XVIII, XIX* (Madrid, 1982). For a critique of the criteria that have constructed "Spanish-American colonial literature," see Walter D. Mignolo, "La lengua, la letra, el territorio (o la crisis de los estudios literarios coloniales)," *Dispositio* 11:28–29 (1986): 137–60.

5. For a Foucauldian analysis of Spanish-American historiography and the different historical genres of the so-called chronicles of the Indies, see the indispensable studies of Walter D. Mignolo, "Cartas, crónicas y relaciones del descubrimiento y la conquista," in *Historia de la literatura hispanoamericana, época colonial*, 2 vols., comp. Luis Iñigo Madrigal (Madrid, 1982), 1:57–116, and idem, "El metatexto historiográfico y la historiografía indiana," *MLN* 96 (Spring 1981): 358–402. Also of interest, though not necessarily from a Foucauldian perspective, are Rolena Adorno, "Literary Production and Suppression," and the essays concerned with examining questions of power and representation in *1492–1992: Re/Discovering Colonial Writing*, ed. René Jara and Nicholas Spadaccini, Hispanic Issues 4 (Minneapolis, 1989). For Fou-

cault's understanding of discourse, see *The Archaeology of Knowledge*, trans. A. M. Sheridan Smith, and the included lecture "The Discourse on Language," trans. Rubert Sawyer (New York, 1972), and idem, *Discipline and Punish*, trans. Alan Sheridan (New York, 1979). Also invaluable for this study is the distinction between the sixteenth-century episteme and that of the Classical Age in idem, *The Order of Things: An Archaeology of the Human Sciences* (New York, 1973). I have found particularly helpful for understanding Foucault's overall project the study by Hubert L. Dreyfus and Paul Rabinow, *Michel Foucault: Beyond Structuralism and Hermeneutics* (Chicago, 1982).

6. See Hayden White, "The Value of Narrativity in the Representation of Reality," in *The Content of Form: Narrative Discourse and Historical Representation* (Baltimore, 1987), 1–25. Also of interest are idem, *Metahistory: The Historical Imagination in Nineteenth-Century Europe* (Baltimore, 1973), and idem, *Tropics of Discourse* (Baltimore, 1978). For an appraisal of White's contribution to twentieth-century historiography, see Paul Ricoeur, *Temps et récit*, 3 vols. (Paris, 1983), 1:228–39.

7. Hayden White, "The Question of Narrative in Contemporary Historical Theory," in *The Content of Form*, 45.

8. Cf. González Echevarria, *Isla*, 19–20, and Beatriz Pastor, "Silence and Writing: The History of the Conquest," in *1492–1992: Re/Discovering Colonial Writing*, ed. Jara and Spadaccini, 122–23.

9. On this debate see the numerous exchanges in the Mexican press in the last few years between Edmundo O'Gorman and Miguel León-Portilla.

10. See Pierre Chaunu, *L'expansion européenne du XIIIe au XVe siècle* (Paris, 1969).

11. Michel de Certeau, "The Politics of Silence: The Long March of the Indians," in *Heterologies: Discourse on the Other*, trans. Brian Massumi, Theory and History of Literature 17 (Minneapolis, 1986), 226–27.

12. Michel de Certeau, *The Writing of History*, trans. Tom Conley (New York, 1988), xxvii.

13. Friedrich Nietzche, *The Use and Abuse of History*, trans. Adrian Collins (Indianapolis, 1957), 37.

14. The contemporary literature on rhetoric is immense. For a systematic exposition and review of contemporary rhetoric, see Paolo Valesio, *Novantiqua: Rhetorics as a Contemporary Theory* (Bloomington, 1980). For a continuous view of the *ancient rhetoric*, see Roland Barthes, "L'ancienne rhétorique: Aide-mémoire," *Communications* 16 (1970): 172–245. On the "effect of the real," see Barthes, "The Discourse of History," trans. Peter Wexler, in *Structuralism: A Reader*, ed. Michael Lanek (London, 1970), 145–55; idem, "L'effet du réel," *Communications* 11 (1968), 84–89.

15. See Angel Rama, *Transculturación narrativa en America Latina* (Mexico City, 1982), and Edward Said, "Traveling Theory," in *The World, the Text, and the Critic* (Cambridge, Mass., 1983), 226–47. Also of interest is the chapter "Replacing Theory" in Bill Ashcroft, Gareth Griffiths, and Helen Tiffin, *The Empire Writes Back: Theory and Practice in Post-Colonial Literatures* (London and New York, 1989), 155–94.

16. See Edward Said, *Orientalism* (New York, 1979), 3; Peter Hulme, *Colonial Encounters: Europe and the Native Caribbean, 1492–1797* (London

and New York, 1986), 2; idem, "Subversive Archipelagos," 1–8, and passim; and the essays from the 1984 conference "Europe and Its Others," in Francis Barker et al., eds., *Europe and Its Others*, 2 vols. (Colchester, 1984). Also of interest are the proposal for the formation of a Group for the Critical Study of Colonial Discourse in *Inscriptions* 1 (1985), and the special issue on *Feminism and the Critique of Colonial Discourse*, ed. Deborah Gordon, *Inscriptions* 3–4 (1988). For colonial Mexico, see J. Jorge Klor de Alva, "Language, Politics, and Translation: Colonial Discourse and Classic Nahuatl in New Spain," in *The Art of Translation: Voices from the Field*, ed. Rosanna Warren (Boston, 1989), and idem, "Contar vidas: la autobiografía y la reconstrucción del ser nahua," *Arbor* 515–16 (1988): 49–78. For a substitution of the term "colonial discourse" with "colonial semiosis," see Walter D. Mignolo, "Colonial Situations, Geographic Discourses, and Territorial Representations: Toward a Diatopical Understanding of Colonial Semiosis," *Dispositio* 14:36–38 (1989): 93–140. As Mignolo correctly remarks, the term *discourse* is bound to "alphabet-oriented notions of text." The term *semiosis*, as I see it, complements by attending to differences in semiotic systems, but does not necessarily entail the understanding of discourse and power that we have learned to analyze with Foucault. Colonial semiosis, as Mignolo points out, may define a field of study that could complement other existing ones such as "colonial history" ("Afterword," *Dispositio* 14:36–38 [1989]: 333–37, esp. 334–35). I wonder, however, if "colonial discourse" is not an object of study that is produced in the intersection of different disciplines and fields, rather than a specific type of object that would define a field, such as art, economics, history, and semiosis in the colonial period.

17. Said, *Orientalism*, 23–24. For a critique of Said's reading of Foucault, see James Clifford, review of *Orientalism* by Edward Said, *History and Theory* 19:2 (1980): 204–23. For a response to Clifford (without direct mention) and other critics, see Edward Said, "Orientalism Reconsidered," in Barker et al., eds., *Europe and Its Others*, 1:14–27.

18. For Said's critique of Foucault's theoretical overtotalization in the context of his discussion of theory and travel, see "Traveling Theory," 246–47.

19. Said, *Orientalism*, 25.

20. See Gayatri Chakravorty Spivak, "The New Historicism: Political Commitment and the Postmodern Critic," in *The New Historicism*, ed. H. Aram Veeser (New York and London, 1989), 291.

21. Foucault quoted in Spivak, "Can the Subaltern Speak?" in *Marxism and the Interpretation of Cultures*, ed. Cary Nelson and Lawrence Grossberg, (Urbana, Ill., 1987), 271–313, 274.

22. See Homi Bhabha, "Signs Taken for Wonder: Questions of Ambivalence and Authority Under a Tree Outside Delhi, May 1817," in *"Race," Writing, and Difference*, ed. Henry Louis Gates, Jr. (Chicago, 1986), 163–84.

23. See Rolena Adorno, *Guamán Poma: Writing and Resistance in Colonial Peru* (Austin, Tex., 1986), 111, 79; also consult Adorno's analysis of Guamán's invention of a pictorial code to represent Spanish culture in "On Pictorial Language and the Typology of Culture in a New World Chronicle," *Semiotica* 36:1–2 (1981): 51–106. On Guamán Poma, see also Roger Zapata, *Guamán Poma, indigenismo y estética de la dependencia en la cultura peruana* (Minneapolis, 1989).

24. Frank Salomon, "Chronicles of the Impossible: Note on Three Peruvian Indigenous Historians," in *From Oral to Written Expression: Native Andean Chroniclers of the Early Colonial Period*, ed. Rolena Adorno (Syracuse, N.Y., 1982), 9–39. On Indian and mestizo historians from the colonial period also consult Raquel Chang-Rodríguez, *La apropiación del signo: Tres cronistas indígenas del Perú* (Tempe, Ariz., 1988).

25. See Rolena Adorno, "Literary Production and Suppression: Reading and Writing about Amerindians in Colonial Spanish America," *Dispositio* 11:28–29 (1986): 1–25.

26. Spivak, "Can the Subaltern Speak?" 291–94.

27. Bhabha, "Signs Taken for Wonder," 172.

28. See Serge Gruzinski, *Man-Gods in the Mexican Highlands* (Stanford, Calif., 1987), 17.

29. Spivak, "The New Historicism," 290.

30. Cf. the use of *métissage*, or *mestizaje*, to formulate a cultural politics in Françoise Lionnet, *Autobiographical Voices: Race, Gender, Self-Portraiture* (Ithaca, N.Y., 1989), esp. 3–18.

31. See Mignolo, "Colonial Situations."

32. Jean Franco, *Plotting Women: Gender and Representation in Mexico* (New York, 1989).

33. Bryan S. Turner, *Marx and the End of Orientalism* (London, 1978), 9.

34. For a tentative universal alternative to Eurocentric development theories, see Samir Amin, *Eurocentrism* (New York, 1989), esp. 136–52. Also see Val Moghadam, "Against Eurocentrism and Nativism: A Review Essay on Samir Amin's *Eurocentrism* and Other Texts," *Socialism and Democracy* 9 (Fall/Winter 1989): 81–104.

35. For an extended discussion of territorial claims and the field of the discipline, see Mignolo, "La lengua, la letra, el territorio."

36. See, for instance, Ashcroft, Griffiths, and Tiffin, *The Empire Writes Back*; Gayatri Chakravorti Spivak, *The Post-Colonial Critic* (New York, 1990); Abdul R. JanMohammed and David Lloyd, eds., *The Nature and Context of Minority Discourse* (New York, 1990).

37. See Talal Asad, "The Concept of Cultural Translation in British Social Anthropology," in *Writing Culture: The Poetics and Politics of Ethnography*, ed. James Clifford and George E. Marcus (Berkeley and Los Angeles, 1986), 141–64, esp. 160–63.

CHAPTER 1. THE NAKEDNESS OF AMERICA?

1. Clifford Geertz, *The Interpretation of Cultures* (New York, 1973), 16. In the course of publishing this book an article came to my attention that seems to have benefited from my argument by which I am mildly pleased.

2. As far as I know the drawing has appeared only once before, and then without significant commentary, in Robert F. Berkhofer, *The White Man's Indian* (New York, 1978).

3. Wilma George, *Maps and Animals* (Berkeley and Los Angeles, 1969), 62.

4. Ibid., 83–84, 206.

5. Michel de Certeau, "History: Ethics, Science, and Fiction," in *Social Science as Moral Inquiry*, ed. Norman Hahn (New York, 1983), 133.

6. See Bern Dibner, "The 'New Discoveries' of Stradanus," in Jan van der Straet, *Nova reperta* (Norwalk, Conn., 1953).

7. Walter Ong, *Ramus, Method, and the Decay of Dialogue* (Cambridge, 1958), and Johannes Fabian, *Time and the Other: How Anthropology Makes Its Object* (New York, 1983), 109–23. For a study of images and propaganda during the baroque, see José Antonio Maravall, "Objectivos sociopolíticos del empleo de medios visuales," an appendix to his *La cultura del Barroco*, 3d ed. (Barcelona, 1983).

8. Antonello Gerbi, *Nature in the New World: From Christopher Columbus to Gonzalo Fernández de Oviedo*, trans. Jeremy Moyle (Pittsburgh, 1985), 43, n. 55. After quoting Dante, Vespucci adds: "It seems to me that the poet in these verses wishes to describe by the 'four stars' the pole of the other firmament, and I have no reason to doubt that what he says may be true" ("Letter to Lorenzo di Pier Francesco di Medici" [1500], in Frederick J. Pohl, *Amerigo Vespucci: Pilot Major* [New York, 1966], 79).

9. Jacques le Goff, *La naissance du purgatoire* (Paris, 1981), 13–14. Cf. Henri Baudet, *Paradise on Earth: Some Thoughts on European Images of Non-European Man*, trans. Elisabeth Wentholt (New Haven, Conn., 1965), 11–12.

10. "By that I mean *a persistent and systematic tendency to place the referent(s) of anthropology in a time other than the present of the producer of anthropological discourse*" (Fabian, *Time and the Other*, 31, Fabian's italics).

11. Peter Hulme, "Polytropic Man: Tropes of Sexuality and Mobility in Early Colonial Discourse," in *Europe and Its Others*, 2:17 (Hulme's italics); Stradanus's allegory also functions as an emblem in his *Colonial Encounters* (see Introduction, n. 16).

12. Rosalie L. Colie, *Paradoxia Epidemica: The Renaissance Tradition of Paradox* (Princeton, N.J., 1966), 38.

13. Charles S. Peirce, *The Philosophy of Peirce: Selected Writings*, ed. Justus Buchler (London, 1956), 115.

14. See the section on linear perpective in *The Notebooks of Leonardo da Vinci* 2 vols., ed. Jean Paul Richter (New York, 1970), 2:27–65.

15. See Pierre Francastel, *La figure et le lieu: L'ordre visuel du quattrocento* (Paris, 1967), 318–24, for a discussion of errant images with respect to realism, marvelous locations, and allegories in Leonardo's notebooks.

16. Foucault, *The Order of Things* (see Introduction, n. 5), 65; Foucault's emphasis.

17. Ibid., 51.

18. See Chester M. Cate, "De Bry and the *Index exporgatorius*," *Bibliographical Society of American Papers* X (1916): 136–40.

19. See Bernadette Bucher, *Icon and Conquest: A Structural Analysis of the Illustration of de Bry's Great Voyages*, trans. Basia Miller Gulati (Chicago, 1981), for a detailed analysis of de Bry's ideological manipulation of the Spanish relations and borrowed iconographical materials. For a study of Léry's *Histoire* in the context of what Bataillon called the "Huguenot corpus on America" and the reaccommodation of the *Histoire* in the Enlightenment, see Frank Lest-

ringant, "The Philosophers Breviary: Jean de Léry in the Enlightenment," *Representations* 33 (1991): 200–209.

20. Urs Bitterli, *Los "salvajes" y los "civilizados": El encuentro de Europa y Ultramar*, trans. Pablo Zorozábal (Mexico City, 1982), 79; idem, *Die "Wilden" und die "Zivilisierten": Grundzü einer Geistes- und Kulturgeschichte der europäisch-überseeischen Begegnung* (Munich, 1976), 72. Hereafter page numbers of the German edition follow those of the Spanish version.

21. Ibid., 83/75.

22. Ibid., 25/27.

23. Ibid., 89/80.

24. Ibid., 536/439.

25. Said, *Orientalism*, 3.

26. Bitterli, *Los "salvajes,"* 536/*Die "Wilden,"* 439.

27. James A. Boon, "Comparative De-enlightenment: Paradox and Limits in the History of Ethnology," *Daedalus* 109 (1980): 73–91; James Clifford, "On Ethnographic Authority," *Representations* I (1983): 118–46; Fabian, *Time and the Other*.

28. Daniel Defert, "The Collection of the World: Accounts of Voyages from the Sixteenth to Eighteenth Centuries," *Dialectical Anthropology* 7:1 (1982): 19.

29. White, "The Noble Savage Theme as Fetish," in *Tropics* (see Introduction, n. 6).

30. On O'Gorman's refutation of a discovery by Columbus on the basis that "discovery" always presupposes an intention, see the polemic between Marcel Bataillon and Edmundo O'Gorman, *Dos concepciones de la tarea histórica con motivo de la idea del descubrimiento de América* (Mexico City, 1955). With respect to a discovery by Vespucci the sources are overwhelmingly numerous. Among the most forceful arguments, see Roberto Leviller, *América la bien llamada* (Buenos Aires, 1948), and Fredrik Pohl, *Amerigo Vespucci, Pilot Major* (New York, 1966). Also of interest are the distinct readings of the "real" Vespucci and the pseudo Vespucci in Antonello Gerbi, *Nature in the New World*, 35–49. Cf. the questioning of a timeless meaning of discovery in W. E. Washburn, "The Meaning of Discovery in the Fifteenth and Sixteenth Centuries," *American Historical Review* 68:1 (1962): 1–21.

31. Jean Amsler, *La renaissance*, in L. M. Parias, *Histoire universelle des explorations*, 3 vols. (Paris, 1955), 2:89.

32. Hugh Honour, *The New Golden Land: European Images of America from the Discovery to the Present Time* (New York, 1975), 41.

33. Ibid., 89.

34. Amsler, *La renaissance*, 88.

35. Michel de Certeau, *L'écriture de l'histoire* (Paris, 1975), title page. This indication is left out in the English version, *The Writing of History*, trans. Tom Conley (New York, 1988). Hereafter all quotations are from Conley's English version, with French terms included within brackets when necessary; page numbers of the French edition follow those of the English version.

36. Ibid., xxv/3.

37. W. G. L. Randles, *De la terre plate au globe terrestre* (Paris, 1980), 71–72.

38. De Certeau, *Writing*, xxv/*L'écriture*, 3.
39. Michel de Certeau, "The Scriptural Economy," chapter 10 of his *The Practices of Everyday Life*, trans. Steven F. Rendall (Berkeley and Los Angeles, 1984), 131–53.
40. For a differentiation between Spanish and English views of the New World as a *tabula rasa*, see Stephen J. Greenblatt, "Learning to Curse: Aspects of Linguistic Colonialism in the Sixteenth Century," in *First Images of America*, 2 vols., ed. Fredi Chiappelli (Berkeley and Los Angeles, 1976), 2:562.
41. Take for instance Michael T. Ryan's appeal to de Certeau: "Although it is overstated and filled with its share of Parisian mumbo, Michel de Certeau's essay, 'Ethnographie. L'oralité, ou l'espace de l'autre: Léry' in his *L'écriture de l'histoire* is worth consulting as an approach to travel literature in general" ("Assimilating New Worlds in the Sixteenth and Seventeenth Centuries," *Society for Comparative Studies in Society and History* 23:4 [1980]: 519–38, 522). If one takes away the "overstated" importance of Léry in the history of ethnography and the "Parisian mumbo," one easily winds up with a domesticated de Certeau for confirming Ryan's thesis of an assimilation of "new worlds." Ryan assumes the "new worlds" and "exoticism" were natural entities ready for observation, and never wonders in his essay how *newness* itself was produced before it could be assimilated, if that was ever the case. See also the adoption of the "blank page" metaphor in Louis Montrose, "The Work of Gender in the Discourse of Discovery," *Representations* 33 (1991): 1–41. On the other hand, without mentioning de Certeau, Hulme gives, in *Colonial Encounters*, a more sophisticated reading of the topos of the "virgin" land. Hulme sees in "the gesture of 'discovery' a ruse of concealment," where, in what he calls the "Classic colonial triangle," the connection between "native" and "land" is dissimulated in Stradanus's allegorical "America" (1). Hulme traces in the ruses of the colonial triangle an anxiety that presupposes an awareness, if not an acknowledgement, of a native text, rather than an unmediated reduction of the land to a "blank page."
42. De Certeau, *Writing*, xxv/*L'écriture*, 3.
43. For a sustained argument against an interpretation of his work as structuralist, see Foucault's introduction to *The Archaeology of Knowledge* (see Introduction, n. 5), 3–17. Also consult Dreyfus and Rabinow, *Beyond Structuralism* (see Introduction, n. 5), 79–103.
44. De Certeau, *Writing*, 210/*L'écriture*, 216.
45. De Certeau, *Writing*, 211–12.
46. Claude Lévi-Strauss, *Tristes tropiques*, trans. John Weightman and Doreen Weightman (New York, 1977), 79, 76.
47. De Certeau, *Writing*, 212.
48. Ibid.
49. Quoted in ibid., 215.
50. Ibid., 232.
51. Ibid., 234.
52. De Certeau appeals to Francastel, *La figure et le lieu*. The following statement by Francastel on Leonardo and the quattrocento, however, seems to contradict de Certeau's observation on Botticelli: "The transformation of the

real universe waits for science; indeed, painting is, for him, the perfect instrument of the mind for those who want to exteriorize the secrets of thought; therefore, we do not find in Leonardo an awareness of the dialectic of the real and the imaginary, nor of a sensualist empirism" (338). This objectification of thought, however, also entails the possibility of objectifying the world; it seems to me that Francastel is questioning the existence of a specific type of empiricism that confines objectivity to one particular set of rules that were slowly defined and became dominant in the modern West. By opening the possibility of reading different modes of objectification in sixteenth-century historiography we may avoid imposing a grid that keeps us from understanding how the world was written in the early modern period in ways that are still influential today. In passing I would like to point out the affinities between Francastel's study of the transition from the invention of elements in the early quattrocento to the formation of a new system in Leonardo with my approach to the invention of America. De Certeau himself takes Francastel in this direction in *La fable mystique XVI–XVII siècle* (Paris, 1982), 34.

53. De Certeau, *Writing*, 211.

54. Ibid., 218.

55. Ibid., 228/*L'écriture*, 238.

56. Cf. Christian Marouby, *Utopie et primitivisme: Essai sur l'imaginaire anthropologique à l'âge classique* (Paris, 1990); Margaret Hodgen, *Early Anthropology in the Sixteenth and Seventeenth Centuries* (Philadelphia, 1964).

57. De Certeau, *Writing*, 225–26.

58. Karl-Otto Apel, "Intentions, Conventions, and Reference to Things: Dimension of Understanding Meaning in Hermeneutics and in Analytic Philosophy of Language," in *Meaning and Understanding*, ed. Herman Parret and Jacques Bouveresse (Berlin and New York, 1981), 109.

CHAPTER 2. COLUMBUS AND THE NEW SCRIPTURAL ECONOMY OF THE RENAISSANCE

1. Jacques Heers, *Christophe Colomb* (Paris, 1981), 7; all English versions from this source are my translations.

2. See Heers's discussion of the first letter with respect to its different versions, addressees, and translations (332–37). There is the possibility that Columbus intended his letters not solely for a particular addressee but for a general audience. Noteworthy is Heers's comment on the literary status the letter assumes with the versification and enrichment by Giuliano Dati as early as June 1493: "This is also the proof that Columbus's *Relation* or *Letter* received in a way a consecration, it acquired the dignity of a literary genre, that of an epic narrative, worthy of being placed next to all the others" (336). Dati's versification implies not only the transformation of the letter into an epic narrative but also its reception as a "literary" document. As Hayden White remarked in "The Question of Narrative in Contemporary Historical Theory," the notions of the poetic and the prosaic are more complex than the traditional differentiation on the basis of message and form: "The form of the poetic text produces a 'meaning' quite other than whatever might be represented in any prose paraphrase of its literal verbal content. But the same can be said of the various

genres of *Kunstprosa* (oratorical declamation, legal brief, prose romance, novel, and so on), of which the historical narrative is undeniably a species; only here the patterning in question is not that of sound and meter so much as that of the rhythms and repetitions of motific structures which aggregate into themes, and of themes which aggregate into plot-structures" (*History and Theory* 23 [1984]: 1–33, 20). While Dati's versification transforms Columbus into a legendary figure, White's clarification opens a vista for reading Columbus's writings as literary artifacts. Reading his writings as literary and rhetorical artifacts, of course, does not mean canonizing Columbus as a literary figure. See the important dismantling of "romantic," noncritical "literary" readings of Columbus, and of Spanish-American historiography in general, in Mignolo, "Cartas, crónicas y relaciones" (see Introduction, n. 5).

3. Heers, *Christophe Colomb*, 8.

4. Ibid.

5. Roland Barthes, "Myth Today," in *Mythologies*, trans. Annette Lavers (New York, 1982), 113 and passim.

6. This assumption of the New World as a given "natural entity" is obviously not exclusive to Heers but prevails in New World historiography. Heers's understanding of a "rejection" is consistent with his explanation of the genesis of the "discovery" with Columbus's intent to travel to China and Japan. Heers forms part of a group of scholars who assert that Columbus "discovers" America in spite of believing he had reached Asia; among the most notable are Samuel Elliot Morison, *Admiral of the Ocean Sea: A Life of Christopher Columbus* (Boston, 1942), and Paolo Emilio Taviani, *Christopher Columbus: The Grand Design* (London, 1985). For other scholars who have advanced various theses that presume that Columbus sailed to the New World with information about it derived from previous European travelers from the so-called anonymous pilot, or from a mid-Atlantic encounter between a European ship and a canoe with several Amerindian women, see Henry Vignaud, *Histoire critique de la grande entreprise de Christophe Colomb*, 2 vols. (Paris, 1911); Demetrio Ramos, *Los contactos transatlánticos decisivos, como precedentes del viaje de Colón* (Valladolid, 1972); Juan Manzano y Manzano, *Colón y su secreto* (Madrid, 1976); and Juan Pérez de Tudela, *"Mirabilis in Altis": Estudio crítico sobre el origen y significado del proyecto descubridor de Cristobal Colón* (Madrid, 1983). These latter theses about a Columbus who had knowledge about the new lands must again presuppose some notion of the New World as a "natural entity." In particular, I have difficulties picturing a group of Amerindian women informing Europeans about a New World that differed from Asia (Pérez de Tudela, 13–14). For a sustained critique of the idea that there could be a discovery in the first place, see O'Gorman, *La invención de América* (see Introduction, n. 2). Building on O'Gorman's critique, Beatriz Pastor (*Discurso narrativo de la conquista de América* [Cuba, 1983]) forges the semblance of a mistaken Columbus. As Pastor's study assumes that one can distinguish a "real" New World from mythified versions, it evades (in an otherwise admirable study of key figures in the Spanish-American colonial literary canon) the fact that the New World, or the "reality" of America for that matter, consists of a web of references, images, symbols, and legends, if not prejudices and deeply embedded Eurocentric devices, which Columbus inau-

gurates; it cannot be simply dismissed by appealing to some readily identifiable natural entity existing "out there" in some unproblematic fashion. Cf. Walter Mignolo, "La lengua, la letra, el territori" (see Introduction, n. 4), esp. 139–40.

7. See Gerbi, *Nature in the New World* (see chapter 1, n. 8), 3–11.

8. For a study of how from the start Columbus's project entails an apocalyptic geography, see Pauline Moffit Watts, "Prophesy and Discovery: On the Spiritual Origins of Christopher Columbus's 'Enterprise of the Indies,'" *American Historical Review* 90:1 (February 1985): 73–102, and Alain Milhou, *Colón y su mentalidad Mesiánica en el ambiente franciscanista español* (Valladolid, 1983).

9. See de Certeau, "The Scriptural Economy," chapter 10 in *The Practice of Everyday Life* (see chapter 1, n. 39), 131–53, and idem, *The Writing of History* (see chapter 1, n. 35), esp. 215–18. See also Walter Ong's indispensable studies of the printing press and the passage from an oral to a literate culture in *Ramus, Method, and the Decay of Dialogue* (Cambridge, Mass., 1958); idem, *Rhetoric, Romance, and Technology* (Ithaca, N.Y., 1971); and idem, *Orality and Literacy: The Technologization of the Word* (London and New York, 1982).

10. Cf. Claude Lévi-Strauss's critique of Sartre in the last chapter of *The Savage Mind*, trans. George Weidenfeld (Chicago, 1966). For a study of the crown's detailed urban planning in early colonial documents and the colonial legacy of this scriptural economy in Latin Amercian history, see Angel Rama, *La ciudad letrada* (Hanover, N.H., 1984).

11. As Walter Ong has put it: "The ancient oral world knew few 'explorers,' though it did know many itinerants, travelers, voyagers, adventurers, and pilgrims" (*Orality and Literacy*, 73). On the printing press and Columbus see Elisabeth Eisenstein, *The Printing Press as an Agent of Change*, 2 vols. (Cambridge, 1979), 2:582–83.

12. Michel Beaujour, "Some Paradoxes of Description," *Yale French Studies* 61 (1978): 27–59, 37.

13. Tzvetan Todorov, *The Conquest of America: The Question of the Other*, trans. Richard Howard (New York, 1984), 3 (emphasis in translation); cf. idem, *La conquête de l'Amérique: La question de l'autre* (Paris, 1982), 11.

14. Even in those sections on Moctezuma and Cortés that address "the production of discourses and symbols" (ibid., 77–97, 110–23), Todorov examines the actualization of a code and not the production of new signs and consequently the making of a New World code. For a distinction between a semiotics of the code and one of production, see Umberto Eco, *A Theory of Semiotics* (Bloomington, Ind., 1979).

15. Todorov, *Conquest*, 17, 20, 29, 31, 34.

16. Ibid., 23.

17. Defert, "The Collection of the World" (see chapter 1, n. 28), 12. Also of interest about Columbus's art of traveling are Daniel Defert's observations in "Un genre ethnographique profane au XVIe siècle: Les livres d'habits (Essai d'ethno-iconographie)," in *Histoires de l'anthropologie: XVI–XIX siècles*, ed. Britta Rupp Einsenreich (Paris, 1984), 25–41, esp. 33.

18. *Raccolta di documenti e studi pubblicati dalla Reale Commissione Colombiana pel quarto centenario della scoperta dell'America*, ed. Cesare de Lollis, 6 pts. in 14 vols. (Rome, 1892–94), pt. 1, 1:26. I follow the *Raccolta*,

hereafter *Racc.*, for all Spanish quotations of Columbus; however, quoted fragments from the *Diario* are identified in the text by dates, or as located in its "prologue." The *Raccolta* retains Columbus's lowercases; I use ellipses at the beginning of quotations to identify passages taken from the middle of a sentence. Although Columbus kept a journal during the first three voyages (1492–93, 1493–96, 1498–1500), there is no indication that he kept a journal during the fourth (1502–04); only the journal of the first voyage has survived, in a truncated transcript by Bartolomé de Las Casas. The account of the third voyage, also copied by Las Casas, is not in a strict sense a journal. The *Diario* constantly shifts back and forth from the first person of Columbus into a third person elaborated by Las Casas. Within the transcript of the *Diario*, the narrative transformations by Las Casas illuminate the codification of the New World within a mythical and legendary dimension. The "imperfection" of the document bespeaks a "story" that has not received sufficient attention: there is a passage from a notion of a *new world* in Columbus to a New World where the full concrescence of meanings that accompany the proper name are prefigured in the writings of the mariner. Cf. Margarita Zamora, " 'Todas son palabras formales del Almirante': Las Casas y el *Diario* de Colón." *Hispanic Review* 57 (1989): 25–41, and Consuelo Valera's introduction to her edition of Critóbal Colón, *Textos y documentos completos* (Madrid, 1984), esp. xvi–xxiii. For a paleographical description of Las Casas's transcripts of the journal and account of the first and third voyages, see Consuelo Varela, "Observaciones para una edición crítica de los diarios del primero y el tercer viaje colombinos," *Columbeis* 3 (1988): 7–17. The English translations are my own; however, I have consulted and learned a great deal from *The Diario of Christopher Columbus's First Voyage to America 1492–1493*, trans. Oliver Dunn and James E. Kelly, Jr. (Norman, Okla., 1989); *Journals and Other Documents on the Life of Christopher Columbus*, trans. Samuel E. Morison (New York, 1963); and *Select Documents Illustrating the Four Voyages*, 2 vols., trans. Lionel Cecil Jane (London, 1930–33). Since some terms in the Jane and in the Morison translations deviate from the Spanish lexicon of exploration and at times alter the meaning of a statement, I have felt the need to provide my own translations. Dunn's and Kelly's bilingual edition provides a transcription that reproduces to the extent possible the basic structure of Las Casas's manuscript.

19. De Certeau, *The Practice of Everyday Life*, 134, 135; de Certeau's emphasis.

20. On travels to the East in the Middle Ages, see Jean-Paul Roux, *Les explorateurs au Moyen Age*, rev. ed. (Paris, 1985); Michel Mollat, *Les explorateurs du XIIe au XVIe siècle: Premiers regards sur des mondes nouveaux* (Paris, 1984); Pauline Moffit Watts, "Prophesy and Discovery"; Alain Milhou, *Colón y su mentalidad mesiánica*; and John K. Wright, *Geographical Lore of the Time of the Crusades* (New York, 1925).

21. For a detailed study of documents concerning Columbus's privileges and titles, see Antonio Rumeu de Armas, *Nueva luz sobre las capitulaciones de Santa Fe de 1492 concertadas entre los Reyes Católicos y Cristóbal Colón: Estudio institucional y diplomático* (Madrid, 1985).

22. Gerbi, *Nature in the New World*, 13. Heers shares Gerbi's view of the originality of the *Diario* (*Christophe Colomb*, 492, 508, 560).

23. I am here attempting to interrelate two modes of producing novelty that Paul Ricoeur has identified with metaphor and narrative: "Whereas metaphorical redescription reigns mostly in the field of sensorial, pathetic, aesthetic, and axiological values, which make of the world a *habitable* world, the mimetic function of narratives exerts itself preferably in the field of action and its *temporal* values," (*Temps et récit*, [see Introduction, n. 6], 1:13 [Ricoeur's emphasis]; my translation).

24. Cf. the reflections on marvel and legend in Vincent Descombes, *L'inconscient malgré lui* (Paris, 1977), 89–108.

25. For a historical appraisal of Marco Polo's authority, textual variations, and the encyclopedic character of his book, see Jacques Heers, "De Marco Polo à Christophe Colomb: comment lire le *Devisement du monde?*," *Journal of Medieval History* 10:2 (June 1984): 125–43. Also consult Henry Yule, introduction to *The Book of Ser Marco Polo*, 2 vols., trans. and ed. Henry Yule (London, 1875), 1:124–35. All quotations from Marco Polo follow Yule's translation. For editions and translations to Spanish and English of Columbus's marginal notes to his Latin copy of Marco Polo, see Marco Polo, *El libro de Marco Polo*, Juan Gil, ed. and trans. (Madrid, 1986), and idem., *The Book of Marco Polo* (Madrid, 1986). Gil has also edited Columbus's annotated copy of Rodrigo de Santaella's Spanish version of Marco Polo, *El libro de Marco Polo anotado por Cristóbal Colon* (Madrid, 1987). The differences between these two variants are relatively small. I have chosen Yule's variant because it includes details not present in Gil's edition that further document Marco Polo's style of writing and mode of traveling. For a study of the uses and receptions of Marco Polo in the context of sixteenth-century Seville, see Gil, "Libros, descubridores y sabios en la Sevilla del Quinientos," introductory remarks to *El libro de Marco Polo*, i–lxix.

26. As Heers points out about Marco Polo, and Mandeville as well: "One would look in vain . . . for the least touch of interest in landscape, a light, a color; there is nothing about the mountains, or the plains, or the travails. Nor is there a tint of emotion, nor a trace of sensibility" (*Christophe Colomb*, 492; my translation). Cf. Leonardo Olschki, *Marco Polo's Asia: An Introduction to His "Description of the World" Called "Il Milione"* (Berkeley and Los Angeles, 1960), 130–34, 147–77.

27. *The Book of Ser Marco Polo*, 2:266.

28. Ibid., 2:289, 282.

29. The question of the fantastic and the real in New World accounts had a brief polemic during the 1940s. For the most part the debate concerned the fictive status of chivalry novels. See Leonardo Olschki, "Ponce de León's Fountain of Youth: History of a Geographic Myth," *Hispanic American Historical Review* 21 (1941): 361–85; Irving Leonard, "Conquerors and Amazons in Mexico," *Hispanic American Historical Review* 24 (1944): 562–79; idem, *Books of the Brave* (Cambridge, Mass., 1949); and Rodolfo Schevill, "La novela histórica, las crónicas de Indias, y los libros de caballería," *Revista de las Indias* 56–60 (1944): 173–96. For a summary of the polemic see Gerbi, *Nature in the New World*, 203–5. Gerbi correctly remarks, following Schevill, that chivalry novels had been branded as immoral and plagued with lies since the late fifteenth century. We are concerned here not with the discrimination of

fable and history, however, but with the status of the real and the fantastic. After all, as Leonard points out, the Amazons and the island of Calafias described in the *Sergas de Esplandián* (1510) by Reinaldos de Montalvan mapped out the discovery of California in the instructions given by official documents. In this context, it is pertinent to quote Michel Foucault's assessment of the sixteenth-century episteme: "The division . . . the great tripartition, apparently so simple and so immediate, into *Observation*, *Document*, and *Fable*, did not exist" (*The Order of Things* [see Introduction, n. 5], 129 [Foucault's emphasis]).

30. Whether "cannibals" existed or not need not concern us. Their anthropophagy eventually becomes factual for Columbus. For our purposes, either form (denial or affirmation) semiotically corroborates the code. For a study of Columbus's fabrication of anthropophagy among the Caribs as a justification of slavery, see W. Arens, *The Man-Eating Myth: Anthropology and Anthropophagy* (New York, 1979). With respect to the validity of Arens's hypothesis, see *The Ethnography of Cannibalism*, ed. Paula Brown and Donald Tuzin (Washington, D.C., 1983). One must also consult Peter Hulme, *Colonial Encounters* (see Introduction, n. 16), esp. 13–43, 45–87. The invention of anthropophagy and the monstrous have been interpreted as early forms of racism by Christian Delacampagne, *L'invention du racisme: Antiquité et Moyen Age* (Paris, 1983).

31. The Portuguese exploration of the coast of Africa is, perhaps, the only counterpart to this condition in the literature of exploration. Translation, even if faulty, was not a problem for medieval travelers in the East. For the Portuguese, linguistic breakdowns and "indomitable savagery" marked the limits of their trade-oriented explorations. For instance, the Venetian Alviso da Ca'da Mosto, or Cadamosto, sailing under Henry the Navigator, sets forth the frontier of interest and the sayable in the following terms: "Little or nothing can be said. . . . [T]he people of the coast were so rude and savage that we were unable to have speech with them on land, or to treat anything" (*The Voyage of Cadamosto*, ed. and trans. G. R. Crone [Nedeln, Liechtenstein, 1967], 63). Whether because of an unfriendly reception or on account of a linguistic barrier, Cadamosto stops where Columbus's relations begin: "Reflecting that we were come to a new country of which we could not learn anything, we decided to continue farther would be useless, for we judged that we should be continually encountering new dialects, and should not be able to achieve any good results" (ibid., 76). Cadamosto remains closer to the themes of Marco Polo than to Columbus, regardless of nautical affinities with the latter. As is well known, Henry the Navigator's initial explorations of the coast of Africa were based on descriptions of landmarks and information about the population derived from Arab scholars during the Conquest of Ceuta. Knowledge of the coast of Africa and the interior was built on a progressive accumulation of data and the training of native interpreters. There was nothing as discontinuous as Columbus's landfall in the New World. The limits of Cadamosto's account illustrate the ground-breaking quality of Columbus's descriptions. Cf. Pierre Chaunu, *L'expansion européenne du XIIIe au XVe siècle* (Paris, 1969), 104–65.

32. See de Certeau, "Ethno-Graphy," chapter 5 in *The Writing of History* (see chapter 1, n. 35).

33. The sign Virgo could further evoke the return of Astraea and the coming of a golden age in Virgil's *Fourth Eclogue*. On Astraea, empire, and the millennium in the Renaissance see Frederick A. de Armas, *The Return of Astraea: An Astral-Imperial Myth in Calderón* (Lexington, Ky., 1986); Frances A. Yates, *Astraea: The Imperial Theme in the Sixteenth Century* (London and Boston, 1975).

34. See W. G. L. Randles, *De la terre plate au globe terrestre: Une mutation épistémologique rapide, 1480–1520* (Paris, 1980), 41–68.

35. Claude Kappler, *Monstres, démons et merveilles à la fin du Moyen-Age* (Paris, 1980), 84.

36. J. H. van den Berg, *The Changing Nature of Man*, trans. H. F. Croes (New York, 1975), makes the following amusing commentary about the description of landscapes: "Almost unnoticed—for everybody was watching the inner self—the landscape changed. It became estranged, and consequently it became visible. In April, 1335, Petrarch climbs Mont Ventoux near Avignon, and was surprised and delighted at the view; he was seeing the landscape behind Mona Lisa, the 'first landscape.' But he apologized, afraid of having earned God's wrath; what he saw was Luther's robes, the jewels of Savonarola" (232–33). We have grown so accustomed to descriptions of landscape that we tend to miss Columbus's innovation. Cf. Leonardo Olschki, *Storia letteraria delle scoperte geographiche* (Florence, 1937).

37. It is not the sense of *gallo* as dory that is implied here, but the description of colors like the rooster's. Cf. the general question of description and the reading of this passage in Alejandro Cioranescu, "El descubrimiento de América y el arte de la descripción," in *Colón humanista: Estudios de humanismo atlántico* (Madrid, 1967), 65; also of interest is Leonardo Olschki, "What Columbus Saw on Landing in the West Indies," *Proceedings of the American Philosophical Society* 84 (1941): 633–59.

38. Consider the following fragment from a speech by Galgacus, a leader of the Britons: "To us who dwell on the uttermost confines of the earth and of freedom, this remote sanctuary of Britain's glory has up to this time been a defence. Now, however, the furthest limits of Britain are thrown open, and the unknown always passes for the marvellous. But there are not tribes beyond us, nothing indeed but waves and rocks, and the yet more terrible Romans from whose oppression escape is vainly sought by obedience and submission. Robbers of the world, having by their universal plunder exhausted the land, they rifle the deep. If the enemy be rich, they are rapacious; if he be poor, they lust for dominion; neither the east nor the west has been able to satisfy them. Alone among men they covet with equal eagerness poverty and riches. To robbery, slaughter, plunder, they give the lying name of empire; they make a solitude and call it peace" (*The Life of Cnaeus Julius Agricola*, in *Complete Works of Tacitus*, trans. Moses Hadas [New York, 1942], 694–95).

39. Bartolomé de Las Casas, *Historia de las Indias*, ed. Augustín Millares Carlo, 3 vols. (Mexico City, 1965), 1:343.

40. For an analysis of the theme of the noble savage, and the contradictory character the notion of nobility assumes in Rousseau, see Hayden White, "The Noble Savage Theme as Fetish," in *Tropics of Discourse* (see Introduction, n. 6).

41. For images, commonplaces, and the location of the earthly paradise, see A. Bartlett Giamatti, *The Earthly Paradise and the Renaissance Epic* (Princeton, N.J.), and Harry Levin, *The Golden Age in the Renaissance* (Bloomington, Ind., 1969).

42. See Randles, *De la terre plate*, 82.

43. For an analysis of the name America as a pun, see Harold Janz, "Images of America in the German Renaissance," in *First Images of America*, (see chapter 1, n. 29), 1:98–100.

44. "uenient annis saecula seris, / quibus Oceanus uincula rerum / laxet et ingens pateat tellus / Tethysque nouos detegat orbes / nec sit terris ultima Thule" (L. Annaei Seneca, *Medea*, 375–79). On the different textual families of Seneca's *Medea* and Columbus's modification, see Gabriella Moretti, "*Nec si terris ultima Thule. (La profezia di Seneca sulla scoperta del Nuovo Mondo),*" *Columbeis* I (1986): 95–106, esp. 101–4.

45. See B. B. Ashcom, "The First Builder of Boats in *El Burlador,*" *Hispanic Review* II (1943): 328–33.

46. On the utopian wish-horizon and Columbus's Eldorado, see Ernst Bloch, *The Principle of Hope*, 3 vols., trans. Neville Plaice, Stephen Plaice, and Paul Knight (Cambridge, Mass., 1986), 2:746–94.

47. See Kappler, *Monstres, démons et merveilles*, 198.

48. Cf. Martin Heiddeger, "The Age of the World Picture," in *The Question Concerning Technology and Other Essays*, trans. William Lowitt (New York, 1977), 115–54); Foucault, *The Order of Things*, 50; and de Certeau, *The Practice of Everyday Life*, 134.

CHAPTER 3. DIALOGUE AS CONQUEST IN THE CORTÉS–CHARLES V CORRESPONDENCE

1. Pedro Calderón de la Barca, *El príncipe constante*, ed. Alberto Porqueras Mayo (Madrid, 1975).

2. Hernán Cortés, *Cartas y documentos* (Mexico City, 1963), 63. The English versions of quoted passages from Cortés's letters are my translations. I have, however, consulted and learned from the versions in *Letters from Mexico*, ed. and trans. Anthony Pagden (New Haven, Conn., 1986), and *Five Letters of Cortés to the Emperor*, trans. J. Bayard Morris (New York, n.d.).

3. For a study of the *Abencerraje* as a prototype of the Moorish genre, see Claudio Guillén, "Literature as Historical Contradiction: *El Abencerraje*, the Moorish Novel, and the Eclogue," in *Literature as System: Essays toward the Theory of Literary History* (Princeton, N.J., 1971), 159–217. My observations on Calderón's lines, and the tradition that draws from the *Abencerraje*, I owe to Israel Burshatin, "Power, Discourse, and Metaphor in the *Abencerraje,*" *MLN* 99 (March 1984): 195–213. Also of interest is Burshatin, "The Moor in the Text: Metaphor, Emblem, and Silence," *Critical Inquiry* 12 (Autumn 1985): 98–118.

4. Johannes Fabian, *Time and the Other* (see chapter 1, n. 7), 1.

5. For an assessment of functional anthropology as an aid to colonial administration, see the essays included in *Anthropology and the Colonial Encounter*, ed. Talal Asad (London 1973). The polemic argued in these essays is centered on such issues as direct filiation or the misuse of knowledge.

6. James Clifford, "Power and Dialogue in Ethnography: Marcel Griaule's Initiation," in *Observers Observed: Essays on Ethnographic Fieldwork*, ed. George Stocking, (Madison, Wis., 1983), 131.

7. Quoted in ibid., 141.

8. Quoted in Michel Foucault, "Nietzsche, Genealogy, History," in *Language, Counter-Memory, Practice*, trans. Donald F. Bouchard and Sherry Simon (Ithaca, N.Y., 1977), 142.

9. I am drawing the notion of deterritorialization and its application to minor discourse from Gilles Deleuze and Félix Guattari, "What Is a Minor Literature?" trans. Robert Brinkley, *Mississippi Review* 22:3 (Spring 1983): 13–33.

10. James Clifford, "On Ethnographic Authority" (see chapter 1, n. 20), 119.

11. For a study of the different version, printings, and possible draftsmen of the map, see Manuel Toussaint, "El plano atribuido a Cortés," in Manuel Toussaint, Federico Gómez de Orozco, and Justino Fernández, *Planos de la ciudad de México siglos XVI y XVII: Estudio histórico, urbanístico y bibliográfico* (Mexico City, 1938), 91–105. See also the descriptions of the plan of the city and the chart of the Gulf Coast in José Luis Martínez, *Hernán Cortés*, 2d ed. (Mexico City, 1990), 304–16.

12. See, for instance, Inga Clendinnen, " 'Fierce and Unnatural Cruelty': Cortés and the Conquest of Mexico," *Representations* 33 (1991): 65–100, esp. 91–94.

13. See Burshatin, "The Moor in the Text."

14. For a description of the letters and the manuscripts, see Martínez, *Hernán Cortés*, 147–56 and passim; Pagden, translator's introduction to *Letters from Mexico*, liii–lx; Morris, introduction to *Five Letters*, xli–xlvii.

15. Marcel Bataillon, "Hernán Cortés, autor prohibido," in *Libro jubilar de Alfonso Reyes* (Mexico City, 1959), 77–82.

16. George E. Marcus and Dick Cushman, "Ethnographies as Texts," *Annual Review of Anthropology* 11 (1982): 25–65, 30 (Marcus and Cushman's emphasis). See also Johannes Fabian, "Presence and Representation: The Other and Anthropological Writing," *Cultural Critique* 16:4 (Summer 1990): 753–72; esp. 760–67.

17. For a detailed overview of contemporary anthropology, see Sherry B. Ortner, "Theory in Anthropology since the Sixties," *Society for Comparative* *Study of Society and History* 26:1 (1984): 126–66.

18. See M. T. Hodgen, *Early Anthropology in the Sixteenth and Seventeenth Centuries* (see chapter 1, n. 56); Bitterli, *Los "salvajes" y los "civilizados"* (see chapter 1, n. 20). For a critique, see Boon, "Comparative De-enlightenment" (see chapter 1, n. 27). Also of interest is Ryan, "Assimilating New Worlds" (see chapter 1, n. 41). For an appraisal of Sahagún as a modern ethnographer, see J. Jorge Klor de Alva, "Sahagún and the Birth of Modern Ethnography: Representing, Confessing, and Inscribing the Native Other," in *The Work of Bernardino de Sahagún: Pioneer Ethnographer of Sixteenth-Century Aztec Mexico*, ed. J. Jorge Klor de Alva, H. B. Nicholson, and Eloise Quiñones Keber (Austin, Tex., and Albany, N.Y., 1988).

19. See Jeanne Favret-Saada's discussion of this transformation in terms of Emile Benveniste's observations on the nature of pronouns in *Deadly Words*

(Cambridge, 1980), 25–28; Emile Benveniste, "The Nature of Pronouns," in *Problèmes de linguistique générale*, 2 vols. (Paris, 1966, 1974), 1:251–57.

20. Burshatin, "Power, Discourse, and Metaphor," 207.

21. Ibid.

22. Kevin Dwyer, *Morrocan Dialogues: Anthropology in Question* (Baltimore, 1982); idem, "The Dialogic of Ethnology" and "On the Dialogic of Field Work," *Dialectal Anthropology* 4:3 (1979): 205–24, and 2:2 (1977): 143–51. Vincent Crapanzano, *Tuhami: Portrait of a Moroccan* (Chicago, 1980); idem, "On the Writing of Ethnography," *Dialectical Anthropology* 2:1 (1977): 69–73. For a discussion of dialogical authority, see Clifford, "On Ethnographic Authority," 133–35 and passim. My thinking in this essay is indebted to Clifford's study. Also consult Johannes Fabian's discussion of dialogue and ethnography in "Presence and Representation: The Other and Anthropological Writing," *Critical Inquiry* 16:4 (Summer 1990): 753–72, esp. 760–66.

23. Clifford, "On Ethnographic Authority," 134–35.

24. Crapanzano, *Tuhami*, 11.

25. Dwyer, "On the Dialogic," 147, 148.

26. See Paul Rabinow, "Discourse and Power: On the Limits of Ethnographic Texts," *Dialectical Anthropology* 10:1–2 (1985): 1–13, esp. 7.

27. In this regard Elizabeth Burgos's editing of her conversations with Rigoberta Menchú as a first-person narrative is paradoxically more dialogic than Dwyer's verbatim record of his conversations with Faqir (see prologue to *Me llamo Rigoberta Menchú y así me nació la conciencia* [Mexico City, 1985], 9–19). I say paradoxically because it is in spite of Burgos's editing that Rigoberta Menchú manages to convey her story in and on her own terms. Burgos tells how Menchú would ignore her questions and go on to elaborate at length on topics and aspects of her life that she felt were more significant. The form of the story is ultimately Menchú's, and it obeys an epistemology that might be at odds with anthropology's criteria of truth and objectivity. This perhaps explains criticisms of Menchú's trustworthiness that disclaim her version of the events on the grounds that they never occurred as she tells them. For a critique of these attacks on Menchú's credibility, see John Beverly's introduction to the special issue on *testimonio* in *Revista de crítica literaria latinoamericana* 18:36 (1992): 7–18. Rigoberta Menchú also hs been a target in the backlash against cultural studies and the so-called leftist McCarthyism of "political correctness"; the power of her story—of her breaching the bounds of acceptable speech—threatens not only the discipline of anthropology but, it would seem, the fabric of Western culture and liberal education. It should be underscored that Menchú intended to produce a plausible story that would convey the horrors of hundreds of massacres that have plagued Guatemalan Indians during the last decades and not a detailed, realistic account of one single event. Factual disclaimers convey a different understanding of ethnographic dialogue to the speech genre favored by Burgos and Menchú, one in which Menchú's first-person narrative questions Western discourse along with the authority of the ethnographer. My observations on speech genres, dialogue, and the active paticipation of listeners are derived from M. M. Bakhtin, "The Problem of Speech Genres," in *Speech Genres and Other Late Essays*, trans.

Vern W. Macgee and ed. Caryl Emerson and Michael Holquist (Austin, Tex., 1986), 60–102.

28. Obviously, I am here adapting, not merely applying, the definition of communication given by Roman Jakobson in "Linguistics and Poetics," in *Style in Language*, ed. Thomas A. Sebeok (New York, 1960), 350–77. Following Jacques Derrida, we may add: "It is therefore *the game of the world* that must first be thought; before attempting to understand all forms of play in the world" (*On Grammatology*, trans. Gayatri Spivak [Baltimore, 1976], 50). As signs lose traces of their motivation, of their cultural specificity, and become arbitrary, they paradoxically naturalize a worldview. On the notion of worlding and colonial discourse, see Gayatri Spivak, "The Rani of Sirmur," in *Europe and Its Others*, (see Introduction, n. 16), 1:128–51. Also informing the notion of dialogue as violent and power-ridden are M. M. Bakhtin's reflections on dialogism in "Discourse and the Novel," in *The Dialogic Imagination: Four Essays*, trans. Caryl Emerson and Michael Holquist (Austin, Tex., 1981), 314–15 and passim.

29. Roy Wagner, *The Invention of Culture*, rev. ed. (Chicago, 1981), 107.

30. See the stimulating discussions of hybridization in Homi Bhabha, "Of Mimicry and Man: The Ambivalence of Colonial Discourse," *October* 28 (1984): 125–33, and idem, "Signs Taken for Wonders." In reading Bhabha, one must take into account Abdul JanMohammed's critique in "The Economy of Manichean Allegory: The Function of Racial Difference in Colonialist Literature," *Critical Inquiry* 12 (Autumn 1985): 59–87, esp. 56–61. See also my observations on Elizabeth Burgos and Rigoberta Menchú in note 27.

31. For Las Casas consider the ample circulation and translations of the *Brevíssima relación de la destruyción de las Indias*, ed. Manuel Ballesteros Gaibrois, (1552; facsimile ed., Madrid, 1977). On Theodore de Bry's translation of Las Casas and the Black Legend in general, see M. S. Giuseppi, F.S.A., "The Work of Theodore de Bry and His Sons, Engravers," *Proceedings of the Huguenot Society of London* 11 (1915–17): 204–27, and Rómulo D. Carbia, *Historia de la Leyenda Negra Hispano-Americana* (Buenos Aires, 1943). For a recent example of a denunciation of ideological manipulation, see W. Arens's interpretation of cannibalism as an invention for the justification of the conquest in *The Man-Eating Myth: Anthropology and Anthropophagy* (see chapter 2, n. 24). Insofar as Todorov's point of departure for a semiotic and moral explanation of the conquest consists of an evaluation of attitudes, and a reduction of the success to the superiority of phonological writing, the benevolent facade of the conquest is undermined in *The Conquest of America* (see chapter 2, n. 11), esp. 57–139. Todorov's classification of Mesoamerican culture as presymbolic because of a lack of phonological writing defeats the moral question of dialogue—the *Other* ends up engrossed in a monologue where symbols cannot be differentiated from reality. For Todorov the success of the conquest is a result of the technological superiority of phonetic writing. Not only is it questionable that there was an absence of phonetic writing in Mesoamerica, but more importantly, the supposedly inferior understanding of symbolism that Todorov adscribes to Mexican culture betrays, in the final analysis, a refusal to account for the Amerindians' creativity. For a discussion of writing in pre-Columbian America and Todorov's position, see Gordon

Brotherston, "Towards a Grammatology of America: Lévi-Strauss, Derrida, and the Native New World Text," in *Europe and Its Others* (see Introduction, n. 16), 2:61–77, esp. 63.

32. Ramón Iglesias, "Hernán Cortés," in his *Cronistas e historiadores de la conquista de México*, ed. Juan A. Ortega y Medina (Mexico City, 1972), 119.

33. For a reading of how Cortés mythicizes himself as a conquistador and a model of conquest, see Beatriz Pastor, "Hernán Cortés: La ficcionalización de la conquista y la creación del modelo de conquistador," in *Discurso narrativo de la conquista de América* (Havana, 1983), 113–233. On autobiography in Cortés's second letter, see Stephanie Merrim, "Ariadne's Thread: Autobiography, History, and Cortés' *Segunda Carta-Relación*," *Dispositio* 11:28–29 (1986): 57–83.

34. The most elaborate Spanish treatise on war during the Middle Ages is found in the "Partida segunda" of Alfonso X el Sabio, *Las siete partidas* (c. 1294; Madrid, 1807), vol. 2. The fundamental question beyond the justification of war concerns the nature of guerdons, *don de guerre*, as the French etymology reminds us. There is a code of guerdoning not only with respect to nobility (i.e., the admiralcy of Columbus) but also for granting conquered property ranging from a kiln to a territory. The popular image of conquest as loot misses the point: conquest must preserve the economic and social structure of the conquered in order to maintain control and derive usufruct. For a particular case in the early *Reconquista*, see Clara Estour, "The Economic Development of the Order of Calatrava, 1158–1336," *Speculum* 57:2 (1982): 267–88. Even Isabel la Católica, whom school manuals represent as a religious fanatic, when she writes the capitulation after the fall of Granada, forbids forced conversions and retains the laws and officials of the conquered. There is a reprint of the document in *New Iberian World: A Documentary History of the Discovery and Settlement of Latin America to the 17th Century*, ed. John H. Parry and Robert G. Keith (New York, 1984). On the breakdown of the truce that eventually led to the expulsion of the Moriscos, see Antonio Domínguez Ortiz and Bernard Vincent, *Historia de los moriscos: Vida y tragedia de una minoría* (Madrid, 1978), and Julio Caro Baroja, *Los moriscos del Reino de Granada* (Madrid, 1976). On the medieval heritage of the New World, see Antonio Garrido Aranda, *Organización de la Iglesia en el Reino de Granada y su proyección en Indias* (Sevilla, 1979), and Luis Weckmann, *La herencia medieval de México*, 2 vols. (Mexico City, 1984).

35. Martín Fernández de Navarrete, *Colección de viajes que hicieron los españoles por la mar desde fines del siglo XV*, 3 vols. (1825–37); reprint, Madrid, 1954–55), 2: 209.

36. Lewis Mumford, *The City in History* (New York, 1961). Also consult Angel Rama, "La ciudad ordenada," in *La ciudad letrada* (Hanover, N.H., 1984).

37. Navarrete, *Colección*, 2: 212.

38. For a metaphorical use of the term *palimpsest* in geography, see André Corbox, "Land as Palimpsest," *Diogenes* 121 (1983): 12–34.

39. Cortés, *Cartas* (see n. 2), 20; page references are hereafter given in the text.

40. Juan Ginés de Sepúlveda, *Hechos de los españoles en el Nuevo Mundo y México*, ed. Demetrio Ramos y Lucio Mijares (Valladolid, 1976), 192, 193. For a study of the debates between Sepúlveda and Las Casas, see Lewis Hanke, *Aristotle and the American Indians* (Bloomington, Ind., 1975).

41. I derive the term "oppositional practices" from the late Michel de Certeau, "On the Oppositional Practices of Everyday Life," *Social Text* 3 (Fall 1980): 3–43. That essay summed up for an English audience some of the main arguments developed in his *L'invention du quotidien. Arts de faire*, vol. 1 (Paris, 1980); translated as *The Practice of Everyday Life* (see chapter 1, n. 28). As de Certeau points out in *The Practices of Everyday Life*, he draws his inspiration from the Amerindians who, "even when they were subjected, indeed even when they accepted their subjection . . . often used the laws, practices, and representations that were imposed on them by force or by fascination to ends other than those of their conquerors; they made something else out of them; they subverted them from within — not by rejecting them or by transforming them (though that occurred as well), but by many different ways of using them in the service of rules, customs or convictions foreign to the colonization which they could not escape. They metaphorized the dominant order: they made it function in another register" (31–32). I believe that one might further illuminate the above, vastly studied question with de Certeau's categories.

42. De Certeau, "On the Oppositional," 5.

43. Bernardino de Sahagún, *Florentine Codex: General History of the Things of New Spain*, 13 vols., trans. and ed. Arthur J. O. Anderson and Charles E. Dibble (Santa Fe and Salt Lake City, 1950–82), 13:47. Hereafter all English versions of the Florentine Codex are by Anderson and Dibble and page references are given in the text.

44. For the editing of information by Sahagún and the Nahua authors in the different versions and stages in the production of the *Historia general*, see Jorge Klor de Alva, "Sahagún and the Birth of Modern Ethnography," esp. 46–52.

45. See Fabian's critique (*Time and the Other*, 82–87) of Emile Benveniste's study of temporal verb forms, "Les relations de temp dans le verbe français," in *Problèmes*, 1:237–50.

46. G. W. F. Hegel, *The Phenomenology of Mind*, trans. J. B. Baillie (New York, 1967), 236, 240. My usage of this passage is inspired by the poststructuralist readings of Jacques Lacan, "Aggressivity in Psychoanalysis" and "The Subversion of Subject and the Dialectic of Desire in the Freudian Unconscious," in *Ecrits*, trans. Alan Sheridan (New York, 1977), 292–325; Jacques Derrida, "From Restricted to General Economy: A Hegelianism without Reserve," in *Writing and Difference*, trans. Alan Bates (Chicago, 1978), 251–77; and André Glucksmann, *Le discours de la guerre: Théorie et stratégie* (Paris, 1967). Glucksmann's reading of Hegel in the light of Roman Jakobson, Emile Benveniste, and Jacques Lacan has been particularly useful. As Glucksmann points out: "The struggle to death does nothing but describe the a priori conditions of all communication, whether it is of love or the most harsh injunction" (80; my translation). Beyond the idealism of the linguists, war without respite lies on the horizon of Hegel's formulation. My point for

235

bringing in Hegel is to chart a terrain for arresting the dialectic and thus warding off the "cunning of reason."

47. G. W. F. Hegel, *The Philosophy of History*, trans. J. Sibree (New York, 1956), 33.

48. Hegel, *Phenomenology of Mind*, 229 (Hegel's emphasis).

49. Cf. Michael Taussig on the formation of what he calls the strategic points of convergence and codependancy in the culture of colonization: "As such they were in effect new rituals, rites of conquest and colony, mystiques of race and power, little dramas of civilization tailoring savagery which did not mix or homogenize ingredients from the two sides of the colonial divide but instead bound Indian understandings of white understandings of Indians to white understandings of Indian understandings of whites" (*Shamanism, Colonialism, and the Wild Man: A Study in Terror and Healing* [Chicago, 1987], 109).

50. On writing and the inscription of the law on the body, see Michel de Certeau, *The Practice of Everyday Life*, 131–65. J. H. Elliot has traced in this undressing of Moctezuma the following passage in Luke, 24:39: "Behold my hands and my feet, that it is I myself: handle me, and see: for a spirit hath not flesh and bones, as ye see me have" ("The Mental World of Hernán Cortés," *Transactions of the Royal Historical Society*, 5th ser., 17 (1967): 41–58, 52. As a repetition of Luke's verses Moctezuma's words would further reinforce the semblance of a noble savage in his complete submission to Charles V. For a discussion of Cortés's allusions to the New Testament, chivalry novels, episodes in Spanish history, characters in classical history, and legal precepts, see Martínez, *Hernan Cortés*, 848–53.

51. See Glucksmann, *Le discours de la guerre*, 78; Benveniste, "La philosophie analytique et le language," in *Problèmes*, 1:267–76, esp. 274–75.

52. See Alfredo López Austin, *Hombre-Dios: Religión y política en el mundo náhuatl* (Mexico City, 1973). Also consult Serge Gruzinski, *Man-Gods in the Mexican Highlands* (see Introduction, n. 28), esp. 21–30. For a study of the different Spanish versions of "the Cortés-Quetzalcoatl myth," see Ross Frank, "The Codex Cortés: Inscribing the Conquest of Mexico," *Dispositio* 14:36–38 (1989): 187–211.

53. See Miguel León-Portilla, introduction to *Visión de los vencidos: Relaciones indígenas de la conquista*, trans. Angel María Garibay K. (Mexico City, 1972), xxiii; "Quetzalcóatl-Cortés en la conquista de México," *Historia mexicana* 24:1 (1974): 13–35. Sahagún felt the need to revise this "indigenous vision" of the conquest in 1585 because "certain mistakes were made, namely that some things were improperly included in the narrative of the conquest while others were improperly left out" (quoted in S. L. Cline, "Revisionist Conquest History: Sahagún's revised Book XII," in *Bernardino de Sahagún*, ed. Klor de Alva, Nicholson, and Keber, 93). As Cline points out, it is a commonplace in Sahaguntian scholarship to attribute the motivations behind the revisions of the Florentine Codex version to its having been "composed, not merely copied, by Indians" (93). An independent history and perspective on the colonial order to those written or collected by missionaries has surfaced as a result of the publications, and insistence on research based on documents in Nahuatl, by Arthur Anderson, Frances Berdan, Frances Kartunnen and James

Lockhart, just to name those who have collaborated in such influential books as *Beyond the Codices* (Berkeley and Los Angeles, 1976), *Nahuatl in the Middle Years* (Berkeley and Los Angeles, 1976), and the *Tlaxcalan Actas* (Salt Lake City, 1986). Worth mentioning is Stephanie Wood's recent work on the representation of the conquest and evangelization in primordial titles, *títulos*, laying claims to land and the political legitimacy of local elites, "The Cosmic Conquest: Late-Colonial Views of the Sword and Cross in Central Mexican *Títulos*," *Ethnohistory* 38:2 (Spring 1991): 176–95. We must differentiate the Florentine Codex version of the conquest, which was solicited by Sahagún for his *Historia general*, from the other documents in Nahuatl, which were primarily written by and for Indians and have functioned up to the present as a history of local consciousness. Insofar as Cortés and the evangelization are depicted in favorable terms, the *títulos* would also differ from the Florentine Codex, where the emphasis is placed on the destruction of the old order. However, the positive depiction, hence adoption, of Spanish political and religious structures does not mean that the dominant motifs in the representations in the *títulos* do not assume different, perhaps contradictory, meanings and functions to those intended by secular and religious authorities. In substance these representations may differ from those in the Florentine Codex, but in form and function they may reveal similar modes of cultural resistance. This would be especially true if we do not limit resistance to intent, but, following de Certeau, trace forms of oppositional consciousness even in those places where Indians willingly adopt Spanish patterns and beliefs (see n. 45).

54. Homi Bhabha, "Signs Taken for Wonders," 99.

55. See, for instance, Angel María Garibay K., *Panorama literario de los pueblos náhuas* (Mexico City, 1975), 35–41.

56. Deleuze and Guattari, "What Is a Minor Literature?," 22.

57. For a discussion of apes in European literature, apropos of the *ximio* (ape) in *La Celestina*, from the scriptures and the patristic writers to Locke and Voltaire, see Otis H. Green, " 'Lo de tu abuela con el ximio' (*Celestina*, auto I)," *Hispanic Review* 24:1 (January 1956): 1–12.

58. Cf. Donald Robertson, *Mexican Manuscript Painting of the Colonial Period* (New Haven, Conn., 1959), 21–22. Although not concerned specifically with the Florentine Codex, the following provide suggestive ways for approaching the clash of forms in postconquest pictorial manuscripts: Joaquín Galarza and Abraham Zemsz, "Le 'portrait-royal' dans l'écriture aztèque: Les 'tableaux' du codex Tovar," *Communications* 29 (1979): 15–56; Rolena Adorno, "On the Pictorial Language" (see Introduction, n. 23).

59. De Certeau, "On the Oppositional," 40.

60. An early variance from this position appears in Fray Pedro de Gante's letter to the friars of the province of Flanders (1529), where he refuses to acknowledge the religiosity of the natives: "Los nacidos en esta tierra son de bonísima complexión y natural, aptos para todo, y más para recibir nuestra fe. Pero tienen, cierto, de malo ser de condición servil, porque nada hacen sino forzados, y cosa ninguna por amor y buen trato; aunque en esto no parecen seguir su propia naturaleza, sino la costumbre, porque nunca aprendieron a obrar por amor a la virtud, sino por temor y miedo." [Those born in these lands have a very good complexion and nature, capable of everything, and even more

for receiving our faith. But they have, indeed, the flaw of being servile, because they do not do anything except when they are forced, and nothing for love and good treatment; even though this is a result, not of their own nature, but of custom, because they never learned to act for the love of virtue, but through fear and apprehension.] (Joaquín García Icazbalceta, and Agustín Millares Carlo, *Bibliografía mexicana del siglo XVI* [Mexico City, 1981], 103.)

61. See Cortés, *Cartas*, 191, 228, 234 for passages that reveal Cortés's visions of the historical importance of New Spain within the geographic context of the "Spice Islands."

62. Of course, I am here alluding to the self-representations by Cortés and the alternate versions by Francisco López de Gómara, *Historia de las Indias y la conquista de la Nueva España* (1552), and Bernal Díaz del Castillo, *Historia verdadera de la conquista de la Nueva España* (c. 1568). For a displacement of the commonplace discussion of Bernal's criticism of Gómara to Bernal's contentiousness against Las Casas, see Rolena Adorno, "Discourse on Colonialism: Bernal Díaz, Las Casas, and the Twentieth-Century Reader," *MLN* 103:2 (March 1988): 239–58. On Gómara and Bernal, also consult Robert Lewis, "Retórica y verdad: los cargos de Bernal Díaz a López de Gómara," in *De la crónica a la nueva narrativa*, ed. Merlin H. Foster and Julio Ortega (Oaxaca, 1986), 37–47.

63. Foucault, "Nietzsche, Genealogy, History," 146.

64. Claude Lévi-Strauss, *The Savage Mind* (see chapter 2, n. 8), 247.

CHAPTER 4. THE TIME OF THE ENCYCLOPEDIA

1. Augustín Dávila Padilla, *Historia de la fundación y discurso de la provincia de Santiago de México, de la orden de Predicadores* (1595), facsimile ed. Augustín Millares Carlo (Mexico City, 1955), 516–18; my translation.

2. Demographic historians from the Berkeley School have calculated that world population in 1500 was 400 million, of which 80 million lived in the Americas. By the mid-1600s there were only 10 million. In Mexico alone, on the eve of the conquest, the population was about 25 million, and by 1600 it had fallen to 1 million. See Sherburne F. Cook and Woodrow Borah, *The Indian Population of Central Mexico, 1531–1610* (Berkeley and Los Angeles, 1960), and idem, *Essays in Population History*, 3 vols. (Berkeley and Los Angeles, 1971–79). Cf. a chart with lower estimates in William M. Denevan, ed., *The Native Population of the Americas in 1492* (Madison, Wis., 1976), 291, also reproduced in James Lockhart and Stuart B. Schwartz, *Early Latin America: A History of Colonial Spanish America and Brazil* (Cambridge, 1983), 36. For a study of an Indian town during those plague-ridden days, see S. L. Cline, *Colonial Culhuacan, 1580–1600: A Social History of an Aztec Town* (Albuquerque, 1986).

3. Umberto Eco, *Semiotics and the Philosophy of Language* (Bloomington, Ind., 1984), 187.

4. Fray Diego de Durán, *Historia de las Indias de Nueva España e islas de la Tierra Firme*, 2 vols., ed. Angel María Garibay K. (Mexico City, 1967); hereafter cited in the text. English versions are my translations. I have consulted the English versions of Durán's history of Mexico-Tenochtitlan, *The*

Aztecs: The History of the Indies of New Spain, trans. Doris Heyden and Fernando Horcasitas (New York, 1964); and of his ethnographic books, *Book of the Gods and Rites and The Ancient Calendar*, trans. Doris Heyden and Fernando Horcasitas (Norman, Okla., 1971). Ignacio Bernal has pointed out that the title given by José Fernando Ramírez in the first edition of 1854 is paradoxical: "We do not know the title Durán gave his work. On the reverse of the first plate of the Atlas can be read an inscription written by a copyist: 'Historia de las Indias de N. i islas y tierra firme.' . . . Ill luck, which has pursued Durán, does not stop there, since because of an inexplicable confusion, in Ramírez's edition the work is called a 'Historia de la Nueva España i Islas de la Tierra Firme,' or 'History of New Spain and of the Islands of the Mainland.' It is difficult to imagine 'islands' on the mainland; therefore I suppose that this must have been simply an error" (Ignacio Bernal, "Introduction," in *The Aztecs*, xxii–xxiii). The paradox, perhaps, is due to our contemporary definitions of *island*, *continent*, *mainland*, and so on, which up to the last century were not as clearly outlined, from what Ramírez's title leads us to believe.

5. Irving A. Leonard, *Baroque Times in Old Mexico: Seventeenth-Century Persons, Places, and Practices* (Ann Arbor, Mich., 1959), 66.

6. Bernardo de Balbuena, *La grandeza mexicana*, ed. Luis Adolfo Domínguez (Mexico City, 1971), 73; hereafter cited in the text. English versions are my translations.

7. For an analysis of the invention of pre-Hispanic culture as the antiquity of Mexico, and a corresponding negative view of the seventeenth-century indigenous population in the aftermath of a riot in Mexico City, see Ramón Iglesia, "The Disillusionment of Don Carlos," in *Columbus, Cortés, and Other Essays*, trans. Lesley Byrd Simpson (Berkeley and Los Angeles, 1969).

8. See P. J. Bakewell, *Silver Mining and Society in Colonial Mexico: Zacatecas, 1546–1700* (Cambridge, 1971), 235. Cf. Woodrow Borah, "New Spain's Century of Depression," *Ibero-Americana* 35 (1951): 1–58. For a general introduction to colonial Latin America, see Lockhart and Schwartz, *Early Latin America* (Cambridge, 1983).

9. See Bakewell, *Silver Mining*, 226, and Charles Verlinder, "El régimen de trabajo en México: Aumento y alcance de la gañanía, siglo XVII," in *Historia y sociedad en el mundo de habla española*, ed. Bernardo García Martínez (Mexico City, 1970), 225.

10. This process of marginalization that results from the "spiritual conquest" has been carefully documented by Robert Ricard in *La conquista espiritual de México*, trans. Angel María Garibay K. (Mexico City, 1947), 429.

11. See François Chevalier, *Land and Society in Colonial Mexico: The Great Hacienda*, trans. Alvin Eustis (Berkeley and Los Angeles, 1970), 269–70.

12. For the specific characteristics of the *encomienda* in Mexico, see Lesley Byrd Simpson, *The Encomienda in New Spain* (Berkeley and Los Angeles, 1966), 26.

13. See the detailed study of Silvio Zavala, *Los esclavos indios en Nueva España* (Mexico City, 1967), 179–224.

14. See Bakewell, *Silver Mining*, 14.

15. See Charles Gibson, *The Aztecs under Spanish Rule* (Stanford, Calif., 1964), 85.

16. See Francisco de Solano, "La modelación social como política indigenista de los Franciscanos de la Nueva España, 1524–1574," *Historia mexicana* 28:2 (1978): 297–332, for an overview of the early Franciscan transplant of models derived from Castilian communities. The purpose of these town structures was the introduction not only of religion but also of agricultural techniques; they constituted a total "civilizing" effort that completely altered the life of the natives, from the distribution of political and social space to that of diet, clothing, and landscape. Also see George Kubler, *Mexican Architecture of the Sixteenth Century*, 2 vols. (New Haven, Conn., 1948), 1:82–102.

17. See Gibson, *The Aztecs*, 166.

18. Ibid., 193.

19. Georges Baudot has a detailed analysis of the confiscation, prohibition, and monopoly of the crown during the 1570s in his *Utopie et histoire au Mexique: les premiers chroniqueurs de la civilization mexicaine, 1520–1569* (Toulouse, 1977), 475–507.

20. See, for instance, Alberto Salas, *Tres cronistas de Indias: Pedro Mártir de Anglería, Gonzalo Fernández de Oviedo, Fray Bartolomé de las Casas* (Mexico City, 1986).

21. Gonzalo Fernández de Oviedo, *Historia general y natural de las Indias*, 5 vols., ed. Juan Pérez de Tudela Bueso (Madrid, 1959); hereafter cited in the text. English versions are my translations. Oviedo published the *Sumario de la natural historia de las Indias* in 1526, at the insistence of Charles V. Before this brief anticipation of what would become his major work and lifetime project, Oviedo had written a chivalric novel, *Claribalte* (1519). As Gerbi points out, the *Claribalte* "marks the ideological transition from Oviedo's life as a courtier and military adventurer to that as observer, naturalist, and historian of the Americas" (*Nature in the New World* [see chapter 1, n. 8], 201). Also see Stephanie Merrim, "The Castle of Discourse: Fernández de Oviedo's *Don Claribalte* (1519)," *MLN* 97 (1982): 329–46. Oviedo's *Historia* was not published in its entirety until 1851–55 by José Amador de los Ríos (see Gerbi, 129–33, 215–16, for details on the publication of the *Historia*). Only the first part was published during his lifetime, in 1535 and 1547; it was translated into French by Jean Poleur in 1555, and an Italian version was included in the *Raccolta di navigationi e viaggi* of Giovanni Ramusio in 1556. The historiography of Oviedo abounds in vituperous attacks that often simply repeat what Las Casas wrote about him, or, as Gerbi deplores, is limited to "a word or two of hasty and generalized approval" that "charitably spare[s] him the usual bio-bibliographical notes without really studying or evaluating him" (134). Cf. José J. Arrom, "Gonzalo Fernández de Oviedo, relator de episodios y narrador de naufragios," *Ideologies and Literature* 4:17 (1983): 133–45.

22. Gerbi, *Nature in the New World*, 246. On Oviedo's historical pessimism and tragic plot, see ibid., 245, 255–61. At times Oviedo calls human history *tragédica*, and at other *diabólica*; as for sketches of his "social types" in the New World, Gerbi has the appropriate trope: "His 'social types' — the adventurer, the cacique, the priest, the captain, and so on — are forcefully delineated, almost as if they were so many zoological species" (308). The tragic obviously does not exclude the comic in Oviedo's "zoological sociology."

23. J. Huizinga, *The Waning of the Middle Ages* (New York, 1964), 278.

24. See Michele di Cuneo, "Letter on the Second Voyage," 28 October 1495, in *Journals and Other Documents on the Life and Voyages of Christopher Columbus*, ed. Samuel Eliot Morison, 216.

25. Hayden White, "Introduction: Tropology, Discourse, and the Modes of Human Consciousness," in *Tropics* (see Introduction, n. 6), 4: "It also moves 'back and forth' (like a shuttle?) between alternative ways of encoding this reality, some of which may be provided by the traditions of discourse prevailing in a given domain of inquiry and others of which may be idiolects of the author, the authority of which he is seeking to establish."

26. Gerbi, *Nature in the New World*, 241.

27. As Daymond Turner points out: "As a servant of the crown prince he had come to know Flemish painters who frequented the court. During his subsequent travels in Italy he had acquired at least a nodding acquaintance with Leonardo da Vinci, Michelangelo, Mantegna, and other outstanding painters of the renaissance" ("Forgotten Treasure from the Indies: The Illustrations and Drawings of Fernández de Oviedo," *Huntington Library Quarterly* 48:1 [Winter 1985]: 1–46, 1–2). See also Gerbi, *Nature of the New World*, 181–83.

28. Quoted in Honour, *The New Golden Land* (see chapter 1, n. 32), 46.

29. Ludwig Wittgenstein, *Philosophical Investigations*, trans. G. E. M. Anscombe (New York, 1968), 159.

30. On the Scots and Irish, see Steven Mullaney, "Strange Things, Gross Terms, Curious Customs: The Rehearsal of Cultures in the Late Renaissance," *Representations* 3 (1983): 40–67, 49–50. Although the first demonologists in the New World were trained in the Basque countries during the 1520s, the discourse is "enriched" with new information. De Lancre speaks not only about a change of abode but also about forms and ways the devil learned in the New World. For details on the above, consult Julio Caro Baroja, *Las brujas y su mundo* (Madrid, 1966), 187–218.

31. On the monstrous and the question of heredity in the sixteenth century, see François Jacob, *The Logic of Living Systems: A History of Heredity*, trans. Betty E. Spillmann (London, 1970), 19–28.

32. Juxtaposed statements as quoted in Gerbi, *La naturaleza de las Indias Nuevas: De Cristóbal Colón a Gonzalo Fernández de Oviedo*, trans. Antonio Alatorre (Mexico City, 1978), 317, and *Nature in the New World*, 262. My interpretation of these passages differs from that of Gerbi, who labors to smooth out the ideological and practical implications; for Gerbi the exotic is a natural category and not a product of discourse.

33. See Gonzalo Fernández de Oviedo y Valdés, *Historia general y natural de las Indias*, 4 vols., ed. José Amador de los Ríos (Madrid, 1851–55), 1:viii. For reproductions of the drawings I discuss here and a study of the transformations Oviedo's drawings and woodcuts have undergone in different editions, including Oviedo's editions of the *Sumario* and the *Historia*, see Turner, "Forgotten Treasure from the Indies." Gerbi points out that Oviedo's woodcuts are certainly not masterpieces, but adds the following on the modifications of Amador de los Ríos: "They still retain a certain documentary quality and naivety of feature that are altogether lacking in the refined versions" (*Nature in the New World*, 182, n. 216). I owe the information on Oviedo's revised hammock to Kathleen Myers.

34. Cf. Stephanie Merrim, "The Apprehension of the New in Nature and Culture: Fernández de Oviedo's *Sumario*," in *1492–1992: Re/Discovering Colonial Writing*, 165–99, esp. 187; Josefina Zoraida Vázquez, "El indio americano y su circunstancia en la obra de Fernández de Oviedo," *Revista de Indias* 17:69–70 (1957): 483–519, esp. 497 and passim.

35. On the reformist and observant positions as well as on the mystical tradition dominant among the Franciscans in Spain before the Conquest of Mexico, see John Leddy Phelan, *The Millenial Kingdom of the Franciscans in the New World*. 2d ed. (Berkeley and Los Angeles, 1970), and Georges Baudot, *Utopie et histoire*.

36. The instructions by Quiñones that I will quote hereafter are included as supporting documents by Fray Gerónimo de Mendieta, *Historia eclesiástica indiana*, ed. Joaquín García Icazbalceta (Mexico City, 1971), 200; hereafter cited in the text. English versions are my translations.

37. It has been pertinently insisted upon that the parallelism with the apostles should be taken, not in terms of an evangelical method, but as a motif to enhance the Franciscan mission in the Indies, notably by Edwin Edward Sylvest, *Motifs of Franciscan Mission Theory in Sixteenth-Century New Spain Province of the Holy Ghost* (Washington, D.C., 1975), and Pedro Borges, *Métodos misionales en la cristianización de América* (Madrid, 1960).

38. Phelan, *The Millenial Kingdom*, 24.

39. For detailed expositions of the influence exerted by Joachim of Flora, see ibid., 22–25, and Baudot, *Utopie et histoire*, 76–85. Also of interest are Luis Weckmann, "Las esperanzas millenarias de los Franciscanos de la Nueva España," *Historia mexicana* 32:1 (1982): 89–105, and Elsa Cecilia Frost, "El milenarismo franciscano en México y el profeta Daniel," *Historia mexicana* 26:1 (1976): 1–28. On the messianic and apocalyptic climate reigning in Spain during the same period, see Marcel Bataillon, *Erasmo y España: Estudio sobre la historia espiritual del siglo XVI*, trans. Antonio Alatorre (Mexico City, 1950), 51–71. For a study of Joachim of Flora, see Henry Bett, *Joachim of Flora* (London, 1931).

40. This letter from 2 January 1555 is contained in the documentary appendix to Fray Toribio (de Benavente) Motolinía, *Memoriales o libro de la Nueva España y de los naturales de ella*, ed. Edmundo O'Gorman (Mexico City, 1971), 412. Quotations from Motolinía, hereafter cited in the text, correspond to this edition; English versions are my translations.

41. For details on Ramírez de Fuenleal's instructions, see Baudot, *Utopie et histoire*, 34–43.

42. On the city as Paradise, see William Alexander McClung, *The Architecture of Paradise: Survivals of Eden and Jerusalem* (Berkeley and Los Angeles, 1983), and Terry Comito, "Renaissance Gardens and the Discovery of Paradise," *Journal of the History of Ideas* 32:4 (1971): 483–506.

43. See Georges Baudot, "Pretendientes al imperio mexicano en 1576," *Historia mexicana* 20:1 (1970): 42–54.

44. On this negative climate, see Baudot, *Utopie et histoire*, 475–507.

45. Fray Gerónimo de Mendieta, *Historia eclesiástica*, 15 (see n. 36).

46. Joaquín García Icazbalceta, *Nueva colección de documentos para la historia de México*, 3 vols. (Mexico City, 1941), 1:7; my translation.

47. See Phelan, *The Millenial Kingdom*, 56.

48. For a study of the transformations that the image of the natives underwent in Franciscan writings during the sixteenth century, see J. Jorge Klor de Alva, "Christianization and the Concept of Self: The Sixteenth-Century Aztec," *Campo Libre* 1:1 (1981): 25–33.

49. See Baudot, *Utopie et histoire*, 119–25.

50. From a passage quoted and translated by Georges Baudot, "Apariciones diabólicas en un texto náhuatl de Fray Andrés de Olmos," *Estudios de cultura náhuatl* 10 (1972): 349–57, 354.

51. For a study of acculturation as a transformation of the sense of the real and the imaginary, see Serge Gruzinski, *La colonization de l'imaginaire: Sociétés indigènes et occidentalization dans le Mexique espagnol XVIe–XVIIIe siècle* (Paris, 1988).

52. Baudot, "Apariciones diabólicas," 357; my translation.

53. On the colonization of Nahuatl, see Klor de Alva, "Language, Politics, and Translation" (see Introduction, n. 16). For studies of the normalization of family life and sexuality, see Klor de Alva, "Contar vidas" (see Introduction, n. 16); Serge Gruzinski, "Confesión, alianza y sexualidad entre los indios de Nueva España: Introducción al estudio de los confesionarios en lenguas indígenas," in *El placer de pecar y el afán de normar*, (Mexico City, 1987), 171–215; idem, "La 'conquista de los cuerpos'. (Cristianismo, alianza y sexualidad en el altiplano mexicano, siglo XVI)," in *Familia y sexualidad en la Nueva España* (Mexico City, 1982), 177–205.

54. This extraordinary effort to incorporate the voice of the other into the encyclopedia without value judgments and intepretations has prompted an equally striking commentary by Todorov in *The Conquest of America*: "It is as if we were suddenly reading a page from some *nouveau roman* . . .; we are reading pure description" (230). I do not know what "pure" description would be, considering that all descriptions imply a taxonomic grid. Moreover, such purity is inconsequential to our purposes, which are concerned not with evaluating attitudes toward the "Other" but with modes of collecting and assembling information in an encyclopedic compendium. The question of a description by the Indians implies gaining access to the rules informing their system of representation. For a general assessment of the false opposition between description and narrative, and the semiological and taxonomical competence all descriptions imply, see Philippe Hamon, *Introduction à l'analyse du descriptif* (Paris, 1981), 54 and passim.

55. For a study of the methods, scopes, and limits of Sahagún's ethnographic project, see Klor de Alva, "Sahagún and the Birth of Modern Ethnography" (see chapter 3, n. 18), and Alfredo López Austin, "The Research Method of Fray Bernardino de Sahagún: The Questionnaires," in *Sixteenth-Century Mexico: The Work of Sahagún*, ed. Munro Edmonson (Albuquerque, 1974), 111–49.

56. Sahagún, *Florentine Codex* (see chatper 3, n. 41), 13:59; hereafter cited in the text.

57. Although I depart from Edmundo O'Gorman's interpretation of Las Casas, I feel that his introduction and appendices to Bartolomé de Las Casas, *Apologética historia sumaria*, 2 vols., ed. Edmundo O'Gorman (Mexico City,

1967), 1:xiii–cixix, offers an excellent introduction to the works of Las Casas and the critical literature. Since O'Gorman's introduction engages in a polemic with Lewis Hanke over the modernity of Las Casas, see Hanke's response in "Bartolomé de Las Casas historiador," preliminary study to Fray Bartolomé de Las Casas, *Historia de las Indias*, 3 vols., ed. Augustín Millares Carlo (Mexico City, 1965), 1:ix–lxxxvi. I believe it is justified to consider Las Casas the most monumental figure in sixteenth-century Spanish historiography of the New World, inasmuch as his writings were not only influential in Spain but throughout Europe. All English versions of Las Casas are my translations.

58. Bartolomé de Las Casas, *Brevíssima relación de la destruyción de las Indias*, facsimile ed. Manuel Ballesteros Gaibrois (Madrid, 1977), n.p.

59. Las Casas, *Historia de las Indias*, 3:251. For a study of similarities between Cortés's and Las Casas's conceptions of how the New World should be organized, see Helen Nader, "The One World and Two Americas of Hernando Cortés and Bartolomé de Las Casas," *Dispositio* 14:36–38 (1989): 213–23.

60. It is not a question of denying the grounds for the denunciation, as the retractors of the Black Legend do, but of highlighting the motifs as well as their rhetorical function.

61. Las Casas, *Brevíssima*, n.p; see Ballesteros Gaibrois's note 52 for commentary and location of the passage. As Ballesteros Gaibrois states in note 1 to the facsimile edition of the *Brevíssima*: "En la forma hay una constante inseguridad, abultamiento, exageración y sistemática censura, que por sí misma se desacredita como fuente histórica, es decir, que no es lícito científicamente especular con las cifras de Fr. B." [In its form itself there is an insecurity, enlargement, exaggeration, and systematic censorship that in itself discredits itself as historical source; that is, it is not licit to speculate scientifically with the figures of Fr. B.] (172).

62. José Antonio Maravall, "Utopía y primitivismo en el pensamiento de Las Casas," *Revista de occidente* 141 (1974): 311–88, 324; my translation.

63. See ibid., 327–43, for specifics about the utopia of Las Casas and Maravall's version of a secular as well as modern Las Casas. See also Stelio Cros, *Realidad y utopía en el descubrimiento y conquista de América hispánica* (Troy, N.Y., 1983), and "La utopía cristiano-social en el Nuevo Mundo," *Anales de literatura hispanoamericana* 6:7 (1978): 87–129. Lewis Hanke, *The Spanish Struggle for Justice in the Conquest of America* (Philadelphia, 1949).

64. At the risk of making our Dominican a sixteenth-century Foucault, I have used the term "discursive practices" to explicate the tragic perspective Las Casas holds on the discovery of America. For Las Casas, however homicidal his theory might be, the destruction of the Indies is less a result of "evil" individuals than of a whole range of cultural patterns that inform the appropriation and expansion in the Americas. Cf. Miguel León-Portilla, "Quetzalcoatl-Cortés," (see chapter 3, n. 53), 23–24.

65. The *Historia de las Indias* was not published until 1875, but several historians had access to the manuscript as early as the sixteenth century. The *Apologética*, originally intended to form part of the *Historia* and written between 1555 and 1559, had a similar destiny and was not published in its entirety until 1902. O'Gorman and Hanke, in the preliminary studies alluded to in note 57, hold different explications for the rationale that led Las Casas to

separate the two texts. I simply refer the curious reader to these introductory studies, since in this essay we are concerned not with the specific motivations Las Casas had for writing a text but with tropes and formal structures in Las Casas's concept and representation of the New World.

66. Henri Baudet, *Paradise on Earth: Some Thoughts on European Images of Non-European man* (New Haven, Conn., 1965), 32.

67. Las Casas, *Apológetica* 1:49; hereafter cited in the text.

68. White, "The Noble Savage Theme," in *Tropics*, 183.

69. Baudet, *Paradise on Earth*, 32.

70. Cf. Christian Marouby, *Utopie et primitivisme: Essai sur l'imaginaire anthropologique à l'âge classique* (Paris, 1991), 45–50 and passim.

71. For a study of a study of the texts and experiments as well as conflicting interpretations of Cumana and Vera Paz, see Marcel Bataillon, *Estudios sobre Bartolomé de Las Casas*, trans. J. Coderch and J. A. Martínez Schrem (Barcelona, 1976), esp. 137–243. The most complete study to date of Cumana continues to be Manuel Giménez Fernández, *Bartolomé de Las Casas*, 2 vols. (Seville, 1953, 1960).

72. Phelan, "El imperio cristiano de Las Casas," 309.

73. See, for instance, "Carta al Maestro Fray Bartolomé Carranza de Miranda," in *Obras escogidas de Bartolomé de Las Casas: Opúsculos, cartas y memoriales*, ed. Juan Pérez de Tudela (Madrid, 1958). This break is already implicit in the introduction's opening statement to the *Apológetica*: "La causa final de escribilla fue cognoscer todas y tan infinitas naciones desde vastísimo orbe infamadas por algunos . . . [que han publicado] que no eran gentes de buena razón para gobernarse, carecientes de humana policía y ordenadas republicas no por más de por las hallar tan mansas, pacientes y humildes . . ." [The final cause for writing it has been to provide knowledge about all and so infinite nations of this immensely vast orb that have been defamed by some . . . [who have published] that they were not peoples with sufficient reason to govern themselves, lacking human institutions and ordered republics simply on the grounds that they were peaceful, patient, and humble . . .] (1:3). The only possible corollary of this statement is the recognition of the sovereignty and legitimacy of their rulers.

74. For a reading of the *noble savage* and the paradisiacal *natural garden* as utopian discursive practices, see José Rabasa, "Utopian Ethnology in Las Casas's *Apológetica*," in *1492–1992: Re/Discovering Colonial Writing*, 263–89. I derive the notion of utopian discourse from Louis Marin, *Utopics: Spatial Play*, trans. Robert A. Vollrath (Atlantic Highlands, N.J., 1984). On Marin, see Frederic Jameson, "On Islands and Trenches: Naturalization and the Production of Utopian Discourse," *Diacritics* 7 (June 1977): 2–21. I now put *noble savage* and *natural garden* in italics to underscore that they no longer function as a mere theme but as utopian discursive devices.

75. For instance, see Américo Castro, "Fray Bartolomé de Las Casas o Casaus," in *Mélanges à la mémoire de Jean Sarrailh*, 2 vols. (Paris, 1966), 1:211–44. On the *estatutos de sangre* (blood statutes) and the formation of the Spanish nation, see Marc Shell, "Marranos (Pigs); or, From Coexistence to Toleration," *Cultural Inquiry* 17:2 (Winter 1991): 306–35.

76. Marin, *Utopics*, 10.

77. Cf. Anthony Pagden, *The Fall of Natural Man: The American Indian and the Origins of Comparative Anthropology* (Cambridge, 1982), esp. 119–45.

78. In this respect, I believe O'Gorman is incorrect when he states in his preliminary study to the *Apologética*: "En efecto, ya para entonces, todas las mentes más alertas comulgaban en la idea de la independencia e individualidad geográfica de América como un 'continente'; pero el padre Las Casas se empeño, a contrapelo de esa opinión en probar que América era una porción territorial de Asia y por lo tanto, a revelarnos que seguía pensando en términos del antiguo esquema tripartita de la ecumene. Y es que además de ser eso lo que realmente creía al escribir aquel capítulo resultaba así, que el indio americano era un oriental" [In fact, by then all the more alert minds shared the idea of a geographic individuality of America; but Father Las Casas insisted, against the grain of that opinion, to demonstrate that America was a territorial portion of Asia and, therefore, to reveal to us that he continued to think in terms of the tripartite schema of the ecumene. And as a consequence of holding these beliefs when he wrote that chapter, the American Indian ended up being an Oriental] (lxxvii). Unfortunately, either O'Gorman is incorrect or my position on Las Casas's metonymic view of American climate and people goes overboard. I believe O'Gorman's interpretation is too geographically literal, and is obviously concerned with making Las Casas fit into his scheme on the invention of America. Thus he misses the rhetorical gist of the chapter: the enthymeme flows from a vision of America draped with resemblances referring to a legendary India *ultra Gangem* to an exposition of a thesaurus of marvelous things he wants to isolate as pertinent to the Indies.

79. See Delacampagne, *L'invention du racisme* (see chapter 2, n. 30), esp. 233–50.

80. See the line of argumentation in the *Apologética* I:130.

81. See Lewis Hanke, "Introducción, in *Del único modo de atraer a todos los pueblos a la verdadera religión*, 2d ed., trans. Atenógenes Santamaria and ed. Agustín Millares Carlo (Mexico City, 1975).

82. For a feminist argument on values and pluralism in objectivity and science, see Helen Longino, *Science as Social Knowledge: Values and Objectivity in Scientific Inquiry* (Princeton, N.J., 1990).

83. Cf. Anthony Pagden, "*Ius et factum*: Text and Experience in the Writings of Bartolomé de Las Casas," *Representations* 33 (1991): 147–62.

84. Marin, *Utopics*, 195.

CHAPTER 5. ALLEGORIES OF ATLAS

1. See G. R. Crone, *Maps and Their Makers: An Introduction to the History of Cartography* (London, 1968), 110. Atlas is represented as fabricating a celestial sphere in the first title page to the *Atlas*, and, in "The Preface vpon Atlas," where Mercator explains the title, he presents himself as drawing his inspiration from the fabled king of Mauretania: "My purpose then is to followe this Atlas, a man so excelling in erudition, humanite, and wisdome" (Mercator, Hondius, Janssonium, *Atlas: or, Geographicke Description of the World*, 2 vols., facsimile ed. of the English translation by Henry Hexham [Amsterdam, 1968], n.p; hereafter cited in the text). English versions of passages in Latin are my translation.

Notes to pages 180-86

2. After describing the topics pertaining to Creation, Mercator adds: "Afterward I will handle Coelestial things in their ranke: then the Astronomicks; which appertayne to conjecture by the Starrs. Fourthly, treat of things Elementarie, & lastly the Geographicks."

3. See J. Keuning, "The History of an Atlas, Mercator-Hondius," *Imago Mundi* 4 (1947): 37–62.

4. Gérard Genette, *Palimpsestes: La litérature au second degré* (Paris, 1982), 451.

5. See chapter 1 for a full quotation and elaboration of Quintilian's notion of irony as illusion in my analysis of Stradanus's allegory.

6. On the *Relaciones geográficas*, see the studies by Howard F. Cline, Donald Robertson, and H. R. Harvey in the *Handbook of Middle American Indians*, vol. 12, ed. Howard Cline (Austin, Tex., 1972). More recently on a specific *Relación* and the coexistence of different cartographical systems, see Walter Mignolo, "El mandato y la ofrenda: La descripción de la ciudad y provincia de Tlaxcala, de Diego Muñoz Camargo y las Relaciones de Indias," *Nueva revista de filología hispánica* 35:2 (1987): 451–84, and idem, "Colonial Situations" (see Introduction, n. 16), esp. 120–32.

7. Clinton R. Edwards, "Mapping by Questionnaire: An Early Spanish Attempt to Determine New World Geographic Positions," *Imago Mundi* 23 (1969): 17–28, 17.

8. For an analysis of the *Relaciones* as hybrid cartographies, see Mignolo, "Colonial Situations," 120–24 and passim. Gruzinski (*La colonization de l'imaginaire* [see chapter 3, n. 51], 104 and passim), studies the adoption of alphabetical writing and Western pictorial conventions as processes of acculturation.

9. Gayatri Chakravorty Spivak, "Revolutions That as Yet Have No Model: Derrida's Limited Inc.," *Diacritics* 10:4 (1980): 29–49.

10. Paul de Man, *Allegories of Reading* (New Haven, Conn., 1979), 17.

11. Cf. Mignolo, "Colonial Situations," 135, n. 3.

12. De Man dismisses history from different points of view. However, one notion that seems to recur in his work is the impossibility of writing a history of romanticism: "The ultimate 'proof' of the fact that Romanticism puts the genetic pattern of history in question would then be the impossibility of writing a history of Romanticism" (*Allegories of Reading*, 82). Here we are concerned not with romanticism per se but with the questioning of the "genetic pattern." The only historical perspective where de Man seems to feel comfortable corresponds to a sort of monumental history well in accord with the omnipresent idealities that a deconstruction of literature would repeat and collect in the language of criticism.

13. See Foucault, *The Order of Things*, 17–43, for an elucidation of the nature of specularity in sixteenth-century knowledge. The understanding of specular signs as natural is defined in *The Port-Royal Logic* (1662); as Foucault points out, "It is characteristic that the first example of a sign given by the *Logique de Port-Royal* is not the word, nor the cry, nor the symbol, but the spatial and graphic representation—the drawing as map or picture. This is because the picture has no other content in fact than that which it represents, and yet that content is made visible only because it is represented by a representation" (64). We may take the primacy of pictures to exemplify a binary

system as an operation on the nature of cartography itself; as examples of binarism, maps are set in a process of unmotivation where the ideological traces that constituted them disappear. See also the discussion of specular images, portraits, and maps in Louis Marin, "A propos du signe naturel: Cartes et tableaux," in his *Etudes sémiologiques* (Paris, 1971): 162–75.

14. Most studies of cartography have unfortunately separated the appraisals of precision from discussions of the allegories surrounding the maps. Charting is taken as merely the objective positioning of points in space without ideological implications. Notable exceptions among other studies already mentioned are the following: Frank Lestringant, "Fictions de l'espace brésilien à la Renaissance; L'example de Guanabara," in *Arts et légendes d'espaces: Figures de voyage et rhétoriques du monde*, ed. Christian Jacob and Frank Lestringant (Paris, 1981), 295–56; Louis Marin, *Le portrait du Roi* (Paris, 1981), esp. 209–21; and Alpers, "The Mapping Impulse in Dutch Art," chapter 4 in *Art of Describing* (see Introduction, n. 1). Since I first wrote the early version of this chapter (see José Rabasa, "Allegories of the *Atlas*," in Barker et al, eds., *Europe and Its Others* [see Introduction, n. 16], 2:1–16), a series of influential essays by J. B. Harley have elaborated systematic ideological unmaskings of objectivity and positivism in maps, while calling for a postmodern reconstruction of cartography as a discipline; see "Maps, Knowledge, and Power," in *The Iconography of Landscape: Essays on the Symbolic Representation, Design, and Use of Past Environments*, ed. Denis Cosgrove and Stephen Daniels (Cambridge, 1988), 277–312; idem, "Deconstructing the Map," *Cartographica* 26:2 (Summer 1989): 1–20; the responses to J. B. Harley's article "Deconstructing the Map," *Cartographica* 26:3–4 (1989): 89–127; and "Cartography, Ethics, and Social Theory," *Cartographica* 27:2 (Summer 1990): 1–23. Though drawing from deconstruction, these essays offer a different line of argument to the one advanced in this chapter. Here we are much less concerned with unmasking an ideology than with examining self-deconstructive moves in the *Atlas* itself—and ultimately with tracing areas of blindness that have always entailed possible readings and reinventions of the world from indigenous and non-Eurocentric perspectives. Also of interest are the essays in the special edition dedicated to mapping in *Word and Image* (see Introduction, n. 2).

15. Following Genette we may refer the notion of palimpsest to Lévi-Strauss's understanding of bricolage as the art of making the new with the old (*Palimpsestes*, 45). On the adoption of the term *bricolage* for characterizing the formation of structural sets, not directly out of other structured sets, but using odds and ends of events, see Lévi-Strauss, *The Savage Mind* (see chapter 2, n. 10), 16–36. Both the mapmaker and the addressee are *bricoleurs* in an open-ended structuring and restructuring of the world.

16. Such a binary opposition is not rigid, inasmuch as it always calls forth a third term. For instance, the opposition between the eternal and the contingent refers to a continuous creation where chaos and form never have a pure existence within a Christian theology such as the one Mercator exposes. See Gerhart B. Ladner, "Medieval and Modern Understanding of Symbolism: A Comparison," *Speculum* 54:2 (1979): 223–56.

17. Although the world map is on a stereographic projection, the Mercator projection constitutes an integral part of the conceptualization of the *Atlas*

Notes to pages 189–92

since the Map of the World of 1569, where Mercator first explained its use in navigation. For the 1595 edition of the *Atlas* Mercator's heirs drafted a stereographic version of a world map, as well as versions of the different continents, based on the geographic conceptions of the 1569 Map of the World. In the *Atlas* Mercator explains his projection in "An Advice to the Use of Maps" (2:275–76). For information on the antecedents of Mercator, the resistance to the adoption of the projection, the distortions all projections introduce, and the theoretical contributions of Edward Wright, see Crone, *Maps and Their Makers*, 102–7; and Leo Bagrow, *History of Cartography*, trans. D. L. Paisey (Cambridge, 1964), 119. Also of interest are Philip and Juliana Muehrcke, *Map Use: Reading, Analysis, and Interpretation* (Madison, Wis., 1978), and John Wright, "Map Makers are Human: Comments on the Subjective in Maps," *Cartographica* 19 (1977): 8–25.

Marshall Hodgson has referred to the Mercator world map as the "'Jim-Crow' projection because it shows Europe as larger than Africa" ("The Interrelations of Societies in History," *Comparative Studies in Society and History* 5:2 [1963]: 227–50, 228). In order to correct this distortion, Hodgson calls for an equal-area world map. However amusing the "Jim-Crow" trope might be, it seems gratuitous to attribute to Mercator a conscious or even an unconscious desire to aggrandize Europe. Note that in the *Atlas*'s world map the smallness of India with respect to England, for instance, corresponds not only to the projection used but also to a lack of precise information about the coastline of India. Moreover, Mercator may have devised the first equal-area projection, which was first used in a map of South America. For equal-area maps by Mercator, consult Wellman Chamberlin, *The Round Earth on Flat Paper* (Washington D.C., 1947), 73, and Norman J. W. Thrower, "New Geographic Horizons: Maps," in *First Images of America* (see chapter 1, n. 29), 2:662. Beyond a question of center, of size, or of giving every culture its due in the formation of modernity as Hodgson proposes, my analysis of the *Atlas* seeks to show how Eurocentrism permeates the world by means of a semantics of space that reduces the meaning of cartographical representations to the signs Europeans appropriate and project on the surface of the Earth.

18. The difference between Mercator's world map and Juan de la Cosa's chart implies a movement from an organization of space closely associated with the experience of the life-world and a symbolic investment of the different regions, to one ruled by an abstract motivation. See Kappler, *Monstres, démons et merveilles* (see chapter 2, n. 35), 31–43, for symbolic investments and organizations of space in medieval cartography. See also Gilles Deleuze and Félix Guattari, *Capitalisme et schizophrénie: Mille plateaux* (Paris, 1980), 597–602, for a characterization of these cartographical differences in terms of *espace lisse* (smooth space) and *espace strié* (striped space), and their nautical implications.

19. Abraham Ortelius, *Theater of the Whole World*, facsimile of the 1606 ed. (Amsterdam, 1968), n.p.

20. See the national characters depicted at the end of the section dedicated to Europe (*Atlas*, 1:42). The case of the inclusion of Ireland within the British Isles exemplifies forgetfulness within a European territory: "These are the manners of the wild Irish, who since the later reigne of Queene Elyzabeth, and

249

King Jeames, both of blessed memory; & now under the Government of our Soveraigne King Charles, they are much reformed and civilized, and have good orders and manners among them, which they have learned of the English in these peaceable times, that inhabit in most parts of Ireland" (1:84). Passages such as this give us a taste of the "Englishing" of the world brought forth by Hexham's translation.

21. The emblem of the geographer as Atlas represents the task of cartography as moving from one stable global totality to another where details are corrected. As such the *Atlas* is a palimpsest. The copyright and title have been erased and supplanted by Hexham's; the peoples decorating the map are also a later addition. For the original version of the title page of the 1595 edition, see Skelton's introduction to the facsimile edition of Hexham's 1636 translation, 1:xiv.

22. See Randles, *De la terre plate*, 17–20. See also Josephine Waters Bennett, *The Rediscovery of Sir John Mandeville* (New York, 1954), 255–57, and William J. Entwistle, "The Spanish Mandevilles," *Modern Language Review* 17 (1922): 251–57.

23. See John Mandeville, *Mandeville's Travels* (Nendeln, Liechtenstein, 1967), 1–3.

24. Kappler (*Monstres, démons et merveilles*, 71–111) has an excellent exposition of the relationship between romance, eschatology, and travel. See also Bennett, *Sir John Mandeville*, 40–53, and Roux, *Les explorateurs* (see chapter 2, n. 20), 222–55.

25. For a detailed analysis of Mandeville's transformation of passages derived from previous accounts, see Bennett, *Sir John Mandeville*.

26. For a discussion of the narratives used for the construction of the Catalan Atlas, see Crone, *Maps and Their Makers*, 39–49.

27. On the importance of Ptolemy's cartographic method and parallelism with the transformation of visual representation by Brunelleschi and Alberti, see Samuel Y. Edgerton, *The Renaissance Rediscovery of Linear Perspective* (New York, 1975), 91–123. Cf. Alpers, "Mapping Impulse in Dutch Art."

28. Georges Canguilhem, "Monstrosity and the Monstrous," *Diogenes* 40 (1972): 27–42.

29. See Michel Beaujour, "Genus universum," *Glyph* 7 (1980): 15–31, 27–30.

30. Ibid., 27.

31. See Ashcroft, Griffiths, and Tiffin, *The Empire Writes Back* (see Introduction, n. 15). For an elaboration of the notion of "writing back" in the context of Said's *Orientalism*, see Clifford's review essay of *Orientalism* (see Introduction, n. 17).

32. For a theory of cultural decolonization that builds on this point, see Graham Huggan, "Decolonizing the Map: Post-Colonialism, Post-Structuralism, and the Cartograhpic Connection," *Ariel* 20:4 (October 1989): 115–31.

33. For a discussion of differences between postmodernism and the postcolonial experience see Kwame Anthony Appiah, "Is the Post- in Postmodernism the Post- in Postcolonial?" *Cultural Critique* 17:2 (Winter 1991): 336–57, and Ashcroft, Griffiths, and Tiffin, *The Empire Writes Back*, esp. 161–65.

EPILOGUE

1. Acosta, *Historia natural y moral* (see Introduction, n. 3), 13; hereafter cited in the text.

2. See Marc Shell, "From Coexistence to Toleration" (see chapter 4, n. 75). For an analysis of missionary methods and their place in the history of the social sciences, see Claude Bénichou, "A propos d'une 'dette' méthodologique," in *Naissance de l'ethnologie?*, ed. Claude Blanckaert (Paris, 1985): 23–42.

3. See, for example, Linda Y. C. Lim, "Capitalism, Imperialism, and Patriarchy: The Dilemma of Third-World Women Workers in Multinational Factories," in *Women, Men, and the International Division of Labor*, ed. June Nash and María Patricia Fernández-Kelly (Albany, N.Y., 1983), 71–101. For a critique, see Aihwa Ong, "Colonialism and Modernity: Feminist Re-presentation of Women in Non-Western Societies," *Inscriptions* 3–4, special issue on *Feminism and the Critique of Colonial Discourse* (1988): 79–93.

4. See the significance of this quotation of Derrida in the context of an interview of Gayatri Spivak with John Hutnyk, Scott McQuire, and Nicos Papastergiadis, "Strategy, Identity, Writing," in *The Post-Colonial Critic* (see Introduction, n. 36), 44–45 and passim.

5. See de Certeau, "Walking in the City," chapter 7 of *The Practice of Everyday Life* (see chapter 1, n. 28).

Bibliography

Acosta, Joseph de. *Historia natural y moral de las Indias*. Edited by Edmundo O'Gorman. Mexico City: Fondo de Cultura Económica, 1979.

Adorno, Rolena. "Discourse on Colonialism: Bernal Díaz, Las Casas, and the Twentieth-Century Reader." *Modern Language Notes* 103:2 (March 1988): 239–58.

———. *Guamán Poma: Writing and Resistance in Colonial Peru*. Austin: University of Texas Press, 1986.

———. "Literary Production and Suppression: Reading and Writing about Amerindians in Colonial Spanish America." *Dispositio* 11: 28–29 (1986): 1–25.

———. "On the Pictorial Language and the Typology of Culture in a New World Chronicle." *Semiotica* 36:1–2 (1982): 1–31.

———, ed. *From Oral to Written Expression: Native Andean Chroniclers of the Early Colonial Period*. Foreign and Comparative Studies/Latin American Monograph Series, no. 4. Syracuse, N.Y.: Maxwell School of Citizenship and Public Affairs, Syracuse University, 1982.

Ailly, Pierre d'. *Ymago mundi*. 3 vols. Translated by Edmund Buron. Paris: Maisonneuve, 1930.

Alfonso X. *Las siete partidas del rey Alfonso X el Sabio*. Madrid: Imprenta Real, 1807.

Alighieri, Dante. *The Divine Comedy*. Translated by H. R. Huse. New York: Holt, Rinehart and Wilson, 1968.

Alpers, Svetlana. *The Art of Describing: Dutch Art in the Seventeenth Century*. Chicago: University of Chicago Press, 1983.

Alvar, Manuel. "Bernal Díaz del Castillo." In Iñigo Madrigal, ed., *Historia de la literatura hispanoamericana*.

Alvarado Tezozomoc, Hernando. *Crónica mexicana*. Preceded by the *Códice Ramírez*. Preliminary study and notes by Manuel Orosco y Berra. Mexico City: Porrúa, 1980.

Amin, Samir. *Eurocentrism*. Translated by Russell Moore. New York: Monthly Review Press, 1989.

Amsler, Jean. *La Renaissance (1415–1600)*. Vol. 2 of *Histoire universelle des explorations*, edited by L. H. Parias. Paris: Nouvelle librairie de France, 1955.

Anderson, Arthur J. O., Frances Berdan, and James Lockhart. *Beyond the Codices: The Nahua View of Colonial Mexico*. Berkeley and Los Angeles: University of California Press, 1976.

Bibliography

Anderson Imbert, Enrique. *Historia de la literatura hispanoamericana*. Vol. 1. Mexico City and Buenos Aires: Fondo de Cultura Económica, 1962.

Apel, Karl-Otto. "Intentions, Conventions, and Reference to Things: Dimensions of Understanding Meaning in Hermeneutics and in Analytic Philosophy of Language." In *Meaning and Understanding*, edited by Herman Parret and Jacques Bouveresse. Berlin and New York: Walter de Gruyter, 1981.

Appiah, Kwame Anthony. "Is the Post- in Postmodernism the Post- in Postcolonial?" *Critical Inquiry* 17:2 (Winter 1991): 336–57.

Arens, W. *The Man-Eating Myth: Anthropology and Anthropophagy*. New York: Oxford University Press, 1979.

Armas, Frederick A. de. *The Return of Astraea: An Astral-Imperial Myth in Calderón*. Lexington: University Press of Kentucky, 1986.

Arrom, José J. "Gonzalo Fernández de Oviedo, relator de episodios y narrador de naufragios." *Ideologies and Literature* 4:17 (1983): 133–45.

Asad, Talal. "The Concept of Cultural Translation in British Social Anthropology." In Clifford and Marcus, eds., *Writing Culture*.

——, ed. *Anthropology and the Colonial Encounter*. London: Ithaca Press, 1973.

Ashcom, B. B. "The First Builder of Boats in *El Burlador*." *Hispanic Review* 11 (1943): 328–33.

Ashcroft, Bill, Gareth Griffiths, and Helen Tiffin. *The Empire Writes Back: Theory and Practice in Post-Colonial Literatures*. London and New York: Routledge, 1989.

Bagrow, Leo. *History of Cartography*. Translated by D. L. Paisey, revised by R. A. Skelton. Cambridge, Mass.: Harvard University Press, 1964.

Bakewell, P. J. *Silver Mining and Society in Colonial Mexico*. Cambridge: Cambridge University Press, 1971.

Bakhtin, M. M. "Discourse and the Novel." In *The Dialogic Imagination: Four Essays*. Translated by Caryl Emerson and Michael Holquist. Austin: University of Texas Press, 1981.

——. "The Problem of Speech Genres." In *Speech Genres and Other Late Essays*, translated by Vern W. Macgee, edited by Caryl Emerson and Michael Holquist. Austin: University of Texas Press, 1986.

Balbuena, Bernardo de. *La grandeza mexicana*. Edited with the *Compendio apologético en alabanza de la poesía*. Mexico City: Porrúa, 1971.

Barker, Francis, et al., eds. *Europe and Its Others*. 2 vols. Colchester: University of Essex, 1985.

Barthes, Roland. "L'ancienne rhétorique: Aide-mémoire." *Communications* 16 (1970): 172–245.

——. "The Discourse of History." Translated by Peter Wexler. *Structuralism: A Reader*, edited by Michael Lanek. London: Jonathan Cape, 1970.

——. "L'effet du réel." *Communications* 11 (1968): 84–89.

—— *Elements of Semiology*. Translated by Annette Lavers and Colin Smith. New York: Hill and Wang, 1978.

——. "Myth Today." In *Mythologies*, translated by Annette Lavers. New York: Hill and Wang, 1982.

Bibliography

Bataillon, Marcel. *Erasmo y España: Estudio sobre la historia espiritual del siglo XVI*. Translated by Antonio Alatorre. Mexico City: Fondo de Cultura Económica, 1950.

———. "Hernán Cortés, autor prohibido." In *Libro jubilar de Alfonso Reyes*. Mexico City: Universidad Nacional Autónoma de México, 1959.

Bataillon, Marcel, and Edmundo O'Gorman. *Dos concepciones de la tarea histórica con motivo de la idea del descubrimiento de América*. Mexico City: Imprenta Universitaria, 1955.

Baudet, Henri. *Paradise on Earth: Some Thoughts on European Images of Non-European Man*. Translated by Elysabeth Wentholt. New Haven, Conn.: Yale University Press, 1965.

Baudot, Georges. "Apariciones diabólicas en un texto náhuatl de Fray Andrés de Olmos." *Estudios de cultura náhuatl* 10 (1972): 349–57.

———. "Pretendientes al imperio mexicano en 1576." *Historia mexicana* 20:1 (1970): 42–54.

———. *Utopie et histoire au Mexique: Les premiers chroniqueurs de la civilization mexicaine*. Toulouse: Privat, 1977.

Beaujour, Michel. "Genus universum." *Glyph* 7 (1980): 15–31.

———. "Some Paradoxes of Description." *Yale French Studies* 61 (1978): 27–59.

Bénichou, Claude. "A propos d'une 'dette' méthodologique." In Blanckaert, ed., *Naissance de l'ethnologie?*

Bennett, Josephine Waters. *The Rediscovery of Sir John Mandeville*. New York: Modern Language Association of America, 1954.

Benveniste, Emile. *Problèmes de linguistique générale*. 2 vols. Paris: Gallimard, 1966, 1974.

———. *Problems in General Linguistics*. Coral Gables, Fla.: University of Miami Press, 1971.

Benzoni, Girolamo. *History of the New World*. Translated by W. H. Smith. London: Hakluyt Society, 1857.

Berkhofer, Robert F. *The White Man's Indian: Images of the American Indian from Columbus to the Present*. New York: Knopf, 1978.

Bernal, Ignacio. "Introduction." In Fray Diego de Durán, *The Aztecs: The History of the Indies of New Spain*, edited and translated by Doris Heyden and Fernando Horcasitas. New York: Orion Press, 1964.

Bett, Henry. *Joachim of Flora*. London: Methuen, 1931.

Beverly, John. "Introducción." *Revista de crítica literaria latinoamericana* 18:36 (1992): 7–18.

Bhabha, Homi. "Of Mimicry and Man: The Ambivalence of Colonial Discourse." *October* 28 (1984): 125–33.

———. "Signs Taken for Wonders: Questions of Ambivalence and Authority under a Tree Outside Delhi." In Barker et al., eds., *Europe and Its Others*.

———. "Signs Taken for Wonder: Questions of Ambivalence and Authority under a Tree Outside Delhi, May 1817." In Gates, ed., *"Race," Writing, and Difference*.

Bitterli, Urs. *Los "salvajes" y los "civilizados": El encuentro de Europa y Ultramar*. Translated by Pablo Sorozábal. Mexico City: Fondo de Cultura Económica, 1982.

Bibliography

————. *Die "Wilden" und die "Zivilisierten": Gründzu einer Geistes- und Kulturgeschichte der europäisch-überseeischen Begegnung.* Munich: Verlag C. H. Beck, 1976.

Blanckaert, Claude, ed. *Naissance de l'ethnologie?* Paris: Cerf, 1985.

Bloch, Ernst. *The Principle of Hope*, 3 vols. Translated by Neville Plaice, Stephen Plaice, and Paul Knight. Cambridge, Mass.: MIT Press, 1986.

Boelhower, William. "Inventing America: A Model of Cartographic Semiosis." *Word & Image* 4:2, special issue on *Maps and Mapping*, ed. Stephen Bann and John Dixon Hunt (April–June 1988): 475–509.

Boon, James A. "Comparative De-enlightenment in the History of Ethnology." *Daedalus* 109 (1980): 73–91.

Borah, Woodrow. "New Spain's Century of Depression." *Ibero-Americana* 35 (1951): 1–58.

Borges, Pedro. *Métodos misionales en la cristianización de América.* Madrid: Consejo Superior de Investigaciones Científicas, 1960.

Boucher, Bernadette. *Icon and Conquest: A Structural Analysis of the Illustration of de Bry's Great Voyages.* Translated by Basia Miller Gulati. Chicago: University of Chicago Press, 1981.

Bracken, H. M. "Essence, Accident, and Race." *Hermathena* 116 (1973): 81–96. ✓

Brotherston, Gordon. "Towards a Grammatology of America: Lévi-Strauss, Derrida, and the Native New World Text." In Barker et al., eds., *Europe, and Its Others*.

Brown, Paula, and Donald Tuzin, eds. *The Ethnography of Cannibalism.* Washington, D.C.: Society for Psychological Anthropology, 1983.

Burshatin, Israel. "Power, Discourse, and Metaphor in the *Abencerraje*." *Modern Language Notes* 99 (March 1984): 195–213.

————. "The Moor in the Text: Metaphor, Emblem, and Silence." *Critical Inquiry* 12:1 (Autumn 1985): 98–118.

Cadamosto, Alviso. *The Voyages of Cadamosto.* Translated and edited by G. R. Crone. Nedeln, Liechtenstein: Kraus Reprint, 1967.

Calderón de la Barca, Pedro. *El principe constante.* Edited by Alberto Porqueras Mayo. Madrid: Espasa-Calpe, 1975.

Canguilhem, Georges. "Monstrosity and the Monstrous." *Diogenes* 40 (1972): 27–42.

Carbia, Rómulo D. *Historia de la leyenda negra hispanoamericana.* Buenos Aires: Ediciones Orientación Española, 1943.

Caro Baroja, Julio. *Las brujas y su mundo.* Madrid: Alianza Editorial, 1966.

————. *Los moriscos del Reino de Granada.* Madrid: Istmo, 1976.

Castro, Américo. "Fray Bartolomé de Las Casas o Casaus." In *Mélange à la mémoire de Jean Sarrailh*, vol. 1. Paris: Centre de recherches de l'Institut d'études hispaniques, 1966.

Cate, Chester M. "De Bry and the *Index exporgatorius*." *Bibliographical Society of American Papers* 10 (1916): 136–40.

Certeau, Michel de. *L'écriture de l'histoire.* Paris: Gallimard, 1975. ✓

————. *La fable mystique XVI–XVII siècle.* Paris: Gallimard, 1982.

————. *Heterologies: Discourse on the Other.* Translated by Brian Massumi. ✓ Theory and History of Literature, volume 17. Minneapolis: University of Minnesota Press, 1986.

Bibliography

————. "History: Ethics, Science, and Fiction." In *Social Science as Moral Inquiry*, edited by Norman Hahn. New York: Columbia University Press, 1983.

————. *L'invention du quotidien*. Vol. 1. *Arts de faire*. Paris: Union général d'éditions, coll. 10/18, 1980.

————. "On the Oppositional Practices of Everyday Life." *Social Text* 3 (Fall 1980): 3–43.

————. *The Practice of Everyday Life*. Translated by Steven F. Rendall. Berkeley and Los Angeles: University of California Press, 1984.

————. *The Writing of History*. Translated by Tom Conley. New York: Columbia University Press, 1988.

Chamberlin, Wellman. *The Round Earth on Flat Paper*. Washington, D.C.: National Geographic Society, 1947.

Chang-Rodríguez, Raquel. *La apropiación del signo: Tres cronistas indígenas del Perú*. Tempe: Arizona State University Center for Latin American Studies, 1988.

————, ed. *Prosa virreinal hispanoamericana*. Barcelona: Hispam, 1978.

Chaunu, Pierre. *Conquête et exploration des nouveaux mondes*. Paris: Presses universitaires de France, 1969.

————. *L'expansion européenne du XIIIe au XVe siècle*. Paris: Presses universitaires de France, 1969.

Chevalier, François. *Land and Society in Colonial Mexico: The Great Hacienda*. Translated by Alvin Eustis. Berkeley and Los Angeles: University of California Press, 1970.

Chiappelli, Fredi, ed. *First Images of America: The Impact of the New World on the Old*. 2 vols. Berkeley and Los Angeles: University of California Press, 1976.

Cioranescu, Alejandro. "El descubrimiento de América y el arte de la descripción." In *Colón humanista: Estudios de humanismo atlántico*. Madrid: Editorial Prensa Española, 1967.

Clendinnen, Inga. " 'Fierce and Unnatural Cruelty': Cortés and the Conquest of Mexico." *Representations* 33 (1991): 65–100.

Clifford, James. "On Ethnographic Authority." *Representations* 1 (1983): 118–46.

————. "Power and Dialogue in Ethnography: Marcel Griaule's Initiation." In Stocking, ed., *Observers Observed*.

————. Review of Edward Said's *Orientalism*. *History and Theory* 19:2 (1980): 204–23.

Clifford, James, and George E. Marcus, eds. *Writing Culture: The Poetics and Politics of Ethnography*. Berkeley and Los Angeles: University of California Press, 1986.

Cline, Howard F. "The *Relaciones geográficas* of the Spanish Indies." In *Guide to Ethnohistorical Sources*, vol. 12 of *Handbook of Middle American Indians*. Austin: University of Texas Press, 1972.

Cline, S. L. *Colonial Culhuacan, 1580–1600: A Social History of an Aztec Town*. Albuquerque: University of New Mexico Press, 1986.

————. "Revisionist Conquest History: Sahagún's revised Book XII." In Klor de Alva, Nicholson and Keber, eds., *The Work of Bernardino de Sahagún*.

Bibliography

Colie, Rosalie Littel. *Paradoxia Epidemica: The Renaissance Tradition of Paradox*. Princeton, N.J.: Princeton University Press, 1966.

Colón, Cristóbal. *Textos y documentos completos*. Edited by Consuelo Varela. 2d ed. Madrid: Alianza Editorial, 1983.

Comito, Terry. "Renaissance Gardens and the Discovery of Paradise." *Journal of the History of Ideas* 32:4 (1971): 483–506.

Cook, Sherburne F., and Woodrow Borah. *Essays in Population History*. 3 vols. Berkeley and Los Angeles: University of California Press, 1971–79.

———. *The Indian Population of Central Mexico, 1531–1610*. Berkeley and Los Angeles: University of California Press, 1960.

Corboz, André. "The Land as Palimpsest." *Diogenes* 121 (1983): 12–34.

Coronil, Fernando. "Discovering America Again: The Politics of Selfhood in the Age of Post-Colonial Empires." *Dispositio* 14:36–38 (1989): 315–31.

Cortés, Hernán. *Cartas y documentos*. Introduction by Mario Hernández Sánchez Barba. Mexico City: Porrúa, 1963.

———. *Five Letters of Cortés to the Emperor*. Translated by J. Bayard Morris. New York: Norton, n.d.

———. *Letters from Mexico*. Translated by A. R. Pagden. New York: Grossman, 1971.

Crapanzano, Vincent. "On the Writing of Ethnography." *Dialectical Anthropology* 2:1 (1977): 69–73.

———. *Tuhami: Portrait of a Morrocan*. Chicago: University of Chicago Press, 1980.

Crone, G. R. *Maps and their Makers*. 4th ed. London: Hutchinson University Library, 1968.

Cuneo, Michele di. "Letter on the Second Voyage, 28 October 1495." In Morison, ed., *Journals and Other Documents*.

Dávila Padilla, Agustín. *Historia de la fundación y discurso de la provincia de Santiago de México, de la orden de Predicadores*. Facsimile ed. by Agustín Millares Carlo. Mexico City: Academia Literaria, 1955.

Defert, Daniel. "The Collection of the World: Accounts of Voyages from the Sixteenth to the Eighteenth Centuries." *Dialectical Anthropology* 7:1 (1982): 11–21. ✓

———. "Un genre ethnographique profane au XVIe siècle: Les livres d'habits (Essai d'ethno-iconographie)." In *Histoires de l'anthropologie: XVI–XIX siècles*, edited by Brita Rupp Eisenreich. Paris: Klincksieck, 1984.

Delacampagne, Christian. *L'invention du racisme: Antiquité et Moyen Age*. Paris: Fayard, 1983.

Delaunay, Paul. *La zoologie au seizième siècle*. Paris: Hermann, 1962.

Deleuze, Gilles, and Félix Guattari. *Capitalisme et schizophrénie: Mille plateaux*. Paris: Minuit, 1980.

———. "What Is a Minor Literature?" Translated by Robert Brinkley. *Mississippi Review* 22:3 (Spring 1983): 13–33.

Denevan, William M., ed. *The Native Population of the Americas in 1492*. Madison: University of Wisconsin Press, 1976.

Derrida, Jacques. "From Restricted to General Economy: A Hegelianism without Reserve." In *Writing and Difference*.

Bibliography

——. *Of Grammatology*. Translated by Gayatri Chakravorty Spivak. Baltimore: Johns Hopkins University Press, 1978.

——. *Writing and Difference*. Translated by Alan Bass. Chicago: University of Chicago Press, 1978.

Descombes, Vincent. *L'inconscient malgré lui*. Paris: Minuit, 1977.

Díaz del Castillo, Bernal. *Historia verdadera de la conquista de la Nueva España*. Edited by Joaquín Ramírez Cabañas. Mexico City: Porrúa, 1980.

Dibner, Bern. "The 'New Discoveries' of Stradanus." In Jan van der Straet, *Nova reperta*. Norwalk, Conn.: Burndy Library, 1953.

Domínguez Ortiz, Antonio, and Bernard Vincent. *Historia de los moriscos: Vida y tragedia de una minoría*. Madrid: Revista de Occidente, 1978.

Dreyfus, Hubert L., and Paul Rabinow. *Michel Foucault: Beyond Structuralism and Hermeneutics*. Chicago: University of Chicago Press, 1982.

Dunn, Oliver, and James E. Kelley, Jr., eds. and trans. *The "Diario" of Christopher Columbus's First Voyage to America*. Norman: University of Oklahoma Press, 1989.

Durán, Fray Diego de. *The Aztecs: The History of the Indies of New Spain*. Translated by Doris Heyden and Fernando Horcasitas. New York: Orion Press, 1964.

——. *Book of the Gods and Rites and The Ancient Calendar*. Translated by Doris Heyden and Fernando Horcasitas. Norman: University of Oklahoma Press, 1971.

——. *Historia de las Indias de Nueva España e islas de la Tierra Firme*. 2 vols. Edited by Angel María Garibay K. Mexico City: Porrúa, 1967.

Dwyer, Kevin. "The Dialogic of Ethnology." *Dialectical Anthropology* 2:2 (1977): 143–51.

——. *Morrocan Dialogues: Anthropology in Question*. Baltimore: Johns Hopkins University Press, 1982.

——. "On the Dialogic of Field Work." *Dialectical Anthropology* 4:3 (1979): 205–24.

Eco, Umberto. *An Introduction to Semiotics*. Bloomington: Indiana University Press, 1976.

——. "Metaphor, Dictionary, and Encyclopedia." *New Literary History* 15:2 (1983): 255–71.

——. "Pour une reformulation du concept de signe iconique." *Communications* 29 (1978): 141–91.

——. "The Scandal of Metaphor: Metaphorology and Semiotics." *Poetics Today* 4:2 (1983): 217–57.

——. *Semiotics and the Philosophy of Language*. Bloomington: Indiana University Press, 1984.

Edgerton, Samuel Y. *The Renaissance Rediscovery of Linear Perspective*. New York: Basic Books, 1975.

Edwards, Clinton R. "Mapping by Questionnaire: An Early Spanish Attempt to Determine New World Geographic Locations." *Imago Mundi* 23 (1969): 17–28.

Eisenstein, Elisabeth. *The Printing Press as an Agent of Change*. 2 vols. Cambridge: Cambridge University Press, 1979.

Bibliography

Elliot, J. H. *The Old World and the New, 1462–1650.* Cambridge: Cambridge University Press, 1978.

———. "The Mental World of Hernán Cortés." *Transactions of the Royal Historical Society*, 5th ser., 17 (1967): 41–58.

Entwistle, William J. "The Spanish Mandevilles." *Modern Language Review* 17 (1922): 251–57.

Estow, Clara. "The Economic Development of the Order of Calatrava, 1158–1366." *Speculum* 57:2 (1982): 267–88.

Fabian, Johannes. "Presence and Representation: The Other and Anthropological Writing." *Cultural Critique* 16:4 (Summer 1990): 753–72.

———. *Time and the Other: How Anthropology Makes Its Object.* New York: Columbia University Press, 1983.

Favret-Saada, Jeanne. *Deadly Words: Witchcraft in the Bocage.* Translated by Catherine Cullen. Cambridge: Cambridge University Press, 1980.

Fernández de Navarrete, Martin. *Colección de viajes que hicieron los españoles por mar desde fines del siglo XV.* 3 vols. Biblioteca de Autores Españoles 75–76. Madrid: Biblioteca de Autores Españoles, 1954–55.

Fleischmann, Suzanne. "On the Representation of History and Fiction in the Middle Ages." *History and Theory* 22:3 (1983): 278–310.

Foster, Merlin H., and Julio Ortega, eds. *De la crónica a la nueva narrativa.* Oaxaca, Mexico: Oasis, 1986.

Foucault, Michel. *The Archaeology of Knowledge.* Translated by A. M. Sheridan Smith. New York: Harper Torchbooks, 1972.

———. *Discipline and Punish: The Birth of the Prison.* Translated by Alan Sheridan. New York: Vintage Books, 1979.

———. "Nietzsche, Genealogy, History." In *Language, Counter-Memory, Practice.* Translated by Donald F. Bouchard and Sherry Simon. Ithaca, N.Y.: Cornell University Press, 1977.

———. *The Order of Things: An Archaeology of the Human Sciences.* New York: Vintage Books, 1973.

Francastel, Pierre. *La figure et le lieu: L'ordre visuel du quattrocento.* Paris: Gallimard, 1967.

Franco, Jean. *Plotting Women: Gender and Representation in Mexico.* New York: Columbia University Press, 1989.

Freud, Sigmund. *The Future of an Illusion.* Translated by W. D. Robson-Scotts, edited by James Strachey. Garden City, N.Y.: Anchor Books, 1964.

Frost, Elsa Cecilia. "El milenarismo franciscano en México y el profeta Daniel." *Historia mexicana* 26:1 (1976): 1–28.

Galarza, Joaquín, and Abraham Zemsz. "Le 'portrait royal' dans l'écriture aztèque: Les 'tableaux' du codex Tovar." *Communication* 29 (1979): 13–55.

García Gallo, Alfonso. "El derecho común ante el Nuevo Mundo." *Revista de estudios políticos* 53:80 (1955): 133–52.

García Icazbalceta, Joaquín. *Bibliografía mexicana del siglo XVI.* 2d ed., rev. Agustín Millares Carlo. Mexico City: Fondo de Cultura Económica, 1981.

———. *Nueva colección de documentos para la historia de México.* 3 vols. Mexico City: Salvador Chávez Hayhoe, 1941.

Garcilaso de la Vega, Inca. *La Florida del Inca.* Edited by Sylvia Hilton. Madrid: Historia 16, 1986.

Bibliography

Garibay K., Angel María. *Panorama literario de los pueblos nahuas*. Mexico City: Porrúa, 1975.

Garrido Aranda, Antonio. *Organización de la Iglesia en el Reino de Granada y su proyección en Indias, Siglo XVI*. Sevilla: Escuela de Estudios Hispano-Americanos, 1979.

Gates, Henry Louis, Jr., ed. *"Race," Writing, and Difference*. Chicago: University of Chicago Press, 1986.

Geertz, Clifford. *The Interpretation of Cultures*. New York: Basic Books, 1973.

Genette, Gérard. *Palimpsestes: La littérature au second degré*. Paris: Seuil, 1982.

George, Wilma. *Animals and Maps*. Berkeley and Los Angeles: University of California Press, 1969.

Gerbi, Antonello. *The Dispute of the New World: The History of a Polemic*. 2d ed. Translated by Jeremy Moyle. Pittsburgh: University of Pittsburgh Press, 1973.

———. *La naturaleza de las Indias Nuevas: De Cristóbal Colón a Gonzalo Fernández de Oviedo*. Translated by Antonio Alatorre. Mexico City: Fondo de Cultura Económica, 1975.

———. *Nature in the New World: From Christopher Columbus to Gonzalo Fernández de Oviedo*. Translated by Jeremy Moyle. Pittsburgh: University of Pittsburgh Press, 1985.

Giamatti, A. Bartlett. *The Earthly Paradise and the Renaissance Epic*. Princeton, N.J.: Princeton University Press, 1966.

Gibson, Charles. *The Aztecs under Spanish Rule*. Stanford, Calif.: Stanford University Press, 1964.

Gil, Juan. "Libros, descubridores y sabios en la Sevilla del Quinientos." Introductory remarks by Polo, *El libro de Marco Polo*.

Ginés de Sepúlveda, Juan. *Hechos de los españoles en el Nuevo Mundo y México*. Edited by Demetrio Ramos and Lucio Mijares. Valladolid: Seminario Americanista de la Universidad de Valladolid, 1976.

Girard, René. *Violence and the Sacred*. Translated by Patrick Gregory. Baltimore: Johns Hopkins University Press, 1979.

Giuseppi, Montague Spencer. "The Works of Theodore de Bry and His Sons, Engravers." *Proceedings of the Huguenot Society of London* 11 (1915–17): 204–26.

Glucksmann, André. *Le discours de la guerre: Théorie et stratégie*. Paris: l'Herne, 1967.

Goff, Jacques le. *La naissance du purgatoire*. Paris: Gallimard, 1981.

González Echevarría, Roberto. *Isla a su vuelo fugitiva*. Madrid: José Porrúa Turanzas, 1983.

Gordon, Deborah, ed. *Feminism and the Critique of Colonial Discourse*. Special issue of *Inscriptions* 3–4 (1988).

Greenblatt, Stephen J. "Learning to Curse: Aspects of Linguistic Colonialism in the Sixteenth Century." In Chiappelli, ed., *First Images of America*.

Gruzinski, Serge. *La colonization de l'imaginaire: Sociétés indigènes et occidentalization dans le Mexique espagnol XVIe–XVIIIe siècle*. Paris: Gallimard, 1988.

———. "Confesión, alianza y sexualidad entre los indios de Nueva España: Introducción al estudio de los confesionarios en lenguas indígenas." In *El*

260

Bibliography

placer de pecar y el afán de normar. Mexico City: Instituto Nacional de Antropología e Historia/Joaquín Mortiz, 1987.

———. "La 'conquista de los cuerpos'. (Cristianismo, alianza y sexualidad en el altiplano mexicano: siglo XVI)." In *Familia y sexualidad en la Nueva España*. Mexico City: SEP/80, 1982.

———. *Man-Gods in the Mexican Highlands*. Translated by Eilleen Corrigan. Stanford, Calif.: Stanford University Press, 1989.

Guillén, Claudio. "Literature as Historical Contradiction: *El Abencerraje*, the Moorish Novel, and the Eclogue." In *Literature as System: Essays toward the Theory of Literary History*. Princeton, N.J.: Princeton University Press, 1971.

Hamon, Philippe. *Introduction à l'analyse du descriptif*. Paris: Hachette, 1981.

Hanke, Lewis. *Aristotle and the American Indians: A Study in Race Prejudice in the Modern World*. Bloomington: Indiana University Press, 1975.

———. Introduction to *Del único modo de atraer a todos los pueblos a la verdadera religión*. Translated by Atenógenes Santamaria, edited by Agustín Millares Carlo. Mexico City: Fondo de Cultura Económica, 1975.

———. "The Requirement and Its Interpreters." *Revista de Historia de América* 1 (1938): 28–34.

———. *The Spanish Struggle for Justice in the Conquest of America*. Philadelphia: University of Pennsylvania Press, 1949.

Harley, J. B. "Cartography, Ethics, and Social Science." *Cartographica* 27:2 (Summer 1990): 1–23.

———. "Deconstructing the Map." *Cartographica* 26:2 (Summer 1989): 1–20.

———. "Maps, Knowledge, and Power." In *The Iconography of Landscape: Essays on the Symbolic Representation, Design, and Use of Past Environments*, edited by Denis Cosgrove and Stephen Daniels. Cambridge: Cambridge University Press, 1988.

———. Responses to J. B. Harley, "Deconstructing the Map." *Cartographica* 26:3–4 (Summer 1989): 89–127.

Hartog, François. *Le miroir d'Hérodote: Essai sur la représentation de l'autre*. Paris: Gallimard, 1980.

Heers, Jacques. *Christophe Colomb*. Paris: Hachette, 1981.

———. "De Marco Polo à Christophe Colomb: Comment lire le *Devisement du monde*?" *Journal of Medieval History* 10:2 (June 1984): 125–143.

Hegel, George Wilhelm Friedrich. *The Phenomenology of Mind*. Translated by J. B. Baillie. New York: Harper Torchbooks, 1967.

———. *The Philosophy of History*. Translated by J. Sibree. New York: Dover, 1956.

Heidegger, Martin. "The Age of the World Picture." In *The Question of Technology and Other Essays*. Translated by William Lovitt. New York: Harper Torchbooks, 1977.

Hodgen, M. T. *Early Anthropology in the Sixteenth and Seventeenth Centuries*. Philadelphia: University of Pennsylvania Press, 1964.

Hodgson, Marshal G. S. "The Interrelations of Societies in History." *Comparative Studies in Society and History* 5:2 (1963): 227–50.

Honour, Hugh. *The New Golden Land*. New York: Pantheon Books, 1975.

Bibliography

Huggan, Graham. "Decolonizing the Map: Post-Colonialism, Post-Structuralism, and the Cartographic Connection." *Ariel* 20:4 (October 1989): 115–31.

Huizinga, Johan. *The Waning of the Middle Ages: A Study on the Forms of Life, Thought, and Art in France and the Netherlands in the XIVth and XVth Centuries*. Garden City, N.Y.: Anchor Books, 1954.

Hulme, Peter. *Colonial Encounters: Europe and the Native Caribbean, 1492–1797*. London and New York: Methuen, 1986.

——. "Polytropic Man: Tropes of Sexuality and Mobility in Early Colonial Discourse." In Barker et al., eds., *Europe and Its Others*.

——. "Subversive Archipelagos: Colonial Discourse and the Breakup of Continental Theory." *Dispositio* 14:36–38 (1989): 1–23.

Iglesia, Ramón. "The Disillusionment of Don Carlos." In *Columbus, Cortés, and Other Essays*. Translated and edited by Lesley Byrd Simpson. Berkeley and Los Angeles: University of California Press, 1969.

——. "Hernán Cortés." In *Cronistas e historiadores de la conquista de México*, edited by Juan A. Ortega y Medina. Mexico City: Sept/Setentas, 1972.

Iñigo Madrigal, Luis, ed. *Historia de la literatura hispanoamericana*. Vol 1, *Epoca colonial*. Madrid: Cátedra, 1982.

Jacob, Christian, and Frank Lestringant, eds. *Arts et légendes d'espaces: Figures du voyage et rhétoriques du monde*. Paris: Presses del'école normale supérieure, 1981.

Jacob, François *The Logic of Living Systems: A History of Heredity*. Translated by Betty E. Spillman. London: Allen Lane, 1974.

Jakobson, Roman. "Linguistics and Poetics." In *Style in Language*, edited by Thomas A. Sebeok. New York: Technology Press and John Wiley, 1960.

Jane, Lionel Cecil, ed. and trans. *Select Documents Illustrating the Four Voyages*, 2 vols. London: Hakluyt Society, 1930–33.

JanMohammed, Abdul R. "The Economy of Manichean Allegory: The Function of Racial Difference in Colonialist Literature." *Critical Inquiry* 12:1 (Autumn 1985): 59–87.

JanMohammed, Abdul R., and David Lloyd, eds. *The Nature and Context of Minority Discourse*. New York: Oxford University Press, 1990.

Janz, Harold. "Images of America in the German Renaissance." In Chiappelli, ed., *First Images of America*.

Jara, René, and Nicholas Spadaccini, eds. *1492–1992: Re/Discovering Colonial Writing*. Hispanic Issues 4. Minneapolis: The Prisma Institute, 1989.

Kappler, Claude. *Monstres, démons et merveilles à la fin du Moyen-Age*. Paris: Payot, 1980.

Karttunen, Frances, and James Lockhart. *Nahuatl in the Middle Years: Language Contact Phenomena in Texts of the Colonial Period*. University of California Publications in Linguistics 85. Berkeley and Los Angeles: University of California Press, 1976.

Keuning, J. "The History of an Atlas, Mercator-Hondius." *Imago Mundi* 4 (1947): 37–62.

Klor de Alva, J. Jorge. "Christianization and the Concept of the Self: The Sixteenth-Century Aztec." *Campo Libre* 1:1 (1981): 22–33.

——. "Contar vidas: La autobiografía y la reconstrucción del ser nahua." *Arbor* 515–16 (1988): 49–78.

Bibliography

————. "Language, Politics, and Translation: Colonial Discourse and Classic Nahuatl in New Spain." In Warren, ed., *The Art of Translation*.

————. "Sahagún and the Birth of Modern Ethnography: Representing, Confessing, and Inscribing the Native Other." In Klor de Alva, Nicholson and Quiñones, eds. *The Work of Bernardino de Sahagún*.

————. "Spiritual Warfare in Mexico: Christianity and the Aztecs." 3 vols. Ph.D. diss. University of California at Santa Cruz, 1980.

Klor de Alva, Jorge, H. B. Nicholson, and Eloise Quiñones Keber, eds. *The Work of Bernardino de Sahagún: Pioneer Ethnographer of Sixteenth-Century Aztec Mexico*. Austin and Albany: State University of New York–Albany Institute of Mesoamerican Studies and University of Texas Press, 1988.

Kubler, George. *Mexican Architecture of the Sixteenth Century*. 2 vols. New Haven, Conn.: Yale University Press, 1948.

Lacan, Jacques. "Agressivity in Psychoanalysis." In *Ecrits*, edited and translated by Alan Sheridan. New York: Norton, 1977.

————. "The Subversion of the Subject and the Dialectic of Desire in the Freudian Unconscious." In *Ecrits*, edited and translated by Alan Sheridan, New York: Norton, 1977.

Ladner, Gerhart B. "Medieval and Modern Understanding of Symbolism: A Comparison." *Speculum* 54:2 (1979): 223–56.

Las Casas, Fray Bartolomé de. *Apologética historia sumaria*. 2 vols. Edited by Edmundo O'Gorman. Mexico City: Universidad Nacional Autónoma de México, 1967.

————. *Brevíssima relación de la destruyción de las Indias*. Facsimile ed. by Manuel Ballesteros Gaibrois. Madrid: Fundación Universitaria Española, 1977.

————. *Historia de las Indias*. 3 vols. Edited by Agustín Millares Carlo. Mexico City: Fondo de Cultura Económica, 1965.

Leonard, Irving A. *Baroque Times in Old Mexico: Seventeenth-Century Persons, Places, and Practices*. Ann Arbor: University of Michigan Press, 1959.

————. *Books of the Brave: Being an Account of Books and of Men in the Spanish Conquest and Settlement of the Sixteenth-Century New World*. New York: Gordian Press, 1964.

————. "Conquerors and Amazons in Mexico." *Hispanic American Historical Review* 24 (1944): 562–79.

Leonardo da Vinci. *The Notebooks of Leonardo da Vinci*. Edited by Jean Paul Richter. 2 vols. New York: Dover, 1970.

León-Portilla, Miguel. Introduction to *Visión de los vencidos: Relaciones indígenas de la conquista*, translated by Angel María Garibay K. México City: Universidad Nacional Autónoma de Mexico, 1972.

————. "Quetzalcóatl-Cortés en la conquista de México." *Historia mexicana* 24:1 (1974): 13–35.

Lestringant, Frank. "Fictions de l'espace brésilien à la Renaissance: l'exemple de Guanabara." In Jacob and Lestringant, eds., *Arts et légendes d'espaces*.

————. "The Philosopher's Breviary: Jean de Léry in the Enlightenment." *Representations* 33 (1991): 200–209.

Levillier, Roberto. *América la bien llamada*. 2 vols. Buenos Aires: Guillermo Kraft, 1948.

Bibliography

Levin, Harry. *The Golden Age in the Renaissance*. Bloomington: Indiana University Press, 1969.

Lévi-Strauss, Claude. *The Savage Mind*. Translated by George Weidenfeld. Chicago: University of Chicago Press, 1966.

————. *Tristes Tropiques*. Translated by John Weightman and Doreen Weightman. New York: Pocket Books, 1977.

Lewis, Robert. "Retórica y verdad: Los cargos de Bernal Díaz a López de Gómara." In Foster and Ortega, eds., *De la crónica a la nueva narrativa*.

Lim, Linda Y. C. "Capitalism, Imperialism, and Patriarchy: The Dilemma of Third World Women Workers in Multinational Factories." In Nash and Fernández-Kelly, eds., *Women, Men and the International Division of Labor*.

Lionnet, Françoise. *Autobiographical Voices: Race, Gender, Self-Portraiture*. Ithaca, N.Y.: Cornell University Press, 1989.

Llolis, Cesare de, et al. *Raccolta di documenti e studi publicati dalla Reale Commisione colombina*. 15 vols. Rome, 1892–94.

Lockhart, James, and Stuart B. Schwartz. *Early Latin America: A History of Colonial Spanish America and Brazil*. Cambridge: Cambridge University Press, 1983.

Lockhart, James, Frances Berdan, and Arthur J. O. Anderson. *Tlaxcalan Actas: A Compendium of the Records of the Cabildo of Tlaxcala (1545–1627)*. Salt Lake City: University of Utah Press, 1986.

Longino, Helen. *Science as Social Knowledge: Values and Objectivity in Scientific Inquiry*. Princeton, N.J.: Princeton University Press, 1990.

López Austin, Alfredo. *Hombre-Dios: Religión y política en el mundo náhuatl*. Mexico City: Universidad Nacional Autónoma de México, 1973.

McClung, William Alexander. *The Architecture of Paradise: Survivals of Eden and Jerusalem*. Berkeley and Los Angeles: University of California Press, 1983.

Man, Paul de. *Allegories of Reading*. New Haven, Conn.: Yale University Press, 1979.

Mandeville, John. *Mandeville's Travels*. Translated by Malcolm Letts. Nedeln, Liechtenstein: Kraus Reprint, 1967.

Manzano y Manzano, Juan. *Colón y su secreto*. Madrid: Ediciones de Cultura Hispánica, 1976.

Maravall, José Antonio. "Utopía y primitivismo en el pensamiento de Las Casas." *Revista de Occidente* 141 (1974): 311–88.

Marcus, George E., and Dick Cushman. "Ethnographies as Texts." *Annual Review of Anthropology* 11 (1982): 25–69.

Marichal, Juan. "The New World from Within: The Inca Garcilaso." In Chiappelli, ed., *First Images of America*.

Marin, Louis. "A propos du signe naturel: cartes et tableaux." In *Etudes sémiologiques*. Paris: Klincksieck, 1971.

————. *Le portrait du Roi*. Paris: Minuit, 1981.

————. *Utopics: Spatial Play*. Translated by Robert A. Vollrath. Atlantic Highlands, N.J.: Humanities Press, 1984.

Marouby, Christian. *Utopie et primitivisme: Essai sur l'imaginaire anthropologique à l'âge classique*. Paris: Seuil, 1991.

Bibliography

Martínez, José Luis. *Hernán Cortés*. 2d ed. Mexico City: Fondo de Cultura Económica, 1990.

Menchú, Rigoberta, *Me llamo Rigoberta Menchú y así me nació la conciencia*. Edited by Elizabeth Burgos. Mexico City: Siglo XXI, 1985.

Mendieta, Fray Gerónimo de. *Historia eclesiástica indiana*. Edited by Joaquín García Icazbalceta. Mexico City: Porrúa, 1971.

Mercator, Hondius, Janssonius. *Atlas or Geographicke Description of the World*. 2 vols. Facsimile ed. of the 1636 English translation by Henry Hexham. Amsterdam: Theatrum Orbis Terrarum, 1968.

Merrim, Stephanie. "The Apprehension of the New in Nature and Culture: Fernández de Oviedo's *Sumario*." In Jara and Spadaccini, eds., *1492–1992: Re/Discovering Colonial Writing*.

———. "Ariadne's Thread: Autobiography, History, and Cortés' *Segunda Carta-Relación*." *Dispositio* 9:28–29 (1986): 57–83.

———. "The Castle of Discourse: Fernández de Oviedo's *Don Claribalte* (1519)." *Modern Language Notes* 97 (1982): 329–46.

———. "Historia y escritura en las crónicas de Indias: Ensayo de método." *Explicación de textos literarios* 9:2 (1981): 193–200.

Mignolo, Walter. "Cartas, crónicas y relaciones del descubrimiento y la conquista." In Iñigo Madrigal, ed., *Historia de la literatura hispanoamericana*.

———. "Colonial Situations, Geographical Discourses, and Territorial Representations: Toward a Diatopical Understanding of Colonial Semiosis." *Dispositio* 14:36–38 (1989): 93–140.

———. "La lengua, la letra, el territorio (o la crisis de los estudios literarios coloniales)." *Dispositio* 11:28–29 (1986): 137–60.

———. "El mandato y la ofrenda: la descripción de la ciudad y provincia de Tlaxcala, de Diego Muñoz Camargo y las relaciones de Indias." *Nueva revista de filología hispánica* 35:2 (1987): 451–84.

———. "El metatexto historiográfico y la historiografía indiana." *Modern Language Notes* 96 (1981): 358–402.

Milhou, Alain. *Colón y su mentalidad mesiánica en el ambiente franciscanista español*. Valladolid: Seminario Americanista de la Universidad de Valladolid, 1983.

Moghadan, Val. "Against Eurocentrism and Nativism: A Review Essay on Samir Amin's *Eurocentrism* and Other Texts." *Socialism and Democracy* 9 (Fall/Winter 1989): 81–104.

Mollat, Michel. *Les explorateurs du XIIe au XVIe siècle: Premiers regards sur des mondes nouveaux*. Paris: J. C. Lattès, 1984.

Momigliano, Arnaldo. "The Place of Herodotus in the History of Historiography." In *Studies in Historiography*. London: Weidenfeld and Nicolson, 1966.

Montaigne, Michel. *Essais*. In *Oeuvres complètes*. Edited by Albert Thibaudet and Maurice Rat. Paris: Gallimard, 1962.

Montrose, Louis. "The Work of Gender in the Discourse of Discovery." *Representations* 33 (1991): 1–41.

Moretti, Gabriella. "*Nec si Teris ultima Thule*. (La profezia di Seneca sulla scoperta del Nuovo Mondo)." *Columbeis* 1 (1986): 328–33.

Morison, Samuel Eliot. *Admiral of the Ocean Sea: A Life of Christopher Columbus*. Boston: Little, Brown, 1942.

Bibliography

————, ed. and trans. *Journals and Other Documents on the Life and Voyages of Christopher Columbus*. New York: Limited Editions Club, 1963.

Motolinia [Toribio de Benavente]. *Memoriales o libro de las cosas de la Nueva España*. Edited by Edmundo O'Gorman. Mexico City: Universidad Nacional Autónoma de México, 1971.

Muehrcke, Philip and Juliana Muehrcke. *Map Use: Reading, Analysis, and Interpretation*. Madison, Wisc.: JP Publications, 1978.

Mullaney, Steven. "Strange Things, Gross Terms, Curious Customs: The Rehearsal of Cultures in the Late Renaissance." *Representations* 3 (1983): 40–67.

Mumford, Lewis. *The City in History: Its Origins, Its Transformation, and Its Prospects*. New York: Harcourt, Brace and World, 1961.

Nader, Helen. "The One World and Two Americas of Hernando Cortés and Bartolomé de Las Casas." *Dispositio* 14:36–38 (1989): 213–23.

Nash, June, and María Patricia Fernández-Kelly, eds. *Women, Men, and the International Division of Labor*. Albany: State University of New York Press, 1983.

Nelson, Cary, and Lawrence Grossberg, eds. *Marxism and the Interpretation of Cultures*. Urbana: Univesity of Illinois Press, 1987.

Nietzsche, Friedrich. *The Use and Abuse of History*. Translated by Adrian Collins. Indianapolis: Bobbs-Merrill, 1957.

O'Gorman, Edmundo. *La invención de América: Investigación acerca de la estructura histórica del Nuevo Mundo y del sentido de su porvenir*. 2d ed. Mexico City: Fondo de Cultura Económica, 1977.

Olschki, Leonardo. *Marco Polo's Asia: An Introduction to His "Description of the World" Called "Il Milione."* Translated by John A. Scott. Berkeley and Los Angeles: University of California Press, 1960.

————. "Ponce de León's Fountain of Youth: History of a Geographic Myth." *Hispanic American Historical Review* 21 (1941): 631–85.

————. *Storia letteraria delle scorpete geografiche*. Florence: Leo S. Olschki, 1937.

————. "What Columbus Saw on Landing in the West Indies." *Proceedings of the American Philosophical Society* 84:5 (1941): 633–59.

Ong, Aihwa. "Colonialism and Modernity: Feminist Representations of Women in Non-Western Societies." In Gordon, ed. *Feminism and the Critique of Colonial Discourse*.

Ong, Walter J. *Orality and Literacy: The Technologization of the Word*. London and New York: Methuen, 1986.

————. *Ramus: Method and the Decay of Dialogue*. Cambridge, Mass.: Harvard University Press, 1958.

————. *Rhetoric, Romance, and Technology*. Ithaca, N.Y.: Cornell University Press, 1971.

Ortelius, Abraham. *Theater of the Whole World*. Facsimile of the 1606 ed. Amsterdam: Theatrum Orbis Terrarum, 1968.

Ortner, Sherry B. "Theory in Anthropology since the Sixties." *Society for Comparative Study of Society and History* 26:1 (1984): 126–66.

Oviedo y Valdés, Gonzalo Fernández de. *Historia general y natural de las Indias*. 5 vols. Edited by Juan Pérez de Tuleda Bueso. Biblioteca de Autores Españoles 117–21. Madrid: Biblioteca de Autores Españoles, 1959.

———. *Historia general y natural de las Indias*. 4 vols. Edited by José Amador de los Ríos. Madrid: Imprenta de la Real Academia de la Historia, 1851–55.

Pagden, Anthony. "*Ius et factum*: Text and Experience in the Writings of Bartolomé de Las Casas." *Representations* 33 (Winter 1991): 147–62.

———. *The Fall of Natural Man: The American Indian and the Origins of Comparative Anthropology*. Cambridge: Cambridge University Press, 1982.

Parry, John H., and Robert G. Keith, eds. *New Iberian World: A Documentary History of the Discovery and Settlement of Latin America*. Vol. 1. New York: Times Books, 1984.

Pastor, Beatriz. *Discurso narrativo de la conquista de América*. Havana: Casa de las Américas, 1983.

———. "Silence and Writing: The History of the Conquest." In Jara and Spadaccini, eds., *1492–1992: Re/Discovering Colonial Writing*.

Peirce, Charles S. *The Philosophy of Peirce: Selected Writings*. Edited by Justus Buchler. London: Routledge & Kegan Paul, 1956.

Pereyra, Carlos. *Hernán Cortés*. 4th ed. Buenos Aires and Mexico City: Espasa-Calpe, 1947.

Pérez de Tudela, Juan. *"Mirabilis in Altis": Estudio crítico sobre el origen y significado del proyecto descubridor de Cristóbal Colón*. Madrid: Consejo Superior de Investigaciones Cientificas, 1983.

Phelan, John Leddy. "El imperio cristiano de Las Casas, el imperio español de Sepúlveda y el imperio milenario de Mendieta." *Revista de Occidente* 141 (1974): 292–310.

———. *The Millennial Kingdom of the Franciscans in the New World*. 2d ed. Berkeley and Los Angeles: University of California Press, 1970.

Philoponus, Honorius [Gaspar Plautius]. *Nova typis transacta navigatio novi orbis Indiae occidentalis*. Venice, 1621.

Piedra, José. "The Game of Arrival." *Diacritics* (Spring 1989): 34–61.

Pohl, Frederick J. *Amerigo Vespucci, Pilot Major*. New York: Octagon Books, 1966.

Polo, Marco. *The Book of Ser Marco Polo*. 2 vols. Translated and edited by Henri Yule. London: John Murray, 1875.

———. *The Book of Marco Polo*. Edited and translated by Juan Gil. Madrid: Testimonio, 1986.

———. *El libro de Marco Polo*. Edited and translated by Juan Gil. Madrid: Testimonio, 1986.

———. *El libro de Marco Polo anotado por Cristóbal Colón*. Edited by Juan Gil. Madrid: Alianza Editorial, 1987.

Pupo-Walker, Enrique. *Historia, creación y profecía en los textos del Inca Garcilaso de la Vega*. Madrid: José Porrúa Turanzas, 1982.

Quintilian. *The "Institutio Oratoria" of Quintilian*. 4 vols. Translated by H. E. Butler. Cambridge, Mass.: Harvard University Press, 1976.

Rabasa, José. "Allegories of the *Atlas*." In Barker et al., eds., *Europe and Its Others*.

———. "Utopian Ethnology in Las Casas's *Apologética*." In Jara and Spadaccini, eds., *1492–1992: Re/Discovering Colonial Writing*.

Rama, Angel. *La ciudad letrada*. Hanover, N.H.: Ediciones del Norte, 1984.

Bibliography

————. *Transculturación narrativa en América Latina*. Mexico City: Siglo XXI, 1982.

Ramos, Demetrio. *Los contactos transatlánticos decisivos, como precedentes del viaje de Colón*. Valladolid: Casa-Museo de Colón Seminario de Historia de América, 1972.

Randles, W. G. L. *De la terre plate au globe terrestre*. Paris: Librairie Armand Colin, 1980.

Reyes, Alfonso. *Letras de la Nueva España*. Vol. 12 of *Obras completas*. Mexico City: Fondo de Cultura Económica, 1960.

Rifaterre, Michael. "Descriptive Imagery." *Yale French Studies* 61 (1978): 107–25.

Ricard, Robert. *La conquista espiritual de México*. Translated by Angel María Garibay K. Mexico City: Jus, 1947.

Ricoeur, Paul. *Temps et récit*. 3 vols. Paris: Seuil, 1983.

Robertson, Donald. *Mexican Manuscript Painting in the Colonial Period*. New Haven, Conn.: Yale University Press, 1959.

Ross, Frank. "The Codex Cortés: Inscribing the Conquest of Mexico." *Dispositio* 14:36–38 (1989): 187–211.

Roux, Jean-Paul. *Les explorateurs au Moyen Age*. 2d ed. Paris: Fayard, 1985.

Rumeu de Armas, Antonio. *Nueva luz sobre las capitulaciones de Santa Fe de 1492 concertadas entre los Reyes Católicos y Cristóbal Colón: Estudio institucional y diplomático*. Madrid: Consejo Superior de Investigaciones Científicas, 1985.

Ryan, Michael T. "Assimilating New Worlds in the Sixteenth and Seventeenth Centuries." *Society for Comparative Study of Society and History* 23:4 (1981): 519–38.

Sahagún, Bernardino de. *Florentine Codex: General History of the Things of New Spain*. 13 vols. Translated and edited by Arthur J. O. Anderson and Charles Dibble. Santa Fe and Salt Lake City: School of American Research and University of Utah, 1950–82.

————. *Historia de las cosas de la Nueva España*. 4 vols. Edited by Angel María Garibay K. Mexico City: Porrúa, 1969.

Said, Edward. *The World, the Text, and the Critic*. Cambridge, Mass.: Harvard University Press, 1983.

————. *Orientalism*. New York: Vintage Books, 1978.

Salas, Alberto. *Tres cronistas de Indias: Pedro Mártir de Anglería, Gonzalo Fernández de Oviedo, Fray Bartolomé de Las Casas*. 2d ed. Mexico City: Fondo de Cultura Económica, 1986.

Salomon, Frank. "Chronicles of the Impossible: Note on Three Andean Chroniclers of the Early Colonial Period." In Adorno, ed., *From Oral to Written Expression*.

Schevill, Rodolfo. "La novela histórica, las crónicas de Indias y los libros de caballería." *Revista de las Indias* 56–60 (1944): 173–96.

Seneca, L. Annaei. *Medea*. In *Tragoediae*, edited by Otto Zwierlein. New York: Oxford University Press, 1986.

Sewell, Elizabeth. "Bacon, Vico, Coleridge, and the Poetic Method." In *Giambattista Vico: An International Symposium*, edited by Giorgio Tagliacozzo and Hayden White. Baltimore: Johns Hopkins University Press, 1969.

Bibliography

Shell, Marc. "From Coexistence to Toleration." *Cultural Critique* 17:2 (Winter 1991): 306–35.

Simpson, Lesley Byrd. *The Encomienda in New Spain: The Beginning of Spanish Mexico*. Berkeley and Los Angeles: University of California Press, 1966.

Solano, Francisco de. "La modelación social como política indigenista." *Historia mexicana* 28:2 (1978): 297–332.

Spivak, Gayatri Chakravorti. "Can the Subaltern Speak?" In Nelson and Grossberg, eds., *Marxism and the Interpretation of Cultures*.

———. *"The New Historicism: Political Commitment and the Postmodern Critic." In Veeser, ed., The New Historicism*.

———. *The Post-Colonial Critic*. New York: Routledge, Chapman and Hall, 1990.

———. "The Rani of Sirmur." In Barker et al., eds., *Europe and Its Others*.

———. "Revolutions That as Yet Have No Model: Derrida's Limited Inc." *Diacritics* 10:4 (1980): 29–49.

Stocking, George, ed. *Observers Observed: Essays on Ethnographic Fieldwork*. History of Anthropology, vol. 1. Madison: University of Wisconsin Press, 1983.

Sylvest, Edwin Edward. *Motifs of Franciscan Mission Theory in Sixteenth-Century New Spain Province of the Holy Ghost*. Washington, D.C.: Academy of American Franciscan History, 1975.

Tacitus. *The Life of Cnaeus Julius Agricola*. In *Complete Works*, translated by Alfred John Church and William Jackson Brodniff. New York: Modern Library, 1942.

Taussig, Michael. *Shamanism, Colonialism, and the Wild Man: A Study in Terror and Healing*. Chicago: University of Chicago Press, 1987.

Tavianni, Paolo Emilio. *Christopher Colombus: The Grand Design*. London: Orbis, 1985.

Thrower, Norman J. W. "New Geographic Horizons: Maps." In Chiappelli, ed., *First Images of America*.

Todorov, Tzvetan. *La conquête de l'Amérique: La question de l'autre*. Paris: Seuil, 1982.

———. *The Conquest of America: The Question of the Other*. Translated by Richard Howard. New York: Harper and Row, 1984.

Toussaint, Manuel. "El plano atribuido a Cortés." In *Planos de la ciudad de México siglos XVI y XVII: Estudio histórico, urbanístico y bibliográfico*, edited by Manuel Toussaint, Federico Gómez de Orozco, and Justino Fernández. Mexico City: Instituto de Investigaciones Estéticas de la Universidad Nacional Autónoma de México, 1938.

Turner, Bryan S. *Marx and the End of Orientalism*. London: Allen and Unwin, 1978.

Turner, Daymond. "Forgotten Treasure from the Indies: The Illustrations and Drawings of Fernández de Oviedo." *Huntington Library Quarterly* 48:1 (Winter 1985): 1–46.

Valesio, Paolo. *Novantigua: Rhetorics as a Contemporary Theory*. Bloomington: Indiana University Press, 1980.

Van den Berg, J. H. *The Changing Nature of Man*. Translated by H. F. Croes. New York: Delta Books, 1975.

Bibliography

Van 'T Hoff, B. Introduction to *Gerard Mercator's Map of the World* (1569). Rotterdam: Publicaties Van Het Maritiem Museum "Prins Hendrick," 1962.

Varela, Consuelo. "Observaciones para una edición crítica de los diarios del primer y tercer viaje colombinos." *Columbeis* 3 (1988): 7–17.

Vázquez, Josefina Zoraida. "El indio americano y su circunstancia en la obra de Fernández de Oviedo." *Revista de Indias* 17:69–70 (1957): 483–519.

Veeser, H. Aram, ed. *The New Historicism.* New York and London: Routledge, 1989.

Verlinder, Charles. "Aumento y alcance de la gañaría: Siglo XVII." In *Historia y sociedad en el mundo de habla española*, edited by Bernardo García Martínez. Mexico City: El Colegio de México, 1970.

———. *Précédents médiévaux de la colonie en Amérique: Période coloniale.* Mexico City: Instituto Panamericano de Geografía e Historia, 1954.

Vignaud, Henry. *Histoire critique de la grande entreprise de Christophe Colomb.* 2 vols. Paris: H. Welter, 1911.

Wagner, Roy. *The Invention of Culture.* 2d ed. Chicago: University of Chicago Press, 1981.

Warren, Rosanna, ed. *The Art of Translation: Voices from the Field.* Boston: Northeastern University Press, 1989.

Washburn, W. E. "The Meaning of Discovery in the Fifteenth and Sixteenth Centuries." *American Historical Review* 68:1 (1962): 1–21.

Watts, Pauline Moffit. "Prophesy and Discovery: On the Spiritual Origins of Christopher Columbus's 'Enterprise of the Indies.'" *American Historical Review* 90:1 (February 1985): 73–102.

Weckmann, Luis. "Las esperanzas milenaristas de los Franciscanos de la Nueva España." *Historia mexicana* 32:1 (1982): 89–105.

———. *La herencia medieval de México.* 2 vols. Mexico City: El Colegio de México, 1984.

White, Hayden. *The Content of Form: Narrative Discourse and Historical Representation.* Baltimore: Johns Hopkins University Press, 1987.

———. *Metahistory: The Historical Imagination in Nineteenth-Century Europe.* Baltimore: Johns Hopkins University Press, 1973.

———. "The Question of Narrativity in Contemporary Historical Theory." *History and Theory* 23 (1984): 1–33.

———. *Tropics of Discourse.* Baltimore: Johns Hopkins University Press, 1978.

Wittgenstein, Ludwig. *Philosophical Investigations.* 3d ed. Translated by G. E. M. Anscombe. New York: Macmillan, 1968.

Wood, Stephanie. "The Cosmic Conquest: late-Colonial Views of the Sword and Cross in Central Mexican *Títulos*." *Ethnohistory* 38:2 (1991): 176–95.

Wright, John. "Map Makers are Human: Comments on the Subjective in Maps." *Cartographica* 19 (1977): 8–25.

Wright, John K. *Geographical Lore of the Time of the Crusades.* New York: American Geographical Society, 1925.

Yates, Frances A. *Astraea: The Imperial Theme in the Sixteenth Century.* London and Boston: Routledge and Kegan Paul, 1975.

Zamora, Margarita. "'Todas son palabras formales del Almirante': Las Casas y el *Diario* de Colón." *Hispanic Review* 57 (1989): 25–41.

Bibliography

Zapata, Roger A. *Guamán Poma, indigenismo y estética de la dependencia en la cultura peruana*. Minneapolis: Institute for the Study of Ideologies and Literature, 1989.

Zavala, Silvio. *Los esclavos indios en Nueva España*. Mexico City: El Colegio Nacional, 1967.

Index

272

Index

157, 165; condemned by Las Casas, 167. *See also* Barbarism; Cannibalism; Genocide; Massacres; Human sacrifice; Slavery
Avan, tailed men of, 63
Azores, 77
Aztecs: persona of, 237–38n.60; religiosity of, 128–29, 134, 136. *See also* Cortés, Hernán; Cuauhtémoc; Moctezuma; Nahuatl; Quetzalcoatl; Tenochtitlan

Bacon, Francis, 3, 78, 194
Balbuena, Bernardo de, 131–34
Barbarism, 170; European, 47; racism inspired by, 4. *See also* Atrocities; Savagery
Barthes, Roland, 10, 50; Eco on, 126; and "effect of the real," 9–10, 13
Basques, demonology among, 147, 160, 241n.30
Bataillon, Marcel, 88, 221n.30
Baudet, Henri, 161, 170, 172
Baudot, Georges, 120, 136
Beaujour, Michel, 52, 81, 208
Benavente, Toribio de. *See* Motolinía
Berdan, Frances, 236n.53
Bering Strait, "Amerindians" to New World via, 210
Berkhofer, Robert F., 219n.2
Bernal, Ignacio, 239n.4
Betanzos, Domingo de, 125
Bhabha, Homi, 11, 13, 110
Bitterli, Urs, 38–43
Black Legend, 92, 166, 244n.60
"Blank page" metaphor, 42–43, 46, 47, 82, 137, 183, 222n.41
Boabdil, 109
Boon, James, 40
Botticelli, Sandro, 42, 45, 222n.52
Brazil, 29; in *Atlas*, 199
Brazilwood, 65

Brevíssima relación de la destruyción de las Indias (Las Casas), 165–67
Bricolage, 186, 248n.15
Bry, Théodore de, 37, 92, 233n.31
Burgos, Elizabeth, 232n.27

Cadamosto, 228n.31
Caesar, Gaius Julius, 153; in *Atlas*, 205–206
Calderón de la Barca, Pedro, 84, 90
California, discovery of, 228n.29
Canary Islands, 51; as Paradise site, 76
Canguilhem, Georges, 202
Caniba, 66, 67
Cannibalism, New World, 6, 66, 179, 228n.30; conquest justified by, 233n.31; in Stradanus engraving, 26
Captions: to allegorical works, 34; ideological freight of, 37; to Stradanus's work, 26, 30, 33, 37, 41–47
Cardos. See Thistles
Caribbean Sea, fish of, 71–72
Caribs, cannibalism attributed to, 66, 228n.30
Carpini, Giovanni da Pian del, 31, 57, 196, 198, 199
Cartographer: Columbus as, 55, 57, 58, 59, 63, 72; Cortés as, 87, 93, 100 (*see also* Mexico, Gulf of—Cortés map of; Tenochtitlan, Cortes map of)
Cartography, 250n.21; allegory and, 248n.14; binary nature of, 247–48n.13; and bricolage, 248n.15; and ideology, 208; medieval, 61; shifting nature of, 188–89; subjectivity of, 213. *See also* Atlas(es); Map(s); Mercator projection
Castilla del Oro, 96
Catalan Atlas, 198

Cathay, 60, 61. *See also* China
Catholicism: great khan's interest in, 57; Spanish cruelty and, 37. *See also* Conversion, to Catholicism; Holy Land; Missionaries
Cempoala, Cortés and inhabitants of, 165, 166
Central America: mistaken for Mangi, 61; phonological writing in, 233n.31; to New Spain, 85. *See also* Guatemala; Honduras; Mexico; Nicaragua
Certeau, Michel de, 4, 8, 30, 50, 51, 102, 116, 178, 213, 237n.53; and "oppositional practices," 235n.41; on Stradanus's "America," 41–48, 222n.41, 222–23n.52; on writing, 55–56. *See also* "Blank page" metaphor
Ceuta, conquest of, 228n.31
Charles V, Holy Roman emperor, 47; Cortés and, 16, 83–124, 162; Moctezuma's recognition of, 103; Motolinía and, 153; New World strategy of, 104–109; Oviedo and, 240n.21
Chaunu, Pierre, 7
China: as Columbus's goal, 224n.6; conquest of, 208; Cortés on, 121; Cuba as, 61; New World discovered by, 29. *See also* Cathay
Chivalry: Mendieta and, 159; novels of, 227n.29; war and, 109
Christianity: as enhancing, 211; and idolatry, 118; Mercator and, 248n.16; militant, 108; noble savage fit for, 74; Spain as exemplar of, 177; truth equated with, 19. *See also* Catholicism
Christophe Colomb (Heers), 49
Cipango (Japan), 55, 60, 61,

Index

Index

on, 169; thrust of, 57–
59. *See also* Las Casas,
Bartolomé de — as Col-
umbus's annotator
Diaz del Castillo, Bernal,
110, 238n.62
Dibble, Charles E., 111,
235n.43
Dictionaries, Nahuatl, 103,
116, 160
Diodorus Siculus, 169, 175
Discourse: colonial, 10–11,
218n.16; discursive for-
mation, 5; Eurocentrism
and, 14; force and, 90;
"hybridization" of, 13
Discovery: as creation, 38;
disingenuousness of,
222n.41; intention as
critical to, 221n.30; as
term, 40
Divine Comedy, The
(Dante), 31
Divisament dou monde
(Polo), 55
Dominicans. *See* Las Casas,
Bartolomé de
Drawings, Oviedo's, 146,
241n.33. *See also*
Map(s); Woodcuts
Dunn, Oliver, 226n.18
Durán, Diego de, 128–31,
133–34, 238–39n.4
Dwyer, Kevin, 90–91,
232n.27

Eco, Umberto, 126
Edwards, Clinton R., 181
Egypt: Mexico compared to,
155; New World con-
trasted with, 177. *See
also* Nile
Elliot, J. H., 236n.50
Encomienda, 135
Encyclopedias, New World,
75, 126, 136–37, 179,
212; *Atlas* contrasted
with, 208; and *Rela-
ciones geográficas*, 183.
See also *Apologética historia sumaria* (Las Ca-
sas); *Brevíssima relación
de la destruyción de las
Indias* (Las Casas); Franciscans, ethnographers
among; *Historia de las

Indias (Las Casas); *Historia de las Indias de
Nueva España e islas de
Tierra Firme* (Durán);
*Historia general y natu-
ral de las Indias* (Ovi-
edo)
Enthymemes, 171–72
Errancy, semiotic of, 54–59
Eschatology, romance and
Christian, 196, 250n.24
Ethnographic realism, positivism and, 89
Ethnography: climate and,
177; dialogical (*see* Dialogue, ethnographic);
and domination, 90, 123
(*see also* Cortés, Her-
nán — as protoanthropol-
ogist; Léry's place in,
222n.41; millennium
and, 152, 157. *See also*
Franciscans, ethnogra-
phers among
Ethnology, 43–44
Eurocentrism, 3, 6, 10, 20,
48, 181; in Acosta, 211;
in *Atlas*, 192–96, 202,
203, 207–209, 212, 249–
50n.20; and colonial dis-
course, 14; deconstruc-
tion of, 21; defined, 18;
emergence of, 6; in
maps, 249 (*see also* Eu-
rocentrism, in *Atlas*);
New World encyclope-
dias and, 179; slipperi-
ness of, 123; today, 212–
14. *See also* Self,
Eurocentric
Europe, in *Atlas*, 189, 203,
207, 249n.17, 249–
50n.20. *See also* Great
Britain; Holland; Italy;
Portugal; Spain
Exoticism: Franciscan use
of, 154; Oviedo's use of,
139–41, 147, 149, 154,
164, 165
Expansionism, European, 7,
20; Bitterli on, 38–39.
See also Colonialism;
Conquest

Fabian, Johannes, 31, 40,
84

Factualism, defined, 8–9
"Far East," 66; as Colum-
bus's goal, 60, 61; in
Mandeville's *Travels*,
196; New World con-
fused with, 65; as Para-
dise site, 76. *See also*
Cathay; Cipango; Indies;
Orient
Fauna: in *Atlas*, 197, 199;
New World, 6, 28, 140,
148, 163; Oviedo on,
140, 148
Favret-Saada, Jeanne, 90,
231n.19
Fernández de Enciso, Mar-
tin, 98
Fetishism, noble savage's
place in, 172–73
Fish, Caribbean, 71–72
Flora: in *Atlas*, 197; New
World, 6, 140, 144, 163;
Oviedo on, 140, 144
Florentine Codex, 16, 102–
103, 110, 112; revised,
236–37n.53
Florida, Soto's invasion of,
140; Indians of, 19
Fortune telling, Franciscans
vs., 160
Foucault, Michel, 5, 43,
122, 162, 228n.29,
247n.13; and analysis of
discourse, 10–11,
218n.16; and dissolution
of the subject, 12; and
European expansionism,
20; on games, 36; Las
Casas and, 244n.64; and
power, 13; Said influ-
enced by, 19; on signs,
36; on subalternity, 11
Francastel, Pierre, 222–
23n.52
Francis, Saint, 152, 153
Franciscans, 111, 135, 136,
151, 240n.16; as Cortés's
allies, 158, 166; eth-
nographers among, 126,
151–65, 167, 179, 208
(*see also* Mendieta, Gerónimo de; Motolinía;
Olmos, Andrés de; Qui-
ñones; Sahagún, Bernar-
dino de); millenarian, 5,
17, 137, 138, 207; in

Index

Index

Index

contrasted, 177; mystic interpretation of (*see* Franciscans, ethnographers among); as "natural entity," 50, 224–25n.6; Oviedo's exoticizing of, 149; population decline in, 238n.2; Satan resettled in, 147, 152, 160–61, 210, 211, 241n.30; writings on, 16–17. *See also* "Blank page" metaphor; Central America; New Spain; South America; Spanish conquest; West Indies

New World (term), 3; Columbus and, 50–51, 53, 57, 59, 65, 226n.18; replaced by "America," 98

Nicaragua, 178

Nietzsche, Friedrich, 9, 85

Nile, Paradise as located on, 76

Noah, as Amerindian progenitor, 210

Noble savage(s), 6, 15, 17, 40, 67, 82, 149, 172–79, 207, 208, 212, 245n.74; Amerindians as, 171–72, 173; and barbarism, 173; Columbus on, 73–75, 76, 80; Moctezuma as, 109, 236n.50; in New World encyclopedias, 137. *See also* Primitivism, ideal

Nova Mexico. *See* Mexico City

Nova reperta (Stradanus), 23, 26, 31

Nueva Galicia, Indians of, 161

Ockham, William of, 154

Odoric of Pordenone, 57, 196

O'Gorman, Edmundo, 3–5, 215–16n.2, 244n.65, 246n.78; vs. Bataillon, 221n.30; on Columbus, 221n.30; on Las Casas, 243–44n.57; and León-Portilla, 217n.9

Olmos, Andrés de, 160–62, 164

Ong, Walter, 31, 225n.11

Opossums, 28

Order of Things, The (Foucault), 19

Orient, 63; conceptualizing of, 39; as Paradise locale, 78. *See also* China; Japan

Orientalism, 11, 39; Said version of, 10; from within, 40

Orientalism (Said), 19, 39, 90

Orinoco River, Columbus on, 77–79

Ortelius, Abraham, 180, 191

Ottoman Empire, 196

Oviedo y Valdés, Gonzalo Fernández de, 17, 47, 126, 136, 137–51, 162, 164, 165, 178, 179, 207; background of, 137; Las Casas's similarities to, 174; style of, 138, 139, 144–46, 240n.22 (*see also* Metaphor[s], Oviedo's use of; Pineapples, Oviedo on)

Pacific Ocean: Cortés's search for, 120; discovery of, 96

Painting: and cartography contrasted, 189–90; Dutch, 140; Flemish, 146, 241n.27; Italian, 146

Palimpsest(s), 180–81, 211, 248n.15; *Atlas* as, 180, 181, 184–86, 250n.21; cartography and, 182; colonization as foreign icon on, 96, 101, 122

Paradise: as Columbus's concept, 15; Dante on, 31; New World as, 76–80, 93, 156–57. *See also* "Natural garden"

Paradox, 214; irony and, 73; nature of, 33–34

Parousia, 153, 158

Pastor, Beatriz, 224n.6

Peirce, Charles, 35

Pérez de Oliva, Hernán, 3, 4

Perspective, da Vinci on, 35

Peru: colonialism in, 11; "inferiority" of, 211; metropolises of, 95; monkeys of, 148; natives of, 178

Petrarch, 229n.36

Phelan, John, 153, 172

Philip II, king of Spain, 182

Philoponus, Honorius, 69

Pigs, Spanish soldiers as gold-obsessed, 111

Pineapples: Locke on, 147; Oviedo on, 140–46

Pinturas, 182

Piracy, Spanish concern with, 182

Plague, in New World, 125, 135, 136

Pliny the Elder, 78; as Las Casas's source, 175; Oviedo's debt to, 144–45, 162; as Sahagún's model, 162

Plotting Women (Franco), 14

Plutarch, 166

Pocho, 20

Politics, hispanicization of Mexican, 135–36

Polo, Marco, 16, 31, 54, 55, 59, 65, 198, 199, 227n.25; and Columbus contrasted, 62–63; emphases of, 61; and gardens, 71; and "Gran Can," 57; as reference, 53, 61, 65, 196

Popocatepetl, 112

Portugal: African adventures of, 228n.31; Spain and, 76–77, 121, 206, 207

Post-structuralism, 13, 14–15; colonial discourse and, 10

Power, and knowledge equated, 84, 85

Prefaces, underwriting of, 18

Primitivism, 147; anti-primitivism and, 46; ideal, 164–70, 172, 178

Principe constante, El (Calderón), 84, 89

Printing press, impact of, 52

Ptolemy, 189, 198–99; in *Atlas*, 205

Purgatory, 31

<u>travel lit.</u>

45 unveiling of the hidden
5 generic differences reflect authority

is Oviedo really "exotic"
does he exoticize America?